First World War

and Army of Occupation

War Diary

France, Belgium and Germany

36 DIVISION
109 Infantry Brigade,
Brigade Machine Gun Company
23 January 1916 - 31 January 1918

WO95/2511/2

The Naval & Military Press Ltd
www.nmarchive.com
Published in association with The National Archives

Published by

The Naval & Military Press Ltd

Unit 10 Ridgewood Industrial Park,

Uckfield, East Sussex,

TN22 5QE England

Tel: +44 (0) 1825 749494

www.naval-military-press.com

www.nmarchive.com

This diary has been reprinted in facsimile from the original. Any imperfections are inevitably reproduced and the quality may fall short of modern type and cartographic standards.

Contents

Document type	Place/Title	Date From	Date To
Heading	WO95/2511 (2)		
Heading	109th Machine Gun Coy. Jan 1916-Jan 1918		
Heading	109th M.G. Coy Vol.1		
Heading	War Diary Of 109th Brigade Machine Gun Company From 23rd January 1916 To 31st January 1916 (Volume I)		
Heading	War Diary Of 109th Brigade Machine Gun Company From 1st February 1916 To 29th February 1916 (Volume II)		
War Diary	Fienvillers	23/01/1916	05/02/1916
War Diary	Varennes	07/02/1916	10/02/1916
War Diary	Mailly Mallet	11/02/1916	29/02/1916
Heading	War Diary Of 109th Brigade Machine Gun Company. From 1st March 1916 To 31st March 1916		
War Diary	Mailly-Mallet	01/03/1916	06/03/1916
War Diary	Martinsart	07/03/1916	31/03/1916
Heading	War Diary Of 109th Brigade Machine Gun Company From 1st April 1916 To 30th April 1916 (Volume I)		
War Diary	Martinsart	01/04/1916	30/04/1916
Miscellaneous	D.A.G		
Heading	War Diary Of 109th Bde Machine Gun Company From 1st May 1916 To 31st May 1916 (Volume I)		
War Diary	Martinsart	01/05/1916	08/05/1916
War Diary	Varennes	09/05/1916	31/05/1916
Heading	109th Brigade Machine Gun Company June 1916		
War Diary	Varennes	01/06/1916	21/06/1916
War Diary	Thiepval Wood	22/06/1916	30/06/1916
Heading	109th Brigade Machine Gun Company July 1916		
War Diary	Gordon Castle Thiepval Wood	01/07/1916	01/07/1916
War Diary	Thiepval Wood And German Trenches N.E.	01/07/1916	02/07/1916
War Diary	Thiepval Wood	02/07/1916	02/07/1916
War Diary	Martinsart Wood		
War Diary	Hedauville	03/07/1916	05/07/1916
War Diary	Herissart	06/07/1916	09/07/1916
War Diary	Candas	10/07/1916	10/07/1916
War Diary	Conteville	11/07/1916	11/07/1916
War Diary	Berguette		
War Diary	Racquinghem	12/07/1916	12/07/1916
War Diary	Quelmes	13/07/1916	21/07/1916
War Diary	Bollezeele	22/07/1916	23/07/1916
War Diary	Romarin	24/07/1916	31/07/1916
Heading	War Diary Of 109th Company Machine Gun Corps. For Month Of August, 1916.		
War Diary	Romarin	01/08/1916	31/08/1916
Heading	War Diary Of 109th Machine Gun Company From 1st September 1916 To 30th September 1916		
War Diary	Romarin	01/09/1916	03/09/1916
War Diary	Mt Kemmel	04/09/1916	22/09/1916
War Diary	Dranoutre	23/09/1916	30/09/1916

Heading	War Diary Of 109th Machine Gun Company From 1st October 1916 To 31st October 1916 (Volume I)		
War Diary	Dranoutre	01/10/1916	31/10/1916
Heading	War Diary Of 109th Brigade Machine Gun Company. From 1st November 1916 to 30th November 1916		
War Diary	Dranoutre	01/11/1916	30/11/1916
Heading	War Diary Of 109th Brigade Machine Gun Company From 1st December 1916 to 31st December 1916		
Heading	War Diary Of 109th Machine Gun Company From 1st December 1916 To 31st December 1916		
War Diary	Dranoutre	01/12/1916	05/12/1916
War Diary	Kortepyp	06/12/1916	31/12/1916
Heading	War Diary Of 109th Brigade Machine Gun Company. From 1st January 1917 To 31st January1917.		
War Diary	Kortepyp	01/01/1917	31/01/1917
Heading	War Diary Of 109th Brigade Machine Gun Company. From 1st February To 28th February.		
War Diary	Kortepyp	01/02/1917	25/02/1917
War Diary	Fontain Houck	26/02/1917	28/02/1917
Miscellaneous	Operation Orders For Co-Operation Of The 109th Machine Gun Company	20/02/1917	20/02/1917
Miscellaneous	Operation Orders by Capt. P.D. Mulholland Commanding 109th M.Gun Company	22/02/1917	22/02/1917
Miscellaneous	Burn	23/02/1917	23/02/1917
Heading	109th Brigade Machine Gun Company. From 1st March 1917, to 31st March 1917		
War Diary	Moolenacker	01/03/1917	13/03/1917
War Diary	Kemmel	14/03/1917	18/03/1917
War Diary	Moolenacker	19/03/1917	19/03/1917
War Diary	Hazebrouck	20/03/1917	21/03/1917
War Diary	Wizernes	22/03/1917	22/03/1917
War Diary	Zuer Camp	23/03/1917	29/03/1917
War Diary	Quercamp	30/03/1917	31/03/1917
Heading	War Diary Of 109th Brigade Machine Gun Company, From 1st April 1917 Till 30th April 1917		
War Diary	Quercamp	01/04/1917	03/04/1917
War Diary	Onthi March Wizernes	04/04/1917	04/04/1917
War Diary	Hazebrouck	05/04/1917	05/04/1917
War Diary	Kemmel	06/04/1917	27/04/1917
War Diary	Spanbroke Sector	28/04/1917	30/04/1917
Miscellaneous	H.E.G. Operation Order No. 14th April 1917		
Miscellaneous	Machine Gun Defence Scheme.		
Miscellaneous	U.E.G. Operation Order No 6	26/04/1917	26/04/1917
Operation(al) Order(s)	Operation Order No 6 (b)	27/04/1917	27/04/1917
Operation(al) Order(s)	Operation Order No 6 (b)		
Heading	War Diary Of 109th. Machine Gun Company. From 1st. May, 1917. Till 31st. May, 1917		
War Diary	Spanbroeke Sawent	01/05/1917	02/05/1917
War Diary	Spanbroeke Salient	04/05/1917	05/05/1917
War Diary	Tyrone Fm	06/05/1917	13/05/1917
War Diary	Wakefield Lines	13/05/1917	13/05/1917
War Diary	Wakefield Lines Nr Locre Belgium	14/05/1917	18/05/1917
War Diary	Wakefield Camp	19/05/1917	22/05/1917
War Diary	Wakefield Camp Nr Locre Belgium	23/05/1917	28/05/1917
War Diary	Wakefield Camp Nr Locre Belgium	29/05/1917	31/05/1917
Operation(al) Order(s)	109th Machine Gun Coy. Operation Orders No. 8	12/05/1917	12/05/1917

Operation(al) Order(s)	109th Machine Gun Coy Operation Orders No. 7	04/05/1917	04/05/1917
Miscellaneous	109th Machine Gun Company		
Heading	War Diary For The Month Of June, 1917 109th Machine Gun Company, Vol 15		
War Diary	Wakefield Huts Nr Locre Belgium	01/06/1917	11/06/1917
War Diary	Ruddigore Lines Nr Locre Belgium	12/06/1917	12/06/1917
War Diary	Nr Westoutre	13/06/1917	17/06/1917
War Diary	Doncaster Huts Nr Locre	18/06/1917	19/06/1917
War Diary	Wychaete 28 SW 5A 07D41 Grandbois	20/06/1917	22/06/1917
War Diary	Grandbois 013a3590	23/06/1917	26/06/1917
War Diary	O 13 B 15 90	27/06/1917	30/06/1917
Miscellaneous	The Action Of The Machine Guns Of The 109th Machine Gun Company.		
Miscellaneous	109th Machine Gun Coy Operation Order For Releif Of 8 Guns Under Lieut. Lea	03/06/1917	03/06/1917
Miscellaneous	Company Operation Orders 109th Machine Gun Coy.	04/06/1916	04/06/1916
Heading	W.D		
Miscellaneous	Company Operation Order (No11) 109th Machine Gun Coy	05/06/1917	05/06/1917
Heading	War Diary For Month Of July, 1917		
War Diary	Strazeele	01/07/1917	04/07/1917
War Diary	Honeghem	05/07/1917	05/07/1917
War Diary	Arques	06/07/1917	06/07/1917
War Diary	Petit Quercamp	07/07/1917	12/07/1917
War Diary	Petit Quercamp 15k From St Omer	13/07/1917	17/07/1917
War Diary	Petit Quercamp Nr Bouvelinghem	18/07/1917	26/07/1917
War Diary	Nezelea Nr Locre 5 Map From Belgium Boundary	27/07/1917	30/07/1917
War Diary	Near Poperinghe	31/07/1917	31/07/1917
Miscellaneous	69th Machine Gun Coy		
Heading	2nd Command		
Heading	War Diary 109th Machine Gun Company. For Month Of August 17		
War Diary	Watou Area N5 Poperinghe	01/08/1917	03/08/1917
War Diary	G5c44	04/08/1917	06/08/1917
War Diary	Nr Poperinghe	06/07/1917	09/07/1917
War Diary	Wieltje Dugouts	10/07/1917	12/07/1917
War Diary	G 5 C 44	13/07/1917	13/07/1917
War Diary	German Trench System 500 Yilne Qwieltje Nrypres	16/07/1917	16/07/1917
War Diary	C23c6080	16/07/1917	16/07/1917
War Diary	C23c6050	16/07/1917	18/07/1917
War Diary	Winnezeele	19/07/1917	23/07/1917
War Diary	Barastre	24/08/1917	28/08/1917
War Diary	Ytres Area	29/08/1917	30/08/1917
War Diary	J21D. 40,30		
Miscellaneous	Administrative Instructions 109th Machine Gun Company		
Miscellaneous	War Diary		
Operation(al) Order(s)	Operation Order No 1 109th Machine Gun Company.		
Heading	War Diary		
Miscellaneous	Administrative Instructions 109th Machine Gun Company		
Heading	War Diary Of 109th Machine Gun Company, Period 1st September to 30th September 1917		
War Diary	Hermies Sector J21D.40, 35.	01/09/1917	06/09/1917
War Diary	J22c	06/09/1917	26/09/1917
War Diary	J22c Coy St G	27/09/1917	30/09/1917

Heading	109th M.G.Coy War Diary of October 1917		
War Diary	J21c	01/10/1917	26/10/1917
War Diary	Bertencourt	27/10/1917	31/10/1917
Heading	109th Machine Gun Coy. Vol 20 War Diary for period from 1st to 30th November, 1917		
Heading	War Diary of 109th M G Coy to November 1917		
War Diary	Bertincourt P7C. Map of France Sheet' 57C.	01/11/1917	15/11/1917
War Diary	Velu Wood J31d. 00,30.	16/11/1917	18/11/1917
War Diary	Velu Wood	18/11/1917	27/11/1917
War Diary	Hermies	28/11/1917	28/11/1917
War Diary	Beaulencourt	29/11/1917	30/11/1917
Heading	109th Machine Gun Company. Vol 21 War Diary For Month Of December, 1917.		
War Diary	Achiet Le-Petit	01/12/1917	01/12/1917
War Diary	Bancourt Bertincourt	02/12/1917	03/12/1917
War Diary	Trescault	04/12/1917	04/12/1917
War Diary	Line R3c.50,80. (boy HQ.)	05/12/1917	05/12/1917
War Diary	R3c.50,80 Coy HQ.	05/12/1917	08/12/1917
War Diary	In The Line	08/12/1917	11/12/1917
War Diary	Line (Sec Sheet III For The 13.7)	12/12/1917	17/12/1917
War Diary	Humbercourt	18/12/1917	28/12/1917
War Diary	Hancard	29/12/1917	31/12/1917
Heading	109th Machine Gun Company. War Diary For Month Of January 1918		
War Diary	Hangard (S.E. Of Amiens)	01/01/1918	08/01/1918
War Diary	Balatre	09/01/1918	13/01/1918
War Diary	In The Line	14/01/1918	14/01/1918
War Diary	Map France Sheet 66c. NW.	15/01/1918	18/01/1918
War Diary	B25b.30,50	19/01/1918	28/01/1918
War Diary	Happencourt	29/01/1918	31/01/1918

36TH DIVISION
109TH INFY BDE

109TH MACHINE GUN COY.

JAN 1916-JAN 1918

109th M. G. Coy

Vol: I

30

Confidential

War Diary

of

109th Brigade Machine Gun Company

From 23rd January 1916 to 31st January 1916

(Volume I)

36 109th M.G. Coy:
Vol: 2

Confidential

War Diary
of

109th Brigade Machine Gun Company

From 1st February 1916 To 29th February 1916

(Volume II)

Instructions regarding War Diaries and Intelligence Summaries are contained in F. S. Regs., Part II. and the Staff Manual respectively. Title pages will be prepared in manuscript.

WAR DIARY
or
~~INTELLIGENCE~~ SUMMARY.

(*Erase heading not required.*)

Army Form C. 2118.

Page 1

Place	Date	Hour	Summary of Events and Information	Remarks and references to Appendices
	1916		109TH BRIGADE MACHINE GUN COMPANY.	
FIENVILLERS	23rd January		This Company was assembled at FIENVILLERS on the 23rd January 1916	
			Authority: Wire from 36th Divisional Headquarters.	
			Personnel:-	
			CAPT. W. McCONACHIE. B.M.G.O. 109th Brigade of 10th Royal Inniskilling Fusiliers	
			LIEUT. H.M. HEWITT. 9th Do Do Do	
			2nd LIEUT. J.M. HAMPSHIRE. 9th Do Do Do	
			LIEUT. A.W. WAKLEY. 10th Do Do Do	
			2nd LIEUT. W.A. GAUSSEN. 10th Do Do Do	
			2nd LIEUT. R. GRANT 11th Do Do Do	
			2nd LIEUT. A.C. HART 11th Do Do Do	
			LIEUT. E.H. CLOKEY 14th Royal Irish Rifles	
			2nd LIEUT. G.C. WEDGWOOD 14th Do Do Do	

2353 Wt. W2544/1454 700,000 5/15 D. D. & L. A.D.S.S./Forms/C. 2118.

Instructions regarding War Diaries and Intelligence Summaries are contained in F. S. Regs., Part II. and the Staff Manual respectively. Title pages will be prepared in manuscript.

WAR DIARY

~~or~~

~~INTELLIGENCE SUMMARY.~~

(Erase heading not required.) 109th Bde Mach Gun Coy.

Army Form C. 2118.

Page. 2

Place	Date	Hour	Summary of Events and Information	Remarks and references to Appendices
	1916			
FIENVILLERS	23rd January.		The N C O's and men were drawn from the Machine Gun Sections of 9th 10th and 11th Royal Inniskilling Fusiliers and 14th Royal Irish Rifles.	
			Equipment: Four Vickers Machine Guns and spare parts complete were drawn from the Battalions (of the 109th Brigade) mentioned above	
			Transport Two Limbered waggons and eight Mules with harness and Saddlery complete ~~were~~ also drawn from the above mentioned Battalions. Four G. S Limbered Waggons. One Water Cart. One Mess Cart, Eleven L.D Horses in charge of six drivers arrived from No1 section A.S.C Horse Transport Depot Base	
			Good Billets were found for the Horses and Men	
			Lieut E. H. CLOKEY and four N C O's proceeded to the G. H. Q Machine Gun School WISQUES	

2353 Wt. W2544/1454 700,000 5/15 D. D. & L. A.D.S.S./Forms/C. 2118.

Instructions regarding War Diaries and Intelligence Summaries are contained in F. S. Regs., Part II. and the Staff Manual respectively. Title pages will be prepared in manuscript.

WAR DIARY

~~or~~

~~INTELLIGENCE~~ SUMMARY.

(Erase heading not required.)

109th Brigade Mach Gun Coy

Army Form C. 2118.

Page 3.

Place	Date	Hour	Summary of Events and Information	Remarks and references to Appendices
	1916			
FIENVILLERS	January 24th to 29th		The period 24th till 29th was taken up in making good, deficiencies in Equipment, Transport, Kit &c.	
	30th		CAPT W. McCONACHIE proceeded on leave. Command of the Company being taken by Lieut A.W. WAKLEY.	
	31st		Complete inspection of the Company, Equipment and Transport	

2353 Wt. W2544/1454 700,000 5/15 D. D. & L. A.D.S.S./Forms/C. 2118.

Instructions regarding War Diaries and Intelligence Summaries are contained in F. S. Regs., Part II. and the Staff Manual respectively. Title Pages will be prepared in manuscript.

WAR DIARY ~~or~~ ~~INTELLIGENCE SUMMARY~~

(Erase heading not required.) 109th Bde M. G. Coy

Army Form C. 2118

Page 4

Place	Date	Hour	Summary of Events and Information	Remarks and references to Appendices
	1916 February			
FIENVILLERS	1st		Football match was played in afternoon between a Company team and Motor Transport Section A.S.C The Result: a draw	[initials]
	3rd		2 Lieut HAMPSHIRE proceeded to ACHEUX to select billets for the company	[initials]
	5th		Company moved direct to VARENNES and took over new billets. ~~Command of~~	[initials]
VARENNES	7th		Eight Officers chargers arrived to day.	[initials]
	8th		Lieut CLOKEY and four N C O's returned from Machine Gun ~~School~~ WISQUES. Command of the company being taken over by Lieut CLOKEY	[initials]
	9th		Lieuts CLOKEY and WAKLEY visited the trenches E of AUCHONVILLERS to find the position of M.G. Emplacements.	[initials]
	10th		CAPT W. McCONACHIE returned from leave and assumed command. The Company moved into Billets at MAILLY-MALLET Lieut CLOKEY took over duties of Adjutant	[initials]
MAILLY-MALLET	11th		Two men were transferred from 109th Field Ambulance and were taken on the strength of the Company	[initials]

1875 Wt. W593/826 1,000,000 4/15 J.B.C. & A. A.D.S.S./Forms/C. 2118.

Instructions regarding War Diaries and Intelligence Summaries are contained in F. S. Regs., Part II. and the Staff Manual respectively. Title Pages will be prepared in manuscript.

WAR DIARY
or
~~INTELLIGENCE~~ SUMMARY

(~~Erase heading not required.~~) 109th Bde M.G. Coy.

Army Form C. 2118

Place	Date 1916	Hour	Summary of Events and Information	Remarks and references to Appendices
MAILLY-MALLET	February 11th		Capt WOODGATE, BMGCC 107th Brigade took the C.O round all the M.G. emplacements and positions of proposed emplacements in the trenches E of AUCHONVILLERS.	
	"		Thirty N.C.O's and men were sent to do duty with teams of the 107 B.M.G. Coy in the trenches.	[initials]
	12th		C.O. along with Capt WOODGATE and 2/Lieut GRANT picked positions for Emplacements south of our Sector. They were shelled when returning through AUCHONVILLERS and WOODGATE and GRANT were severely wounded. Working party of 20 men were sent to build Emplacements in Support-Trench	[initials]
	13th		Lieut CLONEY and 3 other Ranks proceeded on leave	
	14th		Working party of 20 men were sent to build Emplacements under 107th B.M.G. Coy Mr GAUSSEN and Mr WEDGWOOD were sent with a party to build an emplacement in CLONMEL AVENUE. They were spotted and Machine Guns turned on them	[initials]
	15th		A little rain fell during the night and Trenches in some parts are very muddy. Working parties were sent out as last two nights	[initials]
	16th		Heavy rain fell all day. Trenches impassable in some places	[initials]
	17th		The C.O accompanied Brig-General Hickman and Brigade Major RICHARDSON round the Emplacements. They saw a few Germans in their trenches and RICHARDSON had a shot. The range was 700 yards and the Germans quickly disappeared although its uncertain whether they were hit	[initials]

1875 Wt. W593/826 1,000,000 4/15 J.B.C. & A. A.D.S.S./Forms/C. 2118.

Instructions regarding War Diaries and Intelligence Summaries are contained in F. S. Regs., Part II. and the Staff Manual respectively. Title Pages will be prepared in manuscript.

WAR DIARY

~~or~~

~~INTELLIGENCE SUMMARY~~

(Erase heading not required.)

109th Bde M. G. Coy

Army Form C. 2118

Place	Date 1916	Hour	Summary of Events and Information	Remarks and references to Appendices
MAILLY-MALLET	February 18th	1-30AM	Very heavy shelling was heard on our right. It lasted for over an hour	
			The C.O and Lieut MONAGHAN of the 107th Bde MG Coy visited the Divisional reserve line and got shelled. Two shells fell & burst less than 20 yards from them although the nearest German who could have seen them must have been 2½ miles away.	[initials]
	19th	6PM	The Germans started a heavy bombardment of our trenches paying particular attention to our communication trenches. Our artillery replied immediately on their front line and made splendid shooting. It was evident the Germans intended attacking but our Artillery checked them. The bombardment lasted one hour and a half during which the Germans sent over about 1500 shells Our casualties were Nil	[initials]
	20th		The Emplacement at CLONMEL AV. was found to have been heavily shelled and almost demolished during last nights' bombardment. The C.O. decided to demolish it and build a new one some distance off. Accordinly Mr WEDGWOOD and party were sent out to night and removed all trace of both the Emplacement and dugout	[initials]
	22nd		Bosch Aeroplane passed over and dropped a bomb within 100 yards ~~from~~ of this Orderly room. The bomb did not explode	
	"		Mr WEDGWOOD and a working party went out to night to build a new emplacement 50 yards behind the old one in CLONMEL AVENUE.	[initials]
	"		LIEUT WAKLEY and three other ranks proceeded on leave	

1875 Wt. W593/826 1,000,000 4/15 J.B.C. & A. A.D.S.S./Forms/C. 2118.

WAR DIARY

~~or~~

~~INTELLIGENCE SUMMARY~~

~~(Erase heading not required.)~~

Instructions regarding War Diaries and Intelligence Summaries are contained in F. S. Regs., Part II. and the Staff Manual respectively. Title Pages will be prepared in manuscript.

Army Form C. 2118

109th Bde Mach Gun Coy.

Page 7.

Place	Date 1916	Hour	Summary of Events and Information	Remarks and references to Appendices
MAILLY-MALLET	February 22nd		Two Bosch Aeroplanes passed over the village, dropping a few bombs which caused no damage The C.O. inspected the Intermediate Divisional line and selected positions for new M.G. Emplacements	[illegible]
	23rd		Very heavy snow all day Lieut CLOKEY and three other ranks returned from leave	[illegible]
	24th		Heavy Snowfall continued. Arrangements were made to relieve the 107th B.M.G.Coy to-morrow Wire received from H.Q. "All leave stopped"	[illegible]
	25th		All Emplacements, except two, were taken over from the 107th B.M.G.Coy in daylight The remaining two: ELLES SQUARE and FORT HOYSTEAD had to be relieved after darkness had fallen Weather stormy and Heavy snow fall continued all day	[illegible]
	26th		Gun Teams in the Emplacements seem to have settled down to their work Much better weather – Clear & Frosty	[illegible]
	27th		Thaw has set in, making the Trenches very wet	[illegible]
	28th		Little shelling by the Bosch to-day but our artillery was very active Heavy thaw continues and the trenches are in a terrible state. In some places the water is over 3 ft deep. It is very hard on the men, some of whom have to do 10 days in without relief, owing to the number of Emplacements occupied. The men are very cheerful however	[illegible]

1875 Wt. W593/826/1,000,000 4/15 J.B.C. & A. A.D.S.S./Forms/C. 2118.

Army Form C. 2118

Instructions regarding War Diaries and Intelligence Summaries are contained in F. S. Regs., Part II. and the Staff Manual respectively. Title Pages will be prepared in manuscript.

WAR DIARY
or
~~INTELLIGENCE SUMMARY~~

(Erase heading not required.) 109th Bde Mach Gun Coy . Page 8

Place	Date 1916	Hour	Summary of Events and Information	Remarks and references to Appendices
MAILLY-MALLET	February 29th		The Snow has almost disappeared, but the Thaw has caused considerable inconvenience in the matter of Transport and our Rations are arriving very late	[initials]
			The trenches are worse than ever and some resemble fast running rivers	[initials]

1875 Wt. W593/826 1,000,000 4/15 J.B.C. & A. A.D.S.S./Forms/C. 2118.

109 M.G
Coy
Vol 3

Confidential

War Diary
of
109th Brigade Machine Gun Company.

From 1st March 1916 To 31st March 1916

(~~Volume I~~)

Instructions regarding War Diaries and Intelligence Summaries are contained in F. S. Regs., Part II. and the Staff Manual respectively. Title Pages will be prepared in manuscript.

WAR DIARY ~~or~~ INTELLIGENCE SUMMARY

Army Form C. 2118

~~(Erase heading not required.)~~ 109th Bde Mach Gun Coy

Page 9.

Place	Date 1916	Hour	Summary of Events and Information	Remarks and references to Appendices
MAILLY-MALLET	MARCH 1st		2nd Lieut COTTEL and 16 other ranks of the 24th Battery Motor Machine Gun Corps reported to-day and are attached for instruction to this Company	[illegible]
			A Transport Sergeant reported to day for duty (on transfer from 14th M.G. Coy GRANTHAM)	[illegible]
	2nd		The C O visited line of Trenches in THIEPVAL WOOD and inspected M.G. Emplacements	
			~~The~~ A team of the M.M.G Battery took over one of our emplacements in AUCHONVILLERS. Snow fell during the day.	[illegible]
			2nd Lieut GAUSSEN and 3 other ranks returned from leave.	
	3rd		2nd Lieut GAUSSEN and 2nd Lieut HART proceeded to THIEPVAL WOOD for information regarding position of Emplacements &c in view of our move into that line. Orders received re our being relieved by the 107th Bde M.G.Coy.	[illegible]
			Some snow again to-day.. Lieut WAKLEY and 3 other ranks returned from leave	
	4th		All our positions were taken over to-day by 107th Bde M.G. Coy and the entire Company is now in Billets in MAILLY MALLET.. Heavy snow fell all day to-day	[illegible]
	5th		Orders received to move to MARTINSART on 6th inst, accordingly preparations were made during the day. 2 Lieut COTTEL and other ranks of Motor M.G. Corps are to remain behind with 107th B M G Coy. Snow continued to-day but not so heavily as yesterday.	[illegible]
	6th		The N.C.O's in charge of twelve gun teams paraded at 7-30 AM and proceeded to the Trenches in THIEPVAL WOOD for the purpose of securing all information about the positions which their teams were to take over later in the day	[illegible]

1875 Wt. W593/826 1,000,000 4/15 J.B.C. & A. A.D.S.S./Forms/C. 2118.

Instructions regarding War Diaries and Intelligence Summaries are contained in F. S. Regs., Part II. and the Staff Manual respectively. Title Pages will be prepared in manuscript.

WAR DIARY
or
~~INTELLIGENCE SUMMARY~~
(Erase heading not required.)

Army Form C. 2118

109th Bde Mach Gun Company Page 10

Place	Date 1916	Hour	Summary of Events and Information	Remarks and references to Appendices
MAILLY-MALLET	MARCH 6th	8-45AM	168 Belt Boxes of S.A.A – in 3 Limber'd waggons – were sent in charge of 2nd Lieut WEDGWOOD to HEDAUVILLE. The 146th Bde M G Coy received them there in exchange for an equal number of boxes to be left by them in the Emplacements	
		11 AM	2/Lieut HAMPSHIRE proceeded to MARTINSART to take over Billets	
		2 PM	Company paraded with full transport and marched to MARTINSART via ENGLEBELMER. The C.O was in command.	
MARTINSART		5-45PM	Twelve teams paraded with Guns Tripods &c and marched via AUTHUILLE to the trenches in THIEPVAL WOOD and took over the Emplacements there from the 146th Bde M.G Coy LIEUTS WAKLEY & HEWITT and 2nd Lieut HART & GAUSSEN were in charge of the teams. During the day the weather was dry.	ABG
	7th		40 Officers NCOs and men of the Lewis M G School are now attached to us for rations Teams in reserve were engaged to-day cleaning & improving Billets.	EHL
	8th		The Germans shelled our trenches all day to day with heavy shells. One shell exploded in the entrance to the Officers dug out, severely wounding LIEUT WAKLEY'S servant.	EHL
	9th		The guns from two positions at Q36B40-60 and Q36B60-80 (REF.MAP 57D SE) were withdrawn to day – being out of our Brigade area. These positions were apparently spotted by the enemy as they had been heavily shelled and the Emplacement and dug out were completely destroyed. All trenches in Brigade area were again heavily shelled and those near our position at R31A 07-61 (REF.MAP 57D SE) were demolished. Trenches are now fairly dry.	ABG

1875 Wt. W593/826 1,000,000 4/15 J.B.C. & A. A.D.S.S./Forms/C. 2118.

Instructions regarding War Diaries and Intelligence Summaries are contained in F. S. Regs., Part II. and the Staff Manual respectively. Title Pages will be prepared in manuscript.

WAR DIARY
~~or~~
~~INTELLIGENCE SUMMARY~~
~~(Erase heading not required.)~~

109th Bde M. G. Coy

Army Form C. 2118

Page 11.

Place	Date 1916	Hour	Summary of Events and Information	Remarks and references to Appendices
MARTINSART	MARCH 9th		Two men of the Transport were appointed to-day to be Actg Lnce Cpls.	JMB
	10th		All trenches in the Brigade area were again heavily shelled to day, but during the evening it was fortunately quieter when four of our teams were relieved. The guns at R 25 c 50-35 and R 25 c 25-73 were withdrawn as they were required in another sector	JMB
		11 PM	Before the relieved teams had withdrawn from the trenches the enemy commenced an intense bombardment of our trenches. At first his fire was directed on our Fire trench, and after 10 minutes it was lifted and put on our Support trenches, on all roads leading into the trenches and on the villages in rear. When the enemy's fire was lifted off our fire trenches we opened heavy Infantry and Machine Gun Fire on his front line. It was quite evident that the Germans intended making a raid but our fire prevented ~~[illegible]~~ it. Our Artillery were slow in replying to the enemy bombardment and it was 20 mins before the heavies opened. We had no casualties amongst the men of the M.G. Company.	JMB
	11th		A thorough examination of the Emplacements in our line showed that they suffered no damage in the bombardment	JMB
	12th		Everything was fairly quiet to day	JMB

1875 Wt. W593/826 1,000,000 4/15 J.B.C. & A. A.D.S.S./Forms/C. 2118.

Instructions regarding War Diaries and Intelligence Summaries are contained in F. S. Regs., Part II. and the Staff Manual respectively. Title Pages will be prepared in manuscript.

WAR DIARY
or
~~INTELLIGENCE SUMMARY~~

(Erase heading not required.)

10th Bde M. G. Coy

Army Form C. 2118

Page 12

Place	Date	Hour	Summary of Events and Information	Remarks and references to Appendices
	1916 – MARCH			
MARTINSART	13th		Two N.C.O's proceeded to the Anti Gas School at FORCEVILLE to-day for a course of instruction in the Salvus Breathing Apparatus 2/Lieut W. J. WILGAR reported to-day for duty (from 56th Machine Gun Coy) The enemy were fairly quiet again to-day.	[initials]
	14th		6 Gun teams were relieved to-day Enemy showed no activity to-day	[initials]
	15th		A Bosh Aeroplane passed over early this morning. The weather was glorious to-day The NCO's and men of the Company received their new (M.G.Corps) numbers to-day	[initials]
	16th		Enemy is still quiet. Two of our men were evacuated to-day and were struck off the Strength	[initials]
	17th		Our Artillery shelled the enemy for about an hour — A "St Patrick's Day Straffe". The trenches on our immediate right were heavily shelled to-night. There were thirty one casualties amongst the Infantry but ~~the~~ Our Machine Gun emplacement at R 31A 07-61 escaped untouched. Lieut E. H. CLOKEY was appointed 2nd in command of the Company – authority D.R.O 508. The dug out at our emplacement at Q 30 D 85-85 received a direct hit and was blown in. Five men were buried but escaped unhurt Two NCO's returned from ANTI-GAS School after course of instruction	REF MAP 57 D SE (1&2) 1/10000 [initials]

1875 Wt. W593/826 1,000,000 4/15 J.B.C. & A. A.D.S.S./Forms/C. 2118.

Instructions regarding War Diaries and Intelligence Summaries are contained in F. S. Regs., Part II. and the Staff Manual respectively. Title Pages will be prepared in manuscript.

WAR DIARY ~~or~~ ~~INTELLIGENCE SUMMARY~~

109th Bde Machine Gun Coy

(Erase heading not required.)

Army Form C. 2118

Page 13

Place	Date 1916	Hour	Summary of Events and Information	Remarks and references to Appendices
MARTINSART	MARCH 18th		Enemy Artillery was more active all day to-day. Our Emplact at *R25C 27-70 was hit – no damage. Our Aeroplanes were very conspicuous to-day and did as they liked in the air. The enemy fired an enormous amount of ammunition at them and apparently exhausted their stock in the end. The weather was splendid	[initials]
	19th		Five gun teams were relieved to-day and a sixth team was sent to a new gun position at HAMEL. Enemy machine Guns were active to-day	[initials]
	20th		Enemy were quiet to-day. During the evening our gun at *Q24D 70-15 fired on a party of 12 Germans and dispersed them	[initials]
	21st		9 Trench Mortars were sent over by the enemy this morning at our gun position *R25C 27-70 – no damage was done to the Emplacement. One of our guns fired at intervals to-night on the Station (in *Q 18 B) S.W of BEAUCOURT. The fire apparently worried the enemy. A team was sent to ~~take over~~ build a new emplacement at *Q23B 90-70 and to occupy it. The position is a splendid one as the German Front line can be enfiladed from it. We have now 12 of our ~~[struck out]~~ 16 guns in the line. The names of 2 NCO's for a M.G. Course at Wisques were submitted to-day	[initials] * REF MAP 57D SE (1&2) 1/10.000

1875 Wt. W593/826 1,000,000 4/15 J.B.C. & A. A.D.S.S./Forms/C. 2118.

Instructions regarding War Diaries and Intelligence Summaries are contained in F. S. Regs., Part II. and the Staff Manual respectively. Title Pages will be prepared in manuscript.

WAR DIARY ~~or~~ 109th Bde M. G. Coy
~~INTELLIGENCE SUMMARY~~
(Erase heading not required.)

Army Form C. 2118

Page 14.

Place	Date 1916	Hour	Summary of Events and Information	Remarks and references to Appendices
MARTINSART	MARCH 22nd		Eight Actg Corporals were promoted to-day to the Substantive rank of Corporal dating from 13th February 1916 2nd Lieut HAMPSHIRE and 3 other Ranks proceeded on leave Enemy were quiet to day.	[initials]
	23rd		Four gun teams were relieved to-day The enemy showed no activity	[initials]
	24th		A quiet day to-day but three of our Gun positions were shelled with Shrapnel during the night. Some snow fell to-day.	[initials]
	25th		The enemy and ourselves were both active to-day. Our guns fired on enemy trenches and again on the station SW of BEAUCOURT on a signal from the front line that the Enemy transport was heard. During the day 3 heavy German shells landed beside one of our dugouts but did no damage. During the night the trenches on the right of this Brigade were heavily bombarded by Trench Mortars. The Infantry were compelled to leave the front line for a considerable time during which our gun team, which remained, was entirely unsupported. Our wire in front was badly damaged A particularly bright light was seen in No man's Land to-night. It lasted for several minutes and bright white sparks issued from it accompanied by a hissing noise. Nothing happened when it went out	[initials]

1875 Wt. W593/826 1,000,000 4/15 J.B.C. & A. A.D.S.S./Forms/C. 2118.

Instructions regarding War Diaries and Intelligence Summaries are contained in F. S. Regs., Part II. and the Staff Manual respectively. Title Pages will be prepared in manuscript.

WAR DIARY ~~or~~ 109th Bde M. G. Coy

~~INTELLIGENCE SUMMARY~~

(Erase heading not required.)

Army Form C. 2118

Page 15.

Place	Date 1916	Hour	Summary of Events and Information	Remarks and references to Appendices
	MARCH			
MARTINSART	26th		A team was sent into HAMMERHEAD SAP (R25A 54-28) with a Gun to-day. This means we now have 13 of our 16 guns in the line	[initials] REF MAP 57D SE (1&2) 1/10.000
	27th		Three teams were relieved to-night Orders received posponing Machine Gun course until 10/4/15 An A/L/Cpl and one man from M.G. Corps Base depot reported to-day for duty and were taken on the strength Enemy Machine Guns were active to night against our Trenches	[initials]
	28th		A Bosh Aeroplane was over the village this morning and was shelled by our A.A. guns Four Corporals of the Company were promoted to be Sergeants to complete the Establishment All is quiet in the line	
	29th		Trenches on our right were bombarded slightly with Trench Mortars There was some snow to-day	
	30th		Through the good offices of CANON KING, C.F. we received a very useful telescope to-day from Friends of the Company in LIMAVADY Our Machine guns were very active during the ~~night~~ — One gun fired 750 rounds on the Station S W of BEAUCOURT when a train was heard; another put 500 rounds into a working party of Germans with good results and later engaged & silenced a German Machine Gun. The German Artillery heavily shelled THIEPVAL WOOD in the evening. The weather to-day was fine	[initials]

1875 Wt. W593/826 1,000,000 4/15 J.B.C. & A. A.D.S.S./Forms/C. 2118.

Instructions regarding War Diaries and Intelligence Summaries are contained in F. S. Regs., Part II. and the Staff Manual respectively. Title Pages will be prepared in manuscript.

WAR DIARY ~~or~~ 109th Bde M.G. Company

~~INTELLIGENCE~~ SUMMARY

(Erase heading not required.)

Army Form C. 2118

Page 16

Place	Date	Hour	Summary of Events and Information	Remarks and references to Appendices
MARTINSART	MARCH 31st		Enemy Aeroplane was overhead this morning Two of our machines fired on the Station S.W of Beaucourt and on the road leading from station to the village. Screams, shouts and much galloping was afterwards heard so our fire was apparently effective. Enemy artillery was active against THIEPVAL WOOD during the day and Enemy M Guns were active during the night. Three gun teams were relieved to day Lieut HEWITT and three other ranks proceeded on leave of absence to England to day. Weather very fine	[initials]

1875 Wt. W593/826 1,000,000 4/15 J.B.C. & A. A.D.S.S./Forms/C. 2118.

XXXVI N.E.

109 MG Coy
Vol. 4

Confidential

War Diary

of

109th Brigade Machine Gun Company

From 1st April 1916 To 30th April 1916

(Volume I.)

Army Form C. 2118

Instructions regarding War Diaries and Intelligence Summaries are contained in F. S. Regs., Part II. and the Staff Manual respectively. Title Pages will be prepared in manuscript.

WAR DIARY
or
~~INTELLIGENCE~~ SUMMARY
(~~Erase heading not required.~~)

109th Bde M.G. Coy

Page 17.

Place	Date 1916	Hour	Summary of Events and Information	Remarks and references to Appendices
MARTINSART	APRIL 1st		Our Machine guns co-operated with the Artillery and fired on the Station S.W. of BEAUCOURT. Enemy machine guns were again active as were also their Aeroplanes. One of their Aeroplanes dropped a Red White & Black streamer to which was attached a weighted pocket containing a letter from one of our airmen who had been compelled to descend in the enemy's lines. The weather was good to-day.	[illegible]
	2nd		British and German air craft were very active to-day. The Germans dropped a few bombs. The weather was good	[illegible]
	3rd		The enemy was quiet to-day except for some "Heavies" which he put over during the day at intervals. A good number of Bombs were put over into HAMMERHEAD SAP where we have a gun emplacement but no damage was done. One of our Machine guns silenced a Bosh Gun N of HAMEL to-night. The three gun teams in reserve here did some firing practice on a range about half a mile behind. The weather was very fine and the temperature warm	[illegible]
	4th		The Enemy was fairly quiet to day. Our machine guns were again active. 3 Gun teams were relieved this evening. Weather was dry but it was much cooler than yesterday, and very cloudy	[illegible]

1875 Wt. W593/826 1,000,000 4/15 J.B.C. & A. A.D.S.S./Forms/C. 2118.

Instructions regarding War Diaries and Intelligence Summaries are contained in F. S. Regs., Part II. and the Staff Manual respectively. Title Pages will be prepared in manuscript.

WAR DIARY
or 109th Bde Mach Gun Company
~~INTELLIGENCE SUMMARY~~
(Erase heading not required.)

Army Form C. 2118

Page 18

Place	Date 1916	Hour	Summary of Events and Information	Remarks and references to Appendices
MARTINSART	APRIL 5th		There was little activity shown by the Enemy to-day The weather was dry but cloudy	[initials]
	6th		An A/L/Cpl reported to-day from Grantham for duty During the day the enemy shelled THIEPVAL WOOD intermittently The Brigade Front was shortened this evening and consequently our Machine Gun positions were re arranged, and it was possible to withdraw three guns. We now have 10 guns in the line and 6 in reserve.	
		9 PM	The enemy commenced a heavy bombardment on part of our Front and on the front of the Brigade on our left. The bombardment lasted for 1½ hours and was apparently the preliminary to an attempt to raid our lines. Our Machine guns fired throughout the bombardment on the Enemy's trenches and No man's Land. 16,500 rounds were fired by our Machine guns. Fortunately there were no casualties in this Company —— The weather during the day was good.	[initials]
	7th		After yesterday's activity the enemy was fairly quiet during the day and night. One of our guns fired about 250 rounds on the station SW of BEAUCOURT when transport was heard The weather to-day was good	[initials]

1875 Wt. W593/826 1,000,000 4/15 J.B.C. & A. A.D.S.S./Forms/C. 2118.

Instructions regarding War Diaries and Intelligence Summaries are contained in F. S. Regs., Part II. and the Staff Manual respectively. Title Pages will be prepared in manuscript.

WAR DIARY ~~or~~ 109th Bde Machine Gun Coy
~~INTELLIGENCE~~ SUMMARY
(~~Erase heading not required.~~)

Army Form C. 2118

Page 19.

Place	Date	Hour	Summary of Events and Information	Remarks and references to Appendices
MARTINSART	APRIL 8th		We took over a new Machine Gun position to-day at Q23C 30-56 from the 87th M.G.Coy.	REF MAP. 57PSE 1/10000
			Enemy showed little activity to-day	
			2nd Lieut HART and 1 OR proceeded on leave to-day.	
			The weather was good	[initials]
	9th		Two N.C.O's proceeded to the Machine Gun School at CAMIERS for a course of Instruction.	
			2/Lieut HAMPSHIRE and 3 OR returned from leave	[initials]
			Our machine Guns were active during the night, firing on the Enemy Transport and Enemy M.Guns - one of which was silenced.	
			Details of Priv A Neeley's distinguished conduct on the night of 6th inst were forwarded to Brigade Headquarters to-day on AF W3121	
			Weather is still fine	
	10th "		Enemy shelled our line this morning with Shrapnel and several Rifle Grenades were fired at our Gun position in HAMMERHEAD SAP.	
			6 Gun teams were relieved during the evening	[initials]
			An unserviceable mule was cast to day by order of the D.D.R	
			The weather to day was fine and warm	
	11th "		Enemy are apparently searching for our gun at HAMMER HEAD SAP as numerous Rifle Grenades, nine Trench mortars and 6 Heavy shells were put over beside it this morning	
			Our Machine guns were very active during the night. One fired 500 rounds at a German working party of 60 or 70 men and dispersed them	[initials]
			An arrangement was completed to-day to carry in store one day's rations in preserved meat and biscuits	
			Weather to-day was wet and cold	

1875 Wt. W593/826 1,000,000 4/15 J.B.C. & A. A.D.S.S./Forms/C. 2118.

Instructions regarding War Diaries and Intelligence Summaries are contained in F. S. Regs., Part II. and the Staff Manual respectively. Title Pages will be prepared in manuscript.

WAR DIARY
or
~~INTELLIGENCE SUMMARY~~ 109th Bde Machine Gun Coy
(Erase heading not required.)

Army Form C. 2118

Page 20

Place	Date 1916	Hour	Summary of Events and Information	Remarks and references to Appendices
MARTINSART	APRIL 12th		All guns report a quiet night. R.5 fired one belt at enemy M.G at Q17 b 58.12. R.6 fired at "Stand to" this morning, on enemy trenches. Our patrols & working parties were out most of the night. Weather, wet & cold, trenches very muddy.	REF MAP 57D S.E 1/10.000 AWW
	13th		Numbers of Rifles grenades & trench mortars came over R.1, & into Crater. No damage was done. R.4 fired at Dump & Transport, but ceased early, on account of patrols &c being out. Weather, wet & trenches still very muddy.	AWW
	14th		Generally very quiet. R.4 fired on Dump as usual. Two fresh mounds of chalk are visible on enemy's front line at Q17 b. 8-1. & Q17 b. 6-2. An aeroplane was heard over THIEPVAL WOOD last night at 11 pm. Weather unsettled.	AWW
	15th		Enemy shelled continually yesterday between 10am & 6.30pm, concentrating on front line at THIEPVAL WOOD. Guns R.4. & R.6. had very narrow escapes. At Gun No R.4. a shell burst within a yard, a splinter from it smashed the sentry's bayonet, which was on his rifle. A shell cut down a tree which fell over No R.6. emplacement. Instructions were given to discontinue from these positions for a few nights. Transport was heard going all night at the back of THIEPVAL & a train was heard at Station about 9.pm. Lieut HEWITT was round the trenches with an Officer of the 97th M.G Coy, who are on our right. Weather unsettled & trenches in bad condition.	AWW
	16th		Enemy shelled Crater at Q26a 54.30. all day & sent over showers of Rifle grenades during night. At 7.30am 17th an enemy working party of about 20 men was observed by sentry on R.5 gun at Q18 b. 90.70, he dispersed them with small tripod from parapet. From observation with telescope one man appeared to be hit. Everything else quiet. Trenches in bad condition.	AWW

1875 Wt. W593/826 1,000,000 4/15 J.B.C. & A. A.D.S.S./Forms/C. 2118.

Instructions regarding War Diaries and Intelligence Summaries are contained in F. S. Regs., Part II. and the Staff Manual respectively. Title Pages will be prepared in manuscript.

WAR DIARY
or
~~INTELLIGENCE SUMMARY~~
(Erase heading not required.)

Army Form C. 2118

109th Brigade M. Gun. Company.
Page 21.

Place	Date	Hour	Summary of Events and Information	Remarks and references to Appendices
MARTINSART	APRIL 17th		Enemy fairly quiet, a few shrapnel were sent over about 5 pm yesterday, around no 6 position, no damage was done. Nos. 5 & 6 guns fired on Station & Hamel Trenches, silencing enemy M. G. & disturbing transport.	awd
	18th		Every thing fairly quiet. Enemy have a new quick-firing M. G.	awd.
	19th		Fairly quiet, a little artillery activity by both sides. At 8.15am an enemy working party at Q17 b 3.2 was dispersed by no. B. 6 gun.	awd
	20th		The enemy sent over a lot of heavy trench mortars around GEORGE ST last night between 9 pm & midnight, doing considerable damage. Our trench mortar was blown to pieces & the ammunition supply blown up, the trenches in this district are in a very bad state.	awd
	21st		16 men from Battalions in the Brigade were attached from to-day to the Company for instruction in the Vickers Gun. The enemy did not show much activity. Weather: very wet	[illegible]
	22		The day was fairly quiet but our Artillery commenced a very heavy Bombardment of the Enemy lines opposite THIEPVAL WOOD at 9-20 P.M. It was to cover a raid which was made on the German Salient at R31a 4-2, by the 17th Bn H.L.I. The raid was most successful: 13 prisoners being taken. It was noticed how quickly the Bosh artillery replied to our Bombardment. Weather: good	[illegible]

1875 Wt. W593/826 1,000,000 4/15 J.B.C. & A. A.D.S.S./Forms/C. 2118.

Instructions regarding War Diaries and Intelligence Summaries are contained in F. S. Regs., Part II. and the Staff Manual respectively. Title Pages will be prepared in manuscript.

WAR DIARY
~~or~~
~~INTELLIGENCE SUMMARY~~
(~~Erase heading not required.~~)

109th Bde Mach Gun Coy

Army Form C. 2118

Page 22

Place	Date 1916	Hour	Summary of Events and Information	Remarks and references to Appendices
MARTINSART	APRIL 23		Relief of the teams in the trenches were carried out this evening. The enemy was not very active to-day but our Machine guns were very active after dark and fired on the enemy Transport and on the Station S.W. of BEAUCOURT, with some effect. Weather: very good.	
	24th		Enemy was quiet with the exception of a few Trench Mortars, which were replied to by our Heavy guns. Our Machines were again active against the Enemy Transport when it was reported. Weather very fine	
	25th		A few Rifles Grenades were sent over by the Germans during the morning. One of their Machine Guns became rather troublesome and was taken on by one of ours and silenced. Aeroplanes were busy all day. Weather was fine and warm	
	26th		The enemy was busy with Trench Mortars to-day. In the evening we fired about 750 rounds on the Enemy Transport when it was heard. 500 rounds were fired at a German Working Party and they dispersed. Weather still fine and very warm. The trenches are dry	
	27th		Enemy was unusually active to-day and this evening with Trench Mortars, Machine Guns and Bombs. Our machine guns were active against the Station S.W. of BEAUCOURT.	

1875 Wt. W593/826 1,000,000 4/15 J.B.C. & A. A.D.S.S./Forms/C. 2118.

Instructions regarding War Diaries and Intelligence Summaries are contained in F. S. Regs., Part II. and the Staff Manual respectively. Title Pages will be prepared in manuscript.

WAR DIARY or ~~INTELLIGENCE SUMMARY~~ 109th Bde Machine Gun Coy

(Erase heading not required.)

Army Form C. 2118

Page 23

Place	Date 1916	Hour	Summary of Events and Information	Remarks and references to Appendices
MARTINSART	APRIL 28th		A number of heavy trench Mortars were put over by the Germans to-day, close to one of our Emplacements. We fired a large amount of Ammunition after dusk on Enemy Transport and Machine Guns 2 N.C.O's returned from Course of Instruction at CAMIERS to-day Weather is very fine and warm	[initials]
	29th		The day was quiet but at 11-30 PM the Brigade on our left commenced a heavy Bombardment of the enemy trenches opposite and kept it up for an hour. The German Artillery were slow in replying Later the Germans commenced a heavy Bombardment against the trenches on our right. Our Artillery replied Weather still beautiful and very warm Eight gun teams were relieved to-night	[initials]
	30th		Enemy only sent over a few Trench Mortars to-day otherwise all was quiet. Our Machine Guns were not so active as usual. One of them fired on a German working Party and dispersed it Weather still very fine + warm and the Trenches are very dry	[initials]

1875 Wt. W593/826 1,000,000 4/15 J.B.C. & A. A.D.S.S./Forms/C. 2118.

109th BRIGADE
No. 854
Date 2/6/16.
MACHINE GUN COMPANY

To/
D.A.G.
3rd Echelon G.H.Q.

Enclosed please find War Diary
of the 109th Bde M.G. Coy

E H [illegible] Lieut
COMMANDING
109th BDE. MACHINE GUN COY.

109 MG Coy

Ref map 57D 1/10.000

Vol 2

XXXVI

Confidential.

War Diary

of

109th Bde Machine Gun Company

From 1st May 1916 – To 31st May 1916

(Volume I)

Instructions regarding War Diaries and Intelligence Summaries are contained in F. S. Regs., Part II. and the Staff Manual respectively. Title Pages will be prepared in manuscript.

WAR DIARY of ~~INTELLIGENCE SUMMARY~~ 109th Bde Machine Gun Coy

(Erase heading not required.)

Army Form C. 2118

Page 24

Place	Date 1916	Hour	Summary of Events and Information	Remarks and references to Appendices
MARTINSART	MAY 1st		8 men from each of the Battalions in the Brigade (9th; 10th; and 11th Roy Innis Fus and 14th Royal Irish Rifles) were attached to this Company from to-day for one month's course of Instruction with a view towards having an immediate reserve of trained Machine Gunners in the Brigade During the night our Machine Guns were active against the Enemy trenches and wire N.W of HAMEL and against the BEAUCOURT STATION and Road when Enemy Transport was heard. An enemy Aeroplane dropped a couple of Bombs in MARTINSART WOOD early in the morning The weather was good	[initials]
	2nd		The Enemy was very active to-day with French Mortars and Shrapnel against some of the M.G. Emplacements. Two of our gunners were wounded - one slightly.	[initials]
	3rd	3-30AM	One of our guns dispersed a German working party seen at Q.24 D 9.6, and caused them some casualties. Other Machine Guns were active against the Enemy trenches NW of HAMEL.— French mortar fire and Shrapnel were again directed by the enemy against our Emplacements during the early hours of the morning and again during the afternoon.	[initials]
	4th		Our Machine guns fired intermittently during the early hours on the trenches and wire in front of HAMEL. Enemy was again active to-day with French Mortars &c. Two N C O's and one Driver proceeded on leave to-day. The weather was good	[initials]

1875 Wt. W593/826 1,000,000 4/15 J.B.C. & A. A.D.S.S./Forms/C. 2118.

Instructions regarding War Diaries and Intelligence Summaries are contained in F. S. Regs., Part II. and the Staff Manual respectively. Title Pages will be prepared in manuscript.

WAR DIARY
or
~~INTELLIGENCE~~ ~~SUMMARY~~
(Erase heading not required.)

109th Bde Machine Gun Coy

Army Form C. 2118

Page 25

Place	Date 1916	Hour	Summary of Events and Information	Remarks and references to Appendices
MARTINSART	MAY 5th	4-30AM	An enemy Aeroplane, flying very low, dropped 2 Bombs on the edge of the town killing and wounding some men of the 9th Roy Innis Fus. One of our Mules was killed and also a number of horses and mules belonging to above Battalion. During the early hours - up to "Stand to" this morning - our M. Guns fired about 3000 rounds at intervals on the enemy trenches in front of HAMEL. One belt (250 rounds) was also fired at a Sniper, who was observed endeavouring to take up a position. A few light shells were fired by the enemy into MARTINSART in the afternoon. The relief of our gun teams which should have taken place to night was postponed owing to a Bombardment by our Artillery having been planned. The weather was fine	[initials]
	6th		At midnight last night our Artillery commenced a heavy Bombardment of the enemy lines opposite our right to assist in covering a raid by the 15th Lancashire Fus. The raid was successful, five prisoners being captured. The enemy retaliated very heavily and the HAMMERHEAD SAP was blown in. Our M.G. Emplacement in the Sap was demolished and the gun team along with 7 or 8 men of the Lanc's was buried. One of the gunners - 18674 Priv T. BOTTOMS - who had already dug himself out after being buried in the course of the Bombardment, extricated himself from the débris, and with his entrenching tool then commenced, under a very heavy fire, to dig out the others. He succeeded in rescuing the party and his name has been forwarded for recognition of his gallantry and coolness. The enemy was not very active during to-day. He again fired a few small shells into MARTINSART in the afternoon.	[initials]

1875 Wt. W593/826 1,000,000 4/15 J.B.C. & A. A.D.S.S./Forms/C. 2118.

Instructions regarding War Diaries and Intelligence Summaries are contained in F. S. Regs., Part II. and the Staff Manual respectively. Title Pages will be prepared in manuscript.

WAR DIARY or ~~INTELLIGENCE SUMMARY~~ 109th Bde Machine Gun Coy.

(Erase heading not required.)

Army Form C. 2118

Page 26

Place	Date 1916	Hour	Summary of Events and Information	Remarks and references to Appendices
MARTINSART	MAY 6th		The relief of gun teams, which had been posponed, was carried out to-night The weather was rough. Thunder and Lightening accompanied by heavy showers nearly all day.	JMC
	7th		Our machine gun which was buried in HAMMERHEAD SAP was recovered undamaged early this morning. Enemy was fairly quiet during the day - A few shells were fired into MARTINSART during the afternoon.	
		11.PM	The enemy commenced a very heavy bombardment of the trenches on our right - mostly between HAMMERHEAD SAP and FOXBAR St - The Infantry holding the SAP were compelled to retire and about 45 minutes later our Machine Gun team were also compelled to withdraw owing to the heavy fire. The Bombardment proved to be the preliminary to a raid on our trenches by the enemy, a party of whom about 100 strong entered our trenches and took some prisoners including two men of the Gun team. The N.C.O in charge of the team (18638 Corpl. Miller) was also taken, but when outside our wire he and an officer of the DORSET Regiment showed fight and were bayoneted after a struggle. The confusion caused by this Officer and N.C.O enabled many, who had been captured, to escape. In response to a request from the C.O left Battalion of the Division on our right two of our Machine guns and a party of the 10th ROY. INNIS. FUS. went over and drove the enemy from our lines, killing and wounding a number of them, including one officer, and taking several prisoners also including an Officer. A bombardment by our Artillery had been arranged for 11-45 PM with the object of covering a raid on the Enemy trenches opposite our own Brigade front. The raid was successful	JMC

1875 Wt. W593/826 1,000,000 4/15 J.B.C. & A. A.D.S.S./Forms/C. 2118.

Instructions regarding War Diaries and Intelligence Summaries are contained in F. S. Regs., Part II. and the Staff Manual respectively. Title Pages will be prepared in manuscript.

WAR DIARY
or
~~INTELLIGENCE SUMMARY~~

(*Erase heading not required.*)

109th Bde Machine Gun Coy

Army Form C. 2118

Page 27

Place	Date	Hour	Summary of Events and Information	Remarks and references to Appendices
MARTINSART	1916 MAY 8th		Definite orders were received that this Company will be relieved by the 107th Bde Machine Gun Company to-morrow morning, and that we will move to VARENNES when reliefs are completed.	
			The enemy was quiet to-day from about 4 AM when the bombardments, commenced the previous night, ceased.	
			The men of teams in reserve were engaged in packing and clearing up generally, preparatory to our move	
			The weather was showery	[signature]
	9th	6.30 AM	Machine Gun Emplacements in THIEPVAL WOOD were taken over from us by teams from 107th Bde Machine Gun Coy early this morning.	
		12 noon	The 108th Machine Gun Company took over the billets which we occupied in MARTINSART and we moved out and proceeded to VARENNES at 12-30 PM	
VARENNES		2-30 PM	The Company arrived at VARENNES and took over billets which had been occupied by the 107th Bde M. G. Coy.	
			The afternoon was spent in settling the men in their new quarters	[signature]
			A telegram was received from the G.O.C 32nd Division thanking those concerned for the "very prompt and effective support given to his left Battalion" on the night of the 7th inst. In forwarding the telegram, Brig-Gen T.E. HICKMAN. CB DSO. Commanding the 109th Brigade, congratulated – in a kind message – the Machine Gun Coy and said their conduct reflected credit on the whole Brigade.	
			The weather was much better to-day – very little rain	

1875 Wt. W593/826 1,000,000 4/15 J.B.C. & A. A.D.S.S./Forms/C. 2118.

Instructions regarding War Diaries and Intelligence Summaries are contained in F. S. Regs., Part II. and the Staff Manual respectively. Title Pages will be prepared in manuscript.

WAR DIARY or ~~INTELLIGENCE SUMMARY~~ 109th Bde Machine Gun Coy

(Erase heading not required.)

Army Form C. 2118

Page 28

Place	Date 1916	Hour	Summary of Events and Information	Remarks and references to Appendices
VARENNES	MAY 10th	6 AM	Reveille. To day was occupied with an Inspection of Billets by the C.O: Minute Kit inspections by the Section Officers. and examination of Guns, spare parts and equipment. The weather was fine	[initials]
	11th	6 AM	Reveille. Parades to-day were:- Physical Training; Field Exercises on Dummy Trenches; Advanced Drill; Cleaning & Examination of Guns. A Special Order was issued to-day by the Brig General expressing his "keen appreciation of the behaviour of all ranks whilst in the trenches during the past three months". The order was read to the Company on parade	[initials]
	12th	6 AM	Reveille Parades were from 7AM - 3.30PM and included Physical Training; Field Exercises on Instructional Trenches; Stoppages & "Immediate action" on the Range; Close Order Drill and Cleaning & Examination of Guns. The School of Instruction carried on under the instructors. The weather was good	[initials]
	13th	6 AM	Reveille. Parades for to-day were as above, but very heavy rain fell during the day and it was decided to carry on in Billets with lectures &c. The School of Instruction carried out its usual programme	[initials]
	14th	6 AM	Reveille. Church parades in the morning. In the afternoon the Company proceeded to the Dummy Trenches. Eight men were detailed to attend a Bombing Class at the Brigade Bombing School HARPONVILLE.	

1875 Wt. W593/826 1,000,000 4/15 J.B.C. & A. A.D.S.S./Forms/C. 2118.

Instructions regarding War Diaries and Intelligence Summaries are contained in F. S. Regs., Part II. and the Staff Manual respectively. Title Pages will be prepared in manuscript.

WAR DIARY

~~or~~

~~INTELLIGENCE SUMMARY~~ 109th Bde Machine Gun Coy

(Erase heading not required.)

Army Form C. 2118

Place	Date 1916	Hour	Summary of Events and Information	Remarks and references to Appendices
VARENNES	MAY 15	6AM	Reveille. Parades to-day: Nos 1 & 3 Sections at Field Exercises on Dummy Trenches at CLAIRFAYE Nos 2 & 4 Sections at Firing Practice on the Range School of Instruction as usual	[initials]
	16th	6AM	Reveille: Parades: Physical Training, Instruction on Dummy trenches, and Drill School of Instruction: usual programme	[initials]
	17th	6AM 8.30AM	Reveille. Company paraded at full strength and took part in Brigade Attack practice on the Dummy trenches. The School of Instruction paraded with the Company and acted as ammunition Carriers. One Officer reinforcement (2Lt L.H.CLEVERDON) reported to-day for duty The weather was good	[initials]
	18th	6AM	Reveille. Parades: { Nos 3 & 4 Sections at Field Exercises on the Dummy Trenches { Nos 1 & 2 " at Firing practice on the Range and Drill weather good	[initials]
	19th	6AM 8.30AM 4PM	Reveille: The Company paraded and engaged in Brigade training on the Manoeuvre ground A Brigade Boxing Tournament took place and later the 36th Divisional "Follies" gave a show which was much enjoyed – Many of those present hadn't seen anything like Pierrots for eight or nine months The weather was very fine and warm	[initials]

1875 Wt. W593/826 1,000,000 4/15 J.B.C. & A. A.D.S.S./Forms/C. 2118.

Instructions regarding War Diaries and Intelligence Summaries are contained in F. S. Regs., Part II. and the Staff Manual respectively. Title Pages will be prepared in manuscript.

WAR DIARY or ~~INTELLIGENCE SUMMARY~~

109th Bde Machine Gun Coy

(Erase heading not required.)

Army Form C. 2118

Place	Date 1916	Hour	Summary of Events and Information	Remarks and references to Appendices
	MAY	6 AM	Reveille	
VARENNES	20th		Parades to-day included Gun drill Firing practice on the Range and Lectures by Section Officers.	[initials]
			The weather was good	
	21st	6 AM	Reveille	
			Parades to day were for Divine Service	[initials]
			The weather was fine	
	22nd	6 AM	Reveille	
		7.45 AM	The Company including the class of Instruction paraded at full strength and proceeded to the Dummy trenches to take part in Brigade Attack Practice. Smoke was largely used and Aeroplanes co-operated with the Brigade.	[initials]
			The weather was fine and warm	
	23rd	6 AM	Reveille	
		7.45 AM	The Company and class of Instruction paraded and took part in a repetition of yesterdays Attack practice. Aeroplanes again co-operated with the Brigade	[initials]
			A draft of eight men arrived to day as a reinforcement	
			The following appointments were made to-day 1 Lance Sergeant 5 Lance Corporal (paid) to complete Establishment — Authority AG's Circular A/695 d/18.5.16	
			The weather is still fine and warm	

1875 Wt. W593/826 1,000,000 4/15 J.B.C. & A. A.D.S.S./Forms/C. 2118.

Army Form C. 2118

Instructions regarding War Diaries and Intelligence Summaries are contained in F. S. Regs., Part II. and the Staff Manual respectively. Title Pages will be prepared in manuscript.

WAR DIARY
or
~~INTELLIGENCE SUMMARY~~
(Erase heading not required.)

109 Bde Machine Gun Coy — Page 31

Place	Date 1916	Hour	Summary of Events and Information	Remarks and references to Appendices
VARENNES	MAY 24	6 AM	Reveille. Parades for to-day { Physical Training, Instruction on the Dummy Trenches, Gun Drill &c / Class of Instruction on the Range	
		10.30AM	Wire received from Brigade H.Q. "Brigade will assemble at 12 noon on ground S of CLAIRFAYE." Accordingly orders were issued for the Company to close on that place.	[initials]
		12 noon	The Brigade was formed up in Masse and addressed by Brig Gen T.E. HICKMAN CB DSO preparatory to his handing over the Brigade to Brig Gen R.G SHUTER DSO. In the afternoon the Programme of Training was continued. The weather was fine	
	25th	6 AM	Reveille: Parades to-day included Physical Training, Close Order Drill, Gun Drill, Indication & Recognition of Targets, Semaphore &c. School of Instruction had a similar programme. An addition has been made to the Establishment of 1 Spare Riding horse: 2 Spare draught horses and 1 Spare Driver; The weather to-day was good	[initials]
	26th	6 AM	Reveille	
		8 AM	The company, including Class of Instruction, proceeded to the Manoeuvre Ground and took part in Brigade Attack Practice. The weather was good	[initials]
	27th	6 AM	Reveille.	
		8 AM	Company, including Class of Instruction, proceeded to Manoeuvre ground to witness a Demonstration by the Stokes Gun. After the Demonstration the Company was inspected by the Brig General, who expressed his appreciation of the clean and smart appearance of the parade. In the afternoon Sports were held and this Company had the honour of winning the Brigade Relay race. The weather was fine and warm	[initials]

1875 Wt. W593/826 1,000,000 4/15 J.B.C. & A. A.D.S.S./Forms/C. 2118.

Instructions regarding War Diaries and Intelligence Summaries are contained in F. S. Regs., Part II. and the Staff Manual respectively. Title Pages will be prepared in manuscript.

WAR DIARY
or
~~INTELLIGENCE~~ SUMMARY

109th Brigade Machine Gun Coy

(Erase heading not required.)

Army Form C. 2118

Page 32

Place	Date	Hour	Summary of Events and Information	Remarks and references to Appendices
	1916			
VARENNES	MAY 28th	6AM	Reveille Parades to-day were for Divine Service Orders were received last night regarding Brigade move back into the line on 31st Instructions were issued by Brigade to-day that the 32 men on Course of Instruction were to continue for another week. The weather was fine.	[initials]
	29th	6AM 7.30AM	Reveille The Company proceeded to the manoeuvre ground and Co-operated with the Battalions of the Brigade in their independent practice of the attack over the Dummy Trenches. The Class of Instruction remained at their Studies. In the afternoon the Company was marched to the Div Baths at ACHEUX as arranged but the Baths were closed up, - Some heavy Germans shells having landed in their vicinity during the day To-day Orders were received cancelling the Brigade move.	[initials]
	30th	6AM	Reveille. Parades to-day included Close Order Drill and a usual programme of Machine Gunners Training School of Instruction carried out their usual programme The weather was fine	[initials]
	31st	6AM	Reveille: The Company spent the day at Firing practice on a Range which has been allotted to us. The weather was fine and warm	[initials]

109th Brigade.
36th Division.

109th BRIGADE MACHINE GUN COMPANY

JUNE 1916

Instructions regarding War Diaries and Intelligence Summaries are contained in F. S. Regs., Part II. and the Staff Manual respectively. Title Pages will be prepared in manuscript.

WAR DIARY ~~or~~ ~~INTELLIGENCE SUMMARY~~ 109th Bde Machine Gun Coy

(Erase heading not required.)

Army Form C. 2118

Place	Date 1916	Hour	Summary of Events and Information	Remarks and references to Appendices
VARENNES	JUNE 1st	6AM	Reveille. Parades as per Training Syllabus rendered to Brigade H.Q. A reinforcement draft of 9 men reported to-day for duty. Weather good	[initials]
	2nd	6AM	Reveille. The Company was engaged to-day in a tactical exercise. The School of Instruction carried out its programme of training. The weather was good	[initials]
	3rd	6AM	Reveille. Parades were as per Company Training Syllabus	[initials]
	4th	6AM	Reveille. During the morning:- Divine Service. In the afternoon:- Lecture to the N.C.O's on Tactics	[initials]
	5th	6AM	Reveille. The Company took part in a Brigade Attack practice over the dummy trenches at CLAIRFAYE. Examinations were held for those undergoing Instruction. ~~The~~ CAPTAIN McCONACHIE who proceeded on special leave from 25th May returned to-day and resumed Command of the Company. — Lieut E.H. CLOKEY acted as C.O. in his absence. Weather was showery	[initials]

1875 Wt. W593/826 1,000,000 4/15 J.B.C. & A. A.D.S.S./Forms/C. 2118.

Instructions regarding War Diaries and Intelligence Summaries are contained in F. S. Regs., Part II. and the Staff Manual respectively. Title Pages will be prepared in manuscript.

WAR DIARY
or
~~INTELLIGENCE SUMMARY~~

(Erase heading not required.) 109th Bde Machine Gun Coy

Army Form C. 2118

Page 34

Place	Date 1916	Hour	Summary of Events and Information	Remarks and references to Appendices
VARENNES	June 6th	6 AM	Reveille. The Company proceeded to the Range to-day for Firing Practice which had to be abandoned owing to very heavy rain. The remainder of the day was spent by the men in drying their clothing which was very necessary as all blankets have been withdrawn	[initials]
	7th	6 AM	Reveille The Company took part in a Divisional scheme on the Corps Training Area, to-day. The Class of Instruction was further examined Recommendations for the Military Medal for two of our men were forwarded	[initials]
	8th	6 AM	Reveille The Company including those attached for Instruction took part in a Brigade attack Practice to-day The weather: showery	[initials]
	9th	6 AM	Reveille. Eight men from each Battalion of the Brigade having completed a Course of Instruction were returned to their units to-day. We now have four men from each Battalion still attached to the Company The Company were engaged in a tactical exercise on the Corps Training Area during the day. A man who joined the Company with a draft was returned to the Base to-day as being unlikely to become an efficient machine Gunner The weather was showery	[initials]

1875 Wt. W593/826 1,000,000 4/15 J.B.C. & A. A.D.S.S./Forms/C. 2118.

Instructions regarding War Diaries and Intelligence Summaries are contained in F. S. Regs., Part II. and the Staff Manual respectively. Title Pages will be prepared in manuscript.

WAR DIARY
or
~~INTELLIGENCE~~ SUMMARY
(Erase heading not required.)

109th Bde Machine Gun Coy

Army Form C. 2118

Place	Date 1916	Hour	Summary of Events and Information	Remarks and references to Appendices
VARENNES	June 10th	6AM	Reveille. The Company took part in Brigade attack practice to-day The weather was very wet	[initials]
	11th	6AM	Reveille. Parades were for Divine Service this morning 18726 Priv. G. MONRO was to-day recommended for the Military Medal for conspicuous conduct in the trenches	[initials]
	12th	6AM	Reveille. To-day was again spent in practising the attack The weather was showery	[initials]
	13th	6AM	Reveille. The Company carried out a programme of training The weather was wet	[initials]
	14th	6AM	Reveille. Company training to-day.	[initials]
		11PM	According to orders time was advanced 60 minutes.	
	15th	5AM (new time)	Reveille.	
		6.30AM	The Company proceeded to Brigade Rendezvous and afterwards practised the attack (on the Corps training area) in conjunction with the 96th Brigade of the 32nd Division The weather was good	[initials]

1875 Wt. W593/826 1,000,000 4/15 J.B.C. & A. A.D.S.S./Forms/C. 2118.

Instructions regarding War Diaries and Intelligence Summaries are contained in F. S. Regs., Part II. and the Staff Manual respectively. Title Pages will be prepared in manuscript.

WAR DIARY
or
~~INTELLIGENCE SUMMARY~~

(Erase heading not required.) 109th Bde Machine Gun Coy

Army Form C. 2118

Page 36

Place	Date 1916	Hour	Summary of Events and Information	Remarks and references to Appendices
VARENNES	June 16th	6 AM	Reveille. Company was engaged all day on the Manoeuvre ground. In the evening the Company marched to CLAIRFAYE and witnessed a performance of "the Follies". The weather was good	[initials]
	17th	6 AM	Reveille. Physical Training; Gas Helmet Drill and Gas Helmet Inspection, were on in the morning. In the Afternoon – Football. weather good	[initials]
	18th		Sunday Divine Services weather good	[initials]
	19th	6 AM	Reveille. Half the Company proceeded to the range for Firing practice with their Guns and Rifles. The other half practised Bombing, Rifle Drill & Bayonet Exercises. weather good	[initials]
	20th	6 AM	Reveille. Sections paraded to-day for Gun Drill, Mechanism, Belt Filling &c and minute inspection of Kit & Equipment.	[initials]
		6 PM	Nos 1 & 2 Sections paraded and proceeded fully equipped with their Guns &c to AVELUY WOOD where they bivouaced for the night with orders to carry out work in THIEPVAL WOOD on to-morrow. weather Good.	

1875 Wt. W593/826 1,000,000 4/15 J.B.C. & A. A.D.S.S./Forms/C. 2118.

Instructions regarding War Diaries and Intelligence Summaries are contained in F. S. Regs., Part II. and the Staff Manual respectively. Title Pages will be prepared in manuscript.

WAR DIARY
or
~~INTELLIGENCE~~ SUMMARY
(Erase heading not required.)

Army Form C. 2118

Page 37

Place	Date	Hour	Summary of Events and Information	Remarks and references to Appendices
	1916 June			
VARENNES	21st	6AM	Reveille. Orders having been received to move into THIEPVAL WOOD to-night; the day was occupied in packing up. No 1 & 2 Section returned after finishing emplacements in THIEPVAL WOOD. In the afternoon the Company paraded and marched via MARTINSART to THIEPVAL WOOD. The Guns Ammunition &c were taken in the Limbered Waggons as far as BLACKHORSE ROAD and were carried from there into the trenches by the teams.	JWR
THIEPVAL WOOD	22nd		The Company entered the trenches fully equipped, without suffering any casualties, and occupied the Assembly Trenches which had been allotted. Six Gun teams went to positions which had been prepared for bringing indirect fire to bear on the German Trenches during the Bombardment.	JWR
"	23rd		Early this morning the Enemy shelled the Assembly trenches with Heavy H.E. – Several of our men were buried, a few wounded and one Machine Gun was destroyed. Our men were moved to another position in the wood which we hoped would be safer. The weather was good.	JWR
	24th		The Bombardment, preliminary to our proposed attack, commenced this morning and the troops were greatly encouraged by the sound of so many of our Heavies going over. The Bombardment was steady during the day and much to our surprise the Enemy made a very feeble reply during the morning but later in the day he became more active. We had four men wounded. During the night we carried out the scheme of Indirect firing previously arranged	JWR

1875 Wt. W593/826 1,000,000 4/15 J.B.C. & A. A.D.S.S./Forms/C. 2118.

Instructions regarding War Diaries and Intelligence Summaries are contained in F. S. Regs., Part II. and the Staff Manual respectively. Title Pages will be prepared in manuscript.

WAR DIARY of ~~INTELLIGENCE SUMMARY~~

(Erase heading not required.) 109th Bde Machine Gun Coy

Army Form C. 2118

Page 38

Place	Date	Hour	Summary of Events and Information Ref Map 57D SE 1/20.000	Remarks and references to Appendices
THIEPVAL WOOD	1916 June 25th		The Bombardment continued and the Enemy's Artillery fire was stronger to-day. He was also very active with Trench Mortars and demolished our Gun Emplacement at R25a 30.70 but another position was occupied by us and the Night firing scheme was carried out without interruption. It was observed that our bombardment has not yet silenced the Machine Guns in THIEPVAL. Our casualties in the Company to-day were 1 killed 2 wounded. The weather was showry	[illegible]
	26th		To-day the Enemy retaliated vigorously to our Bombardment. A length of trench near our Gun emplacement at Q30b 90.00 was blown in by Heavies. Our front line was shelled with Shrapnel and GORDON CASTLE with Heavies during the day and especially in the Afternoon, when Gas was emitted from our Front Line – the wind being favourable. A back draught caused some of our Gas to blow back and it filled one of our gun Emplacements. The gunners however were wearing their Box Respirators and continued firing without suffering any ill effects. The enemy's Machine guns were again active The usual Night firing scheme was carried out. Our casualties in the Company were 3 wounded. The weather was wet.	[illegible]

1875 Wt. W593/826 1,000,000 4/15 J.B.C. & A. A.D.S.S./Forms/C. 2118.

Army Form C. 2118

Instructions regarding War Diaries and Intelligence Summaries are contained in F. S. Regs., Part II. and the Staff Manual respectively. Title Pages will be prepared in manuscript.

WAR DIARY or of ~~INTELLIGENCE SUMMARY~~

(Erase heading not required.) 109th Bde Machine Gun Coy — Page 39

Place	Date 1916 June	Hour	Summary of Events and Information	Remarks and references to Appendices
THIEPVAL WOOD	27th		Enemy retaliation to our continued Bombardment was again vigorous. He shelled the wood with Heavies, Sharpnel and Lachrymatory shells, searching it very thoroughly. Our gun emplacement at W end of ROSS Street was destroyed but no damage was done to the gun or team. The scheme of night firing was carried out as usual. As on other days there was a period of intense Bombardment by our artillery. Our casualties in the Company were 4 wounded. The weather was showery.	[initials]
	28th		Our Bombardment continued and the Enemy's Reply seemed to be much stronger. Our gun emplacement in CHATEAU Street was destroyed by shell fire as was also the new emplacement built near W end of ROSS Street to replace the one destroyed yesterday – In the latter case the members of the team were buried, three being wounded. The Personnel of the Company is beginning to feel the strain of the stay in the trenches during the past seven days and many show outward signs of being greatly shaken, especially after hearing, during the afternoon, that the attack which was to take place tomorrow was postponed for two days. The teams which had suffered most were sent back to MARTINSART this afternoon for a little Rest. The night firing was carried out by our guns as usual. Our casualties today were 3 wounded. The weather was showery.	[initials]

1875 Wt. W593/826 1,000,000 4/15 J.B.C. & A. A.D.S.S./Forms/C. 2118.

Instructions regarding War Diaries and Intelligence Summaries are contained in F. S. Regs., Part II. and the Staff Manual respectively. Title Pages will be prepared in manuscript.

WAR DIARY or ~~INTELLIGENCE SUMMARY~~

(Erase heading not required.) 109th Bde Machine Gun Company

Army Form C. 2118

Page 40

Place	Date 1916	Hour	Summary of Events and Information	Remarks and references to Appendices
THIEPVAL WOOD	June 29		Our Bombardment was continued and the Enemy retaliated strongly during the day with Heavies Shrapnel and Lachrymatory shells. At dawn this morning he put a barrage of Shrapnel on our front line. Early this morning Divisional Order No 39 was issued – 7AM – to the effect that Zero had been postponed for 48 hours. To-day was to be known as Y1 day; to-morrow Y2 day and July 1st as Z day – the day of the attack. Casualties Nil.	[initials]
	30th		Enemy shelled the WOOD this morning with a large number of Heavy shells but it was noticed he did not put a Shrapnel Barrage on our front line as usual. During the day and afternoon the Enemy put a large number of Heavies into the Wood and was also active with Lachrymatory shells. In the afternoon the teams which had been out in MARTINSART for a rest returned to the Wood and by 9-30PM all the teams were in the positions allotted to them for the attack, with the exception of those teams doing Night firing – It was arranged that they should fire as usual and take up their positions at Day light. Our casualties to-day (in the Company) were 2/Lieut J.P. HAMPSHIRE Shell-shock and 2 other ranks wounded. The attack is to take place in the morning and "Everybody's Happy"	[initials]

1875 Wt. W593/826 1,000,000 4/15 I.B.C. & A. A.D.S.S./Forms/C. 2118.

36th Division.

109th Brigade.

109th BRIGADE MACHINE GUN COMPANY

JULY 1916

Instructions regarding War Diaries and Intelligence Summaries are contained in F. S. Regs., Part II. and the Staff Manual respectively. Title pages will be prepared in manuscript.

WAR DIARY
or
~~INTELLIGENCE SUMMARY.~~
(*Erase heading not required.*) 109 Machine Gun Coy

Army Form C. 2118.

Page 41

Place	Date	Hour	Summary of Events and Information	Remarks and references to Appendices
Gordon Castle Thiepval Wood	1/7/16		The attack on the enemy trenches commenced today, and beneath I give a copy of the Company Operations issued the previous evening 30-6-16 Operation Orders, by Captn W. McConachie commanding 109th Brigade Machine Gun Coy 30/1/16 Information (a) The company will take part in a general offensive tomorrow Saturday, at an hour which will be issued later. (b) The 96th Brigade of the 32nd Division will attack on our right and the 108th Brigade on our left (c) The right boundary of the 109th Brigade will be a line drawn from the N.E corner of THIEPVAL WOOD to a point (R 20 C. 83.20) 100 yards S. of LISNASKEA (R 20 C 7.4) (d) The left boundary of the Brigade will be a line drawn from the Junction of trenches Q 24/2 (Q 24 D 7.1) near No 3 Emplacement to a point about R 20 A 6.2 Desposition of the Company. Two guns will be attached to each of the four Battalion in the Brigade as under, and will receive orders from the C.Os of those Battalions	Ref Map 57D S.E 1/20000

1577 Wt. W10791/1773 500,000 1/15 D. D. & L. A.D.S.S./Forms/C. 2118.

Instructions regarding War Diaries and Intelligence Summaries are contained in F. S. Regs., Part II. and the Staff Manual respectively. Title pages will be prepared in manuscript.

WAR DIARY
or
~~INTELLIGENCE SUMMARY.~~
(Erase heading not required.) 109th Machine Gun Coy

Army Form C. 2118.

Page 42

Place	Date	Hour	Summary of Events and Information	Remarks and references to Appendices
			Company Orders Continued	
Gordon Castle, Thiepval Wood	1/7/16		Nos 3 & 4 teams under 2nd Lieut. W. Edinborough to the 9th Royal Inniskilling Fusiliers	
			Nos 6 & 8 teams under 2nd Lieut. CLEVERDON to the 10th R. Innis. Fus.	
			Nos 9, 10 teams under 2nd Lieut. HART to the 11th R. Innis. Fus.	
			Nos 11 & 12 teams under Sergt HALLIDAY to the 14th Royal Irish Rifles.	
			Those teams will report to the C.Os of their respective Battalions, two hours before Zero, and will make themselves acquaint with his wishes as early as possible.	
			Nos 1 & 2 teams under Lieut HEWITT, will assemble with the right rear company of the 9th R Innis. Fus and will proceed with them to LISNASKEA and become part of the garrison of that point	
			Nos 5 & 7 teams under Lieut WAKLEY will assemble between the front ranks of the two rear companies of the 10th R. Innis. Fus. (24.25 Assembly trench) and will go forward with them to DUNGANNON (R 20.A. 4.1.) and become part of the Garrison	
			Nos 13 & 14 teams under 2nd Lieut WEDGEWOOD and	
			Nos 15 & 16 teams under Lieut CLOKEY will be reserve guns and will remain	

1577 Wt. W10791/1773 500,000 1/15 D. D. & L. A.D.S.S./Forms/C. 2118.

Instructions regarding War Diaries and Intelligence Summaries are contained in F. S. Regs., Part II. and the Staff Manual respectively. Title pages will be prepared in manuscript.

WAR DIARY
or
~~INTELLIGENCE~~ SUMMARY.
(Erase heading not required.) 109th Machine Gun Coy

Army Form C. 2118.

Page 43

Place	Date	Hour	Summary of Events and Information	Remarks and references to Appendices
			Company Orders Continued	
Gordon Castle. Thiepval Wood	1/7/16		in their present positions (SUTHERLAND AVENUE) (Q36A7.7) until 15 minutes before zero when they will move into position behind the rear Battalions. They will follow the rear Battalions via Paisley Avenue & Inniskilling Av. Nos 13 & 14 teams going to the CRUCIFIX (R19D9.2) where they will form part of the Garrison, and Nos 15, 16 going to B15, where they will consolidate (R19D4.6) and be reserve guns.	
			Carriers. Each Battalion will supply 32 men to act as carriers, each gun team will then have eight carriers. Carriers for Nos 1. 2. 3 & 4 Sections will come from the 9th 10th 11th R. Innis Fus and 14th R. Irish Rifles respectively.	
			Company Details. The Coy Sergt Major, Reserves and R.A.M.C. men will go with Nos 15 & 16 teams under Lieut CLOKEY.	
			The Artificer, Storeman, and Signallers will remain at GORDON CASTLE (Q30.D.1.8) until further orders.	
			The Artificer and Storeman will be responsible for all Stores left there.	
			The Attack. The true bearing of the direction of Attack is 69°.	
			The teams and their carriers will keep in groups as long as possible.	

1577 Wt. W10791/1773 500,000 1/15 D. D. & L. A.D.S.S./Forms/C. 2118.

Instructions regarding War Diaries and Intelligence Summaries are contained in F. S. Regs., Part II. and the Staff Manual respectively. Title pages will be prepared in manuscript.

WAR DIARY
or
~~INTELLIGENCE SUMMARY.~~

(Erase heading not required.) 109th Machine Gun Coy

Army Form C. 2118.

Place	Date	Hour	Summary of Events and Information	Remarks and references to Appendices
			Company Orders	
			The Attack continued	
Gordon Castle. Thiepval Wood	1/7/16		They will keep in the same position in relation to the Infantry as at the commencement of the attack. In the event of the Infantry being held up the teams will get into action in such a position that the advancing Infantry will not mask the fire of their guns	
			When the teams reach the objective, they will at once mount gun and if necessary bring it into action so as to allow the Infantry to have a free hand to consolidate the position	
			Teams appointed to a strong position must remain there at all costs and use the guns boldly.	
			When the Battalions arrive at their objective the teams attached to them should attempt to find positions - such as shell holes - well out in front of the trench being dug.	
			If they get from 100 to 150 yards in front they stand a good chance of escaping shell fire which is bound to be directed on the Infantry at work	
			Teams in such positions should remember the Machine Gunner's Maxim	

Instructions regarding War Diaries and Intelligence Summaries are contained in F. S. Regs., Part II. and the Staff Manual respectively. Title pages will be prepared in manuscript.

WAR DIARY
or
~~INTELLIGENCE SUMMARY.~~

(Erase heading not required.) 109 Machine Gun Coy

Army Form C. 2118.

Page 45

Place	Date	Hour	Summary of Events and Information	Remarks and references to Appendices
			Company Orders	
			The attack continued	
Gordon Castle. Thiepval Wood	1/7/16		Maxim. "Reserve your fire for a suitable target."	
			Guns in strong points should take on targets at long ranges.	
			Some time after 2.38 (after Zero) the 107th Brigade will pass through our lines and attack the D Line. Every effort must be made to support them with covering fire and it may be necessary for teams to move to a flank to give such assistance.	
			Company Headquarters. It is hoped to make B15 Company H.Qtrs and messages for reserves should be sent via that point	
			Ammunition. The Brigade Bombing Officer is arranging to bring S.A.A. to the enemy front trench (A line) and a dump will be established at the Crucifix. S.A.A. for this dump will be brought from our line via St PIERRE DIVION-THIEPVAL ROAD to the cross roads N.E. of HAMMERHEAD SAP and thence by the road to the CRUCIFIX. Team Commanders will send back their Carriers via this route but the N.C.O. or Private in charge of carriers must be competent. If Carriers dont come back in a reasonable time, team commanders will make enquiries. Advanced Dumps have been established in our front and Service trenches in THIEPVAL WOOD	

Instructions regarding War Diaries and Intelligence Summaries are contained in F. S. Regs., Part II. and the Staff Manual respectively. Title pages will be prepared in manuscript.

WAR DIARY
or
~~INTELLIGENCE SUMMARY~~.
(Erase heading not required.) 109th Machine Gun Coy

Army Form C. 2118.

Place	Date	Hour	Summary of Events and Information	Remarks and references to Appendices
			Company Orders	
Gordon Castle: Thiepval Wood.	1/7/16		Equipment of Teams. Teams will carry forward with them:- Gun Tripod First Aid Case, Spare Parts Box, Condenser, 4000 S.A.A. in Belts, 1000 rounds in Box, Two gallon tin of Water, 3 shovels & 2 Picks, Very Pistol & Ammunition. O.C. Sections will inspect above equipment and in addition see that every man has a box respirator, Gas Helmet, First Aid Dressing, Identity disc, Full Water Bottle, 2 Bombs and 3 Sandbags.	
Communications			Teams will send messages back through the Infantry to whom they are attached and only urgent messages will be sent by messenger from the teams.	
			Wounded. It must be impressed on all ranks that on no account will any one fall out to take wounded men to the rear.	
			Stragglers. Any man getting lost must make for B15. In event of a gun being destroyed the team will go to the same place.	
			Rations. Rations for A day &c will be sent to the HAMEL-THIEPVAL ROAD near the Mill. Teams will send their rations parties to B15 on Z/A Night. O.C. B15 will send an N.C.O. and man to Lancashire Dump to guide Transport and Ration Parties to the Mill above mentioned.	
			Signed [illegible] Captn Comdg. 109th Machine Gun Coy	[initials]

T2134. Wt. W708-776. 500000. 4/15. Sir J. C. & S.

Instructions regarding War Diaries and Intelligence Summaries are contained in F. S. Regs., Part II. and the Staff Manual respectively. Title pages will be prepared in manuscript.

WAR DIARY
or
~~INTELLIGENCE~~ SUMMARY.
(*Erase heading not required.*) 109th Machine Gun Coy.

Army Form C. 2118.

Place	Date	Hour	Summary of Events and Information	Remarks and references to Appendices
Gordon Castle Thiepval Wood	1/7/16		During the night all the Infantry of our Division (36th) got into their Assembly Trenches with very few casualties. Our Machine Guns fired as usual all night and after daybreak, they and their carriers, joined the Platoons they were to advance with. Contrary to the usual practice, the enemy didn't put a barrage of fire on our wire this morning. Until the attack, the enemy artillery was rather quieter than usual. It looked as if he expected the attack and was holding his guns in readiness. During the night we were informed Zero would be 7.30 a.m. The final intense bombardment commenced about 6.20 am. It was certainly the heaviest we had heard. At first the enemy artillery didn't make a very vigorous reply but about Zero he was very active. At 7.20 a.m. the whole Division got out of their Assembly trenches and commenced moving forward into no mans land. Almost at once a enemy machine Gun on the north side of the Ancre opened fire. At 7.28 a.m. there was a sudden heavy burst of	[initials]

T2134. Wt. W708—776. 500000. 4/15. Sir J. C. & S.

Instructions regarding War Diaries and Intelligence Summaries are contained in F. S. Regs., Part II. and the Staff Manual respectively. Title pages will be prepared in manuscript.

WAR DIARY
or
~~INTELLIGENCE SUMMARY~~.

(*Erase heading not required.*) 109th Machine Gun Coy

Army Form C. 2118.

Place	Date	Hour	Summary of Events and Information	Remarks and references to Appendices
Thiepval Wood and German trenches N.E	1/4/16		~~machine~~ gun fire from Thiepval ~~Wood~~ village on our right The troops on the right suffered very badly from this fire and the right Division (32nd) never got into the enemy trenches. The 29th Division on our left didn't get much further than their own wire. Our own Division went straight ahead and got to their objectives but suffered very heavily in no man's land.	
			As this isn't a history of the Division, I'll confine it to the movements of each gun as far as we know.	
			Teams Nos 1, 2 3 & 16 with their officers Lieut H ~~Hewitt~~ HEWITT & 2nd Lt N. EDINBOROUGH were completely wiped out in no mans land. A heavy shell burst over No 10 team, in no mans land, killing all the team except Cpl Porter, who was wounded, and destroying the gun. No 4 team got into the enemy trenches with two men but only one belt box and no tripod. This gun went on to LISNASKEA but wasn't able to do much work with only one belt. About midday it was destroyed by shell fire.	
			2nd Lieut WEDGWOOD and his Sergt Owens were killed in our own wire by machine	[initials]

T2134. Wt. W708—776. 500000. 4/15. Sir J. C. & S.

Instructions regarding War Diaries and Intelligence Summaries are contained in F. S. Regs., Part II. and the Staff Manual respectively. Title pages will be prepared in manuscript.

WAR DIARY
or
~~INTELLIGENCE SUMMARY.~~
(Erase heading not required.)

109th Machine Gun Coy

Army Form C. 2118.

Page 49

Place	Date	Hour	Summary of Events and Information	Remarks and references to Appendices
Thiepval Wood and German Trenches N.E.	1/7/16		machine gun fire and 2nd Lt HART was wounded but managed to go on. The rest of the teams got into the enemy trenches with a few casualties but lost the most of the Ammunition Carriers. Nos 5.6.7.8 went on to the third line and took up positions there. Unfortunately No 8 went on with the 107 Brigade and the gun was destroyed by shell fire in the GRANDCOURT - THIEPVAL Road but the two remaining members of the team returned and joined No 6 team. No 12 team also went on to the 4th Line with the 107 Brigade and under L. Cpl FISHER, did some very good work there. He caught the enemy coming up the sunken road from GRANDCOURT and drove them back with very heavy casualties. About midday he came back with the 107 Brigade and took up a position in a shell hole in front of the 3rd line. Although wounded when coming back he remained in this position until dark and helped considerably in driving back counter-attacks, using all his ammunition and all the infantry could spare him	[illegible initials]

T2134. Wt. W708—776. 500000. 4/15. Sir J. C. & S.

Instructions regarding War Diaries and Intelligence Summaries are contained in F. S. Regs., Part II. and the Staff Manual respectively. Title pages will be prepared in manuscript.

WAR DIARY
or of
~~INTELLIGENCE SUMMARY.~~
(Erase heading not required.) 109 Machine Gun Coy

Army Form C. 2118.

Page 50

Place	Date	Hour	Summary of Events and Information	Remarks and references to Appendices
Thiepval Wood and German trenches N.E.	1/7/16		All the other guns got to their objectives and Lieut CLOKEY took charge at B15. When he heard how many guns we had lost on the right flank, he sent No 6 gun under 2nd Lt CLAVERDON up to that flank. Lieut Wakley also went up to this flank but was severely wounded on the way and had to make the best of his way back. Shortly after, 2nd Lt CLAVERDON was wounded and Lieut CLOKEY was now the only M.G. officer left. In addition to taking charge of our own guns, he took charge of guns belonging to other companies who had lost their officers and later on in the evening he collected and reorganized any infantry in his vicinity.	
			Our troops held the third line until dark but after a heavy bombardment we were bombed out, but still held the second line. During the afternoon, we were attacked from the flanks as well as the front and had heavy casualties.	
			During the whole day it was impossible to get any messages over no man's land. The enemy machine guns in Thiepval	[initials]

T2134. Wt. W708-776. 500000. 4/15. Sir J. C. & S.

Instructions regarding War Diaries and Intelligence Summaries are contained in F. S. Regs., Part II. and the Staff Manual respectively. Title pages will be prepared in manuscript.

WAR DIARY
or
~~INTELLIGENCE~~ ~~SUMMARY.~~

(*Erase heading not required.*) 109th Machine Gun Coy

Army Form C. 2118.

Page 51

Place	Date	Hour	Summary of Events and Information	Remarks and references to Appendices
Thiepval	1/7/16		village kept up such an accurate fire that nothing could live there.	
Wood			About 6.0 p.m we got some messages back but unfortunately had no	
and			reinforcements to send over. About 8.0 p.m a brigade of the 49th Division	
German			got orders to reinforce and sent over two companies.	
trenches			Heavy fighting continued all night. Unfortunately some officer gave	
N.E	2/7/16		the order for all our Brigade to retire about 2.0 p.m. A little before	
			this Lieut CLOKEY managed to get back to report the situation to the	
			BRIGADE and get orders. He was so exhausted that he couldn't make	
			his way back to the German trenches.	
		2.0 a.m	The fresh troops of the 49th Division were now taking the trenches over	
			and our infantry retired to THIEPVAL WOOD. With our few remaining	
			guns and men we held positions in the front line until midday	
			Our total Casualties were 4 officers killed. Lieut HEWITT and	
			2nd Lieuts HART. WEDGWOOD. + EDINBOROUGH. wounded Lieut WAKLEY and	
			2 Lt CLAVERDON and 2nd Lt HAMPSHIRE. shell shock.	
			Killed. wounded and Missing in other ranks. 88. and 11 Guns lost.	[initials]

T2134. Wt. W708—776. 500000. 4/15. Sir J. C. & S.

Army Form C. 2118

WAR DIARY
of
~~INTELLIGENCE SUMMARY~~
(Erase heading not required.) 109th Bde Machine Gun Coy

Page 52

Instructions regarding War Diaries and Intelligence Summaries are contained in F. S. Regs., Part II. and the Staff Manual respectively. Title Pages will be prepared in manuscript.

Place	Date 1916	Hour	Summary of Events and Information	Remarks and references to Appendices
THIEPVAL WOOD	July 2nd		All available men were collected and a roll called The gun stores etc were collected also and stored at GORDON CASTLE Orders were received for Our Brigade to move out of the WOOD – The Company was to proceed to MARTINSART WOOD and go into Huts.	[initials]
MARTINSART WOOD		7PM	The Company, with it's strength sadly reduced, arrived in MARTINSART WOOD and took over Huts. The men can be seen proudly strutting about with Bosh Helmets on. The weather to-day was good.	[initials]
–	3rd		Orders were received for the Coy to move to HEDAUVILLE at 3PM	[initials]
HEDAUVILLE		5PM	The Company with Transport arrived at HEDAUVILLE and took over Huts The weather was showery in the evening	
	4th	10AM	The Company paraded with the remainder of the 109th Brigade for inspection by the GOC 36th Division. In his address the GOC expressed his complete satisfaction with the conduct of the men and the achievements of the Brigade as a whole in the attack. He also expressed his sorrow at the heavy losses of Officers and men	[initials]

1875 Wt. W593/826 1,000,000 4/15 J.B.C. & A. A.D.S.S./Forms/C. 2118.

Instructions regarding War Diaries and Intelligence Summaries are contained in F. S. Regs., Part II. and the Staff Manual respectively. Title pages will be prepared in manuscript.

WAR DIARY

~~or~~

~~INTELLIGENCE SUMMARY.~~

(Erase heading not required.) 109th Machine Gun Coy

Army Form C. 2118.

Page 53

Place	Date 1916	Hour	Summary of Events and Information	Remarks and references to Appendices
HEDAUVILLE	July 4th		"A special order of the day" ~~[illegible]~~ Maj Gen O.S.W. NUGENT D.S.O is quoted:- "The General Officer commanding the Ulster Division desires that the Division should know that in his opinion, nothing finer has been done in the war than the attack by the Ulster Division on 1st July. The leading of the Coy Officers, the discipline and courage shewn by all ranks of the Division will stand out in future history of the war as an example of what good troops, well led, are capable of accomplishing. None but troops of the best quality could have faced the fire which was brought to bear on them and the losses suffered during the advance. The advance across the open to the German line was carried out with the steadiness of a parade movement under a fire both from front and flanks which could only have been faced by troops of the highest quality...... The Division captured nearly 600 Prisoners and carried its advance triumphantly to the limits of the objective laid down. There is nothing in the operations carried out by the Ulster Division on the 1st July that will not be a source of pride to all Ulstermen.... the standard of gallantry and devotion attained is one that may be equalled but is never likely to be surpassed. The General Officer commanding deeply regrets the heavy losses of Officers and men. He is proud beyond description, as every Officer and man in the Division may well be of the magnificent example of sublime courage and discipline which the Ulster Division has given to the Army."	[illegible]

1577 Wt. W10791/1773 500,000 1/15 D. D. & L. A.D.S.S./Forms/C. 2118.

Army Form C. 2118.

Instructions regarding War Diaries and Intelligence Summaries are contained in F. S. Regs., Part II. and the Staff Manual respectively. Title pages will be prepared in manuscript.

WAR DIARY
or
~~INTELLIGENCE SUMMARY.~~

(Erase heading not required.)

109th Machine Gun Coy Page 54

Place	Date 1916	Hour	Summary of Events and Information	Remarks and references to Appendices
	July			
HEDAUVILLE	5		Orders were received for the Company to move to HERISSART ~~at~~ to-day During the march to HERISSART a Reinforcement draft of Eighty men joined the Company for duty. On reaching our destination the men were settled in the Billets alloted to the Company The weather was good	[initials]
HERISSART	6		To-day was occupied with: unpacking stores, improving Billets and there was an inspection of the kits of the new men. Limbers were sent to VARENNES to draw Officers' and men's kits which had been dumped there previous to the Active Operations	[initials]
	7th		Further reinforcements to the number of Thirty Other Ranks reported to day for duty. The Kits of Officers and men, wounded missing and deceased, were thoroughly examined by an Officer and dealt with according to Gen Routine Orders. This was in our case unfortunately a very big task. 2nd Lieut P.N. DINGLEY: 2nd Lieut D. WALKER and 2 Lieut E.N. MONIE reported to-night for duty	[initials]

Instructions regarding War Diaries and Intelligence Summaries are contained in F. S. Regs., Part II. and the Staff Manual respectively. Title pages will be prepared in manuscript.

WAR DIARY

or

~~INTELLIGENCE SUMMARY.~~

(Erase heading not required.) 109th Machine Gun Coy Page 55

Army Form C. 2118.

Place	Date	Hour	Summary of Events and Information	Remarks and references to Appendices
	1916 July			
HERISSART	8th		The Office reinforcements were posted to Sections to-day and were engaged in making up teams &c In the afternoon: Pay parade. weather was good	[illegible]
	9th		Sunday: The Company paraded at full strength and attended Brigade Church Parade It was a Combined Service for all denominations. weather - good.	[illegible]
	10th		The Brigade moved by march route to CANDAS ~~and~~ FIENVILLERS this morning - This	
CANDAS			Company being billeted in CANDAS. Orders were received late to-night for the Coy to march to CONTEVILLE early to-morrow morning	[illegible]
CONTEVILLE	11th		The Company arrived here about mid-day with orders to entrain at times specified in the Brigade Entraining Orders. The Company entrained for BERGUETTE	
BERGUETTE			The Coy (including transport) detrained here at about 11 PM. Tea was prepared and served preparatory to commencing our march to RACQUINHEM	[illegible]
	12th	12·30 AM	The Coy "fell in" and marched off.	
RACQUINHEM		6·30 AM	We arrived at our new Billets. The men were free to rest for the rest of the day. 2/Lieut C.M.LEA and 2/Lieut H.W.ROOT joined the Coy for duty this afternoon. weather good	[illegible]
	13th		In accordance with orders the Company paraded at 9 AM and marched with the Brigade to QUELMES via ARQUES, St OMER and TATINGHEM. Outside St OMER	
QUELMES			a long halt was ordered for Dinners. On arrival at QUELMES Billets were taken over, and allotted to the Sections. The weather was splendid	

1577 Wt. W10791/1773 500,000 1/15 D. D. & L. A.D.S.S./Forms/C. 2118.

Instructions regarding War Diaries and Intelligence Summaries are contained in F. S. Regs., Part II. and the Staff Manual respectively. Title pages will be prepared in manuscript.

WAR DIARY
~~or~~
~~INTELLIGENCE SUMMARY.~~
(Erase heading not required.) 109th Machine Gun Coy

Army Form C. 2118.

Page 56

Place	Date 1916	Hour	Summary of Events and Information	Remarks and references to Appendices
QUELMES	July 14th		To-day was principally occupied with "Improving Billets" &c. The weather was good	[initials]
	15th		Parades to day were Physical Training, Inspection by C.O and Cleaning guns &c	[initials]
	16th		SUNDAY. Divine Services to-day. 2nd Lieut S. IDIENS joined the Coy to-day on being granted a Commission from the 19th Hussars.	[initials]
	17th	6AM	REVEILLE ~~[illegible]~~: The new drafts were examined in their knowledge of the Gun and this took up the entire day. Weather fine & warm	[initials]
	18th	6AM	Reveille: 7AM Physical Training. The route march arranged for this morning in our Training Syllabus was postponed owing to very wet weather and lack of arrangements for drying the mens clothes. The men were still further examined with a view to alloting positions on the teams to the proper men. Weather: Bad.	[initials]
	19th	6AM	Reveille. In the morning Physical Training, Gun Drill &c. In the afternoon all available men were marched to the BATHS in ST OMER. Weather: fair.	[initials]
	20th		Orders had been received for a move to day but they were cancelled late last night. The usual drills were carried on. In the evening Orders were received for the Coy to march with the Brigade to BOLLEZEELE early to morrow. Weather: good	[initials]
	21st		We paraded at 8-45AM and commenced our march to new billets. The route was via MORINGHEM, MOULLE; SERQUES; St MOMELIN; BROXEELE; 1½ hours halt was made ½ mile S.W. of St MOMELIN for dinners. Arrived BOLLEZEELE at about 5.30PM and took over new Billets. Weather very fine and warm	[initials]

Instructions regarding War Diaries and Intelligence Summaries are contained in F. S. Regs., Part II. and the Staff Manual respectively. Title pages will be prepared in manuscript.

WAR DIARY
or
~~INTELLIGENCE~~ SUMMARY.
(Erase heading not required.) 109th Machine Gun Coy

Army Form C. 2118.

Page 57

Place	Date 1916	Hour	Summary of Events and Information	Remarks and references to Appendices
	July			
BOLLEZEELE	22nd		Orders were received to day that the 109th Brigade will move by Bus from BOLLEZEELE to ROMARIN, 3 miles N.W of ARMENTIERS on the 23rd and that all 1st line Transport would march to ROUGE CROIX to-day and from ROUGE CROIX to ROMARIN on the 23rd. Our Transport left at 10 AM in charge of 2Lt W.J. WILGAR Transport Officer weather: good	[initials]
	23rd		The Company paraded and boarded the eight Busses alloted to it, At 2 PM we moved off in rear of the long column of Busses occupied by the remainder of the Brigade. After a most interesting journey we reached ROMARIN at about 8 PM and marched to our	[initials]
ROMARIN			new quarters in KORTEPYP CAMP. The Transport had already arrived. weather good.	
	24th		To-day was spent in arranging and improving Billets &c weather: good	[initials]
	25th		The C.O. paid a visit to the trenches to-day to have a look at the Gun Emplacements The Officers divided up their Sections into teams in readiness for taking over a line of trenches	[initials]
	26th		Parades to-day were Physical Training, Gun Drill &c &c. After "Lights out" to night there was a Gas Alarm but fortunately no Gas came our length. The weather is fine and very warm	[initials]
	27th		The C.O visited the trenches today and while there, heard we were taking over from the 122 M. G. Coy so he returned and gave orders for the teams as under.	

1577 Wt. W10791/1773 500,000 1/15 D. D. & L. A.D.S.S./Forms/C. 2118.

Instructions regarding War Diaries and Intelligence Summaries are contained in F. S. Regs., Part II. and the Staff Manual respectively. Title pages will be prepared in manuscript.

WAR DIARY
or
~~INTELLIGENCE SUMMARY.~~ 109 Machine Gun Coy

(*Erase heading not required.*)

Army Form C. 2118.

Place	Date	Hour	Summary of Events and Information	Remarks and references to Appendices
ROMARIN	27/7/16	7.30pm	Look over the undermentioned Emplacements from the 122nd Machine Gun Coy A. U 13 A 95.80. B. U.13 D 15.50 C U14 A 1.8. D. U14 A. 8.45 E U.14 A 8.1. F U 8 D 35.05. G U.14 D 25.80. H. U14 C 50.40 Eight Emplacements. Mr Jacins took charge of Emplacements. A.B.C and has his Dugout at U.13 B 0.6. Mr Roote & Mr Monee took charge of D.E.F.G.H. and stayed in Cellars beneath the ruined Chateau U.14.C 10.45 The C.O. stayed with them until he was satisfied they knew their duties in the trenches which he expected would be in a fortnight.	Ref Map 28. S.W. 4 [initials]
ROMARIN	28/7/16		Teams in the line got settled down and had a quiet night Enemy seem to be quiet here and doesnt appear to have much artillery	[initials]
ROMARIN	29/7/16		Enemy did some Machine Gun Fire at night. His Artillery registered on Chateau with 15 c.m. His second shot was a direct hit	[initials]

T2134. Wt. W708—776. 500000. 4/15. Sir J. C. & S.

Instructions regarding War Diaries and Intelligence Summaries are contained in F. S. Regs., Part II. and the Staff Manual respectively. Title pages will be prepared in manuscript.

WAR DIARY
or
~~INTELLIGENCE SUMMARY~~.
(Erase heading not required.) 109 Machine Gun Coy

Army Form C. 2118.

Page 59 [3]

Place	Date	Hour	Summary of Events and Information	Remarks and references to Appendices
ROMARIN	~~29~~ 30/7/16		Enemy Machine Guns were active all night Our Guns fire 2500 rounds on ASH AVENUE, PLOEGSTEERT – MESSINES Road. The weather was very good but there was a heavy mist in the morning.	[initials]
"	31/7/16		Enemy Machine Guns were very active between 10.0 p.m. & midnight They paid particular attention to Hill 63 Our Guns fired 2000 rounds on enemy communications The weather is still very fine & rather warm	[initials]

T2134. Wt. W708–776. 500000. 4/15. Sir J. C. & S.

C O N F I D E N T I A L

Vol 5

W A R   D I A R Y

of

109TH COMPANY MACHINE GUN CORPS.

FOR MONTH OF AUGUST, 1916.

Instructions regarding War Diaries and Intelligence Summaries are contained in F. S. Regs., Part II. and the Staff Manual respectively. Title pages will be prepared in manuscript.

WAR DIARY
or
~~INTELLIGENCE~~ SUMMARY.
(Erase heading not required.)

No. 109 MACHINE GUN COMPANY.
Page 60

Army Form C. 2118.

Place	Date 1916	Hour	Summary of Events and Information	Remarks and references to Appendices
	AUG		Last night the Enemy appeared nervous and sent up a lot of Very lights, but his Machine Guns were quiet.	
ROMARIN	1st		Our Machine guns fired 2.000 rounds on the MESSINES-PLOEGSTEERT Road: SCHNITZEL FARM and ASH AVENUE.	
			Teams in Reserve had Gun Drill & a Route March to-day.	
		5.30PM	An Enemy Aeroplane flew over our lines. Weather Dry and very warm	
	2nd		Enemy Machine guns were quiet last night. Early in the afternoon the enemy registered with 10 cm Guns on the CHATEAU in U14C. His fourth Shot was a direct hit. Relief of teams in the trenches was carried out this evening. Weather good	
	3rd		During last night it was noticed the Enemy still uses Very Lights largely. His Machine Guns were quiet for the most part. Our M. Guns fired 3000 rounds on MESSINES-PLOEGSTEERT Road. Teams which came into Reserve last night spent to-day in cleaning their guns Equipment &c &c weather fine & warm	
	4th		Enemy Machine Guns were quiet again last night but we fired 1800 rounds on MESSINES-PLOEGSTEERT Road. Enemy Artillery sent over about two dozen 77 cm shells into Hill 63 in the afternoon. Teams in Reserve carried out Gun Drills &c and also had a route march. Weather still fine & warm	

T2134. Wt. W708-776. 500000. 4/15. Sir J. C. & S.

Instructions regarding War Diaries and Intelligence Summaries are contained in F. S. Regs., Part II. and the Staff Manual respectively. Title pages will be prepared in manuscript.

WAR DIARY ~~or~~ INTELLIGENCE SUMMARY.

(Erase heading not required.)

No. 109 MACHINE GUN COMPANY.

No. Page 61

Army Form C. 2118.

Place	Date 1916	Hour	Summary of Events and Information	Remarks and references to Appendices
ROMARIN	AUGUST 5th		Last night was very quiet – Our Machine Guns did no firing Teams in Reserve practised Gun Drill &c during the morning there was Football in the afternoon The weather was good but much cooler	[initials]
	6th		Sunday Teams in Reserve paraded for Divine Service this morning Guns in the trenches did some night firing last night — weather fine & warm	[initials]
	7th		In the trenches, last night was quiet. Teams in Reserve practised Gun Drill and carried out a programme of training weather fine & warm	[initials]
	8th		Nothing unusual was reported from the trenches. Teams in Reserve were occupied in the usual Machine Gun training. weather is still fine and warm	[initials]
	9th		Enemy was quiet last night. Our Machines Guns fired during the night on SCHNITZEL FARM and PLOEGSTEERT–MESSINES Road. 39 Other Ranks – surplus to our Establishment – were returned to the Base to-day Relief of teams in the trenches was carried out this evening	[initials]

T2134. Wt. W708–776. 500000. 4/15. Sir J. C. & S.

Instructions regarding War Diaries and Intelligence Summaries are contained in F. S. Regs., Part II. and the Staff Manual respectively. Title pages will be prepared in manuscript.

WAR DIARY
or
~~INTELLIGENCE SUMMARY.~~
(Erase heading not required.)

Army Form C. 2118.

Place	Date 1916	Hour	Summary of Events and Information	Remarks and references to Appendices
	AUGUST			
ROMARIN	10th		Enemy Machine Guns showed no activity during last night. We fired 4000 rounds on PLOEGSTEERT–MESSINES Road; SCHNITZEL FARM Tramway and enemy trenches around PETIT DOUVE FARM. Teams in Reserve did no outdoor training to-day owing to very heavy showers, but Instruction on the Gun was given to them in the huts.	[initials]
	11th		Nothing unusual was reported from our teams in the trenches. All the available men in Reserve were employed to-day in making Sanitary Arrangements in accordance with orders. Weather was fine and warm again to-day	[initials]
	12th		Enemy Machine Guns were slightly active last night and we did some night firing. Teams in Reserve continued the work of Sanitation. In the afternoon Gas Drill was practised. Weather fine & warm	[initials]
	13th		Sunday Teams in Reserve paraded for Divine Service. Enemy Machine Guns were reported to have been more active last night. We fired on PLOEGSTEERT–MESSINES Road during the night. Weather fine & warm	[initials]

T2134. Wt. W708–776. 500000. 4/15. Sir J. C. & S.

Instructions regarding War Diaries and Intelligence Summaries are contained in F. S. Regs., Part II. and the Staff Manual respectively. Title pages will be prepared in manuscript.

WAR DIARY
or
~~INTELLIGENCE SUMMARY.~~
(Erase heading not required.)

No. 109 MACHINE GUN COMPANY. No. Page 63

Army Form C. 2118.

Place	Date 1916	Hour	Summary of Events and Information	Remarks and references to Appendices
	AUGUST			
ROMARIN	14th		Enemy machine Guns were fairly active last night and our guns fired 1000 rounds on their front line trenches and wire. The teams in reserve carried out usual programme of Instruction. Weather Showery	[initials]
	15th		Enemy M. Guns were quiet last night and ours did the usual night firing. Reserve teams received the usual instruction on the gun but heavy showers prevented much out door work. 2 Lieut J. W. GOLDMAN (3.6.15) reported to the Coy for duty early to-day.	[initials]
	16th		Things were reported as being normal last night: we fired 1000 rounds on MESSINES ROAD Coy Head Qrtrs in the trenches got three light shells on it to-day. Reserve teams prepared for duty in the trenches and carried out reliefs this evening	[initials]
	17th		Enemy M Guns were inactive last night but we fired a little on the MESSINES ROAD Teams which were relieved last night spent the day in washing and cleaning up Weather was showery in the afternoon	[initials]

T2134. Wt. W708—776. 500000. 4/15. Sir J. C. & S.

Instructions regarding War Diaries and Intelligence Summaries are contained in F. S. Regs., Part II. and the Staff Manual respectively. Title pages will be prepared in manuscript.

WAR DIARY
or
INTELLIGENCE SUMMARY.
(*Erase heading not required.*)

No. 109 MACHINE GUN COMPANY.
Page 64

Army Form C. 2118.

Place	Date 1916	Hour	Summary of Events and Information	Remarks and references to Appendices
	AUGUST			
ROMARIN	18th		Teams in the Trenches reported last night as being unusually quiet as regards Enemy action. Our Machine Guns fired a good deal on Enemy trenches and MESSINES ROAD. A good many shells burst close to Coy's Trench H^d Qrtrs during to-day. Weather Showery. Teams in Reserve carried on Gun drill &c &c	JMcL
	19th		Enemy M Guns were active last night. We fired during the night on the enemy trenches and MESSINES ROAD. Small shells were dropping close to our Emplacement at SEAFORTH FARM to-day. Hollonal instruction was given to teams in Reserve. Weather Showery	JMcL
	20th		Sunday. Reserve teams paraded and attended Divine Service to-day. The enemy retaliated smartly to our Artillery Bombardment of LA PETIT DOUVE FARM last night and a good number of shells fell around our Machine Gun Emplacements at SEAFORTH FARM, LA ROSSIGNOL and LA HUTTE CHATEAU. Weather fine & warm	JMcL
	21st		Enemy Machine Guns were very active last night. Early this morning 3 small shells dropped near one of our Emplacements at LA ROSSIGNOL. A working party was sent to the trenches to-day and the remainder of the men practised Gun Drill &c &c. Weather was good	JMcL

Instructions regarding War Diaries and Intelligence Summaries are contained in F. S. Regs., Part II. and the Staff Manual respectively. Title pages will be prepared in manuscript.

WAR DIARY
or
~~INTELLIGENCE SUMMARY.~~
(*Erase heading not required.*)

Page 65

Army Form C. 2118.

Place	Date	Hour	Summary of Events and Information	Remarks and references to Appendices
	1916 AUGUST			
ROMARIN	22nd		Last night Enemy Machine Guns were Active. Our own M Guns carried out the usual night firing.	
			Teams in Reserve carried out a general programme of Instruction.	
			We have received information that 18679 A/Lce Corp FISHER J of this Company has been awarded the D.C.M for his gallant conduct in the offensive operations of 1st July last	[signature]
			Weather: Fine & warm	
	23rd		Enemy Machine Guns were again active during last night we replied by directing about 2000 rounds on the MESSINES ROAD.	
			One ^Gun^ Emplacement was shelled during the afternoon	
			Teams in Reserve were engaged in preparing for their tour of duty in the trenches and late in the evening relieved the teams in the trenches	[signature]
	24th		Last night our guns fired at interval on ROADSIDE REDOUBT & MESSINES ROAD.	
			Late in the afternoon a German Aeroplane tried to cross our lines but after being heavily shelled it turned tail to one of our 'Planes which had gone up in pursuit	
			This afternoon 6 heavy H.E. Shells were fired by the enemy into this Camp – 2 Lieut W.J. WILGAR and 2 OR were wounded (1 slightly)	[signature]
			The weather was good	

Instructions regarding War Diaries and Intelligence Summaries are contained in F. S. Regs., Part II. and the Staff Manual respectively. Title pages will be prepared in manuscript.

WAR DIARY
or
INTELLIGENCE SUMMARY.
(Erase heading not required.)

No. 109 MACHINE GUN COMPANY. No. Page 66

Army Form C. 2118.

Place	Date	Hour	Summary of Events and Information	Remarks and references to Appendices
	1916 AUGUST			
ROMARIN	25th		Our Machine Guns fired during the night on the MESSINES ROAD The enemy fired ~~six~~ heavy HE shell into a field near one of our Emplacements at LA ROSSIGNOL yesterday and he continued the shelling again to-day. We can't make out what his target is — It is was very noticeable that a fair number of his shells were "Duds" The teams in Reserve were engaged in M G Training to-day.	[initials]
	26th		Enemy appeared to be very nervous last night — He fired an unusual number of Very Lights Out of 20 Enemy Shrapnel shells fired at road in front of DEAD COW FARM to-day 10 were blind Our Machine Guns were active during last night against SCHNITZEL FARM and MESSINES ROAD. Teams in Reserve were engaged in usual training to-day Weather Showery	[initials]
	27th		The men in Reserve attended Church Parade in the morning. In the afternoon, Kits were examined. Nothing of importance was reported from the trenches last night. Our Machine Guns fired on the MESSINES ROAD. Several showers during the afternoon.	[initials]

Instructions regarding War Diaries and Intelligence Summaries are contained in F. S. Regs., Part II. and the Staff Manual respectively. Title pages will be prepared in manuscript.

WAR DIARY
or
INTELLIGENCE SUMMARY.
(*Erase heading not required.*)

No. 109 MACHINE GUN COMPANY
No. Page 67

Army Form C. 2118.

Place	Date	Hour	Summary of Events and Information	Remarks and references to Appendices
	1916. AUGUST			
ROMARIN.	28th		Machine Guns were quiet on both sides last night. This evening we sent an extra gun and team to the front line which took up a position near ANTON'S FARM. Heavy showers fell during the day and interrupted instruction at camp.	D.W.
	29th		Last night three Machine Guns were in position in the front line. One at ANTON'S FARM; one at SEAFORTH FARM and the gun from ADVANCED ESTAMINET which fired from a position near DONNINGTON HALL. The extra guns were placed in the front line in preparation for a raid proposed to take place tonight. Two of our reserve guns fired on Schnitzel Farm and Messines Rd. The front line guns opened fire at 1.30 a.m. this morning. At camp this morning, we packed limbers preparatory to moving to our new winter quarters and this afternoon all available men went to prepare the new camp. The morning was dull and later very heavy thunderstorms were the order.	D.W.

T2134. Wt. W708—776. 500000. 4/15. Sir J. C. & S.

Instructions regarding War Diaries and Intelligence Summaries are contained in F. S. Regs., Part II. and the Staff Manual respectively. Title pages will be prepared in manuscript.

WAR DIARY
~~or~~
~~INTELLIGENCE~~ SUMMARY.
(Erase heading not required.)

Army Form C. 2118.

Place	Date	Hour	Summary of Events and Information	Remarks and references to Appendices
	1916. AUGUST			
ROMARIN.	30th		Last night Enemy Machine Guns were unusually active. The enemy seemed to be very nervous using a large number Very Light. Possibly he may have heard that a raid was impending. Yesterday evening it rained heavily and the wind changed till by midnight it was unfavourable for the use of our gas. The raid was postponed to wait for favourable conditions. Our guns were active. From the front line they fired on BARRICADE AVENUE and on a working party opposite ANTON'S FARM. Work apparently ceased. The CHATEAU gun fired on the MESSINES ROAD between 10.0 p.m and 3.0 a.m. Yesterday evening one man was wounded by machine gun fire while carrying water near HYDE PARK CORNER. Rain fell heavily and continuously all day and made the work of taking over our winter quarters very unpleasant. Several days will have to be spent on fatigue work in the new camp. It is about a mile from KORTEPYP and rather cramped.	D.W.
	31st		In the new camp. Last night, conditions being favourable, the raid took place. Our front lines guns did not fire before 1.10 a.m. as patrols were out.	

Instructions regarding War Diaries and Intelligence Summaries are contained in F. S. Regs., Part II. and the Staff Manual respectively. Title pages will be prepared in manuscript.

WAR DIARY
or
~~INTELLIGENCE SUMMARY.~~
(Erase heading not required.)

No. 100 MACHINE GUN COMPANY. No. Page 69 Date

Army Form C. 2118.

Place	Date	Hour	Summary of Events and Information	Remarks and references to Appendices
	1916. AUGUST 31st (Continued.)		Three of our reserve guns fired on points behind the enemy front line between 9:30 p.m and 3:30 a.m.	
			A patrol was reported to be moving in NO MANS LAND at 1:15 a.m. Fire was opened on it by the guns at SEAFORTH FARM and DONNINGTON HALL. Result not known.	
			Gas was released according to programme and the artillery intensely bombarded the enemy's positions from 1:34 a.m to 2:4 a.m. Two of our front line guns had some difficulty in maintaining fire as gas was discharged from their bays.	
			Enemy Machine Guns were active about 3 a.m. firing on the front line and ANSCROFT AVENUE.	
			Official report does not state if gas (or other causes) was responsible for:- "many dead bodies seen in trenches". One of the patrols that ~~who~~ went out after the bombardment remarked that no Machine Gun fire was directed on them. A few of the raiders entered the enemy's front line.	
			The teams in reserve were busy. In this camp, new latrines, harness rooms, cookhouses and a guardroom have to be put up. There are no facilities for washing and cooking as yet.	
			The weather was ~~exce~~ splendid.	D.W.

T2134. Wt. W708—776. 500000. 4/15. Sir J. C. & S.

Original.

Vol 6

Confidential

War Diary

of

109th Machine Gun Company.

From 1st September 1916

To 30th September 1916 (Inclusive)

Instructions regarding War Diaries and Intelligence Summaries are contained in F. S. Regs., Part II. and the Staff Manual respectively. Title pages will be prepared in manuscript.

WAR DIARY
~~or~~ ~~INTELLIGENCE SUMMARY.~~
(Erase heading not required.)

No. 109 MACHINE GUN COMPANY. Page 70.

Army Form C. 2118.

Place	Date	Hour	Summary of Events and Information	Remarks and references to Appendices
	1916.			
	SEPTEMBER			
ROMARIN.	1st		Enemy Machine Guns were very active last night between 9'0 p.m. and 10 p.m. Early this morning our artillery heavily shelled the enemy's front line for about half an hour commencing at 1'34 a.m. and gas was released at 1'45 a.m. The enemy sent up several red flares at this time. An enemy aeroplane passed over the CHATEAU at 4 a.m., its engine making a particularly loud noise.	
			From camp: sections 3 and 4 relieved 1 and 2 which had been in the line nine days.	D.W.
			Weather — very dull.	
	2nd		Last night, Enemy Machine Guns were remarkably inactive and ours were quiet. One of our guns fired on SCHNITZEL FARM. At 1'30 this afternoon, ten shells burst in the vicinity of the CHATEAU.	
			In camp, fatigues were the order and the men were paid in the afternoon. Weather — dull.	D.W.
	3rd		At 11'0 p.m. last night, a sentry, mistaking a mist lying in NO MANS LAND for gas, sounded an alarm. Everyone was roused in our camp and still farther back. Our Machine Guns opened fire immediately on enemy front line. At 11'15 p.m. our artillery opened heavy fire and the enemy retaliated feebly.	

T2134. Wt. W708—776. 500000. 4/15. Sir J. C. & S.

Instructions regarding War Diaries and Intelligence Summaries are contained in F. S. Regs., Part II. and the Staff Manual respectively. Title pages will be prepared in manuscript.

WAR DIARY
or
INTELLIGENCE SUMMARY.
(*Erase heading not required.*)

Army Form C. 2118.

Place	Date	Hour	Summary of Events and Information	Remarks and references to Appendices
	1916. SEPT. 3rd. (Continued.)		At 11·0 a.m this morning, 23 British aeroplanes flew East over our camp and the CHATEAU. About this time, our gun at LA HUTTE fired on an enemy aeroplane flying low. There was no Church Parade at camp. We were warned this morning that a move North was likely and the C.O. went to look at the trenches opposite ~~by~~ WYSCHAETE. We hear that our gas used on Aug 31st and Sept 1st was very effective. A very fine day.	D.W.
MT KEMMEL	4th		In the line, enemy machine guns were inactive last night. Guns fired on SCHNITZEL FARM and MESSINES ROAD. About midnight, the enemy used a large number of red light. Pigeons were observed flying to and from MESSINES. In camp, at midnight, we received ~~a~~ moving orders and left ROMARIN this morning at 9 a.m. We reached our winter quarters (again) on the South West spur of MONT KEMMEL, N.31.B.0,5, at about 1·0 p.m. We marched through NEUVE EGLISE and DANOUTRE and at one point this road was shelled at 3·15 p.m. and 21 casualties were reported from the WORCESTERS. This new camp is a great improvement on the last. It is very high and there is plenty of room. Apparently it is not shelled. There are no horse standings. Dull and showery.	D.W.

T2134. Wt. W708–776. 500000. 4/15. Sir J. C. & S.

Instructions regarding War Diaries and Intelligence Summaries are contained in F. S. Regs., Part II. and the Staff Manual respectively. Title pages will be prepared in manuscript.

WAR DIARY
~~or~~
~~INTELLIGENCE SUMMARY.~~

(*Erase heading not required.*)

No. 109 MACHINE GUN COMPANY.
No. Page 72.

Army Form C. 2118.

Place	Date	Hour	Summary of Events and Information	Remarks and references to Appendices
	1916. SEPT^R			
M^T KEMMEL.	5th		Our 8 guns and their teams are still in the old part of the line and they report that last night was very quiet. Our guns fired at intervals on MESSINES R^D. In camp, we unpacked limbers and in the afternoon 3 teams of No 1 Section took their guns to the new line & relieved 3 guns of the 57th B^de. They occupied positions, all poor & in bad repair at the "CAUSEWAY", the "BOLT COURT", and the "QUADRANT" Emplacements. Mr Wilgar returned this evening from hospital. A very wet day.	D.W.
	6th		Reports from LA HUTTE CHATEAU shew that machine guns were quiet on both sides last night but our artillery shelled the neighbourhood of AVENUE FARM very steadily. The 8 guns in the old sector were relieved this afternoon by the 57th M. G. Coy. Their teams arrived at this camp about 9.0 p.m., after five days in the line. Reports from our three guns in the new line state that they had completed the relief by 4.15 p.m. yesterday afternoon. At 10.30 p.m., men of the N. Staffs Reg^t carried out a bombing raid. Our artillery was active nearly all night. They commenced a steady and fairly intense bombardment at 8.0 p.m. and this they maintained till 3 a.m. this morning. The enemy's reply was very feeble.	

Instructions regarding War Diaries and Intelligence Summaries are contained in F. S. Regs., Part II. and the Staff Manual respectively. Title pages will be prepared in manuscript.

WAR DIARY
or
~~INTELLIGENCE SUMMARY.~~
(*Erase heading not required.*)

No. 109 MACHINE GUN COMPANY.
No. Page 73.

Army Form C. 2118.

Place	Date	Hour	Summary of Events and Information	Remarks and references to Appendices
	1916. SEPTEMBER.			
Mt KEMMEL.	6th (Contd.)		In camp, this morning, we prepared our 5 available guns for work in the trenches and by 4.30 p.m. they had relieved the guns of the 57th M.G. Coy at the following positions:- Piccadilly; Shell Farm; Frenchman's Farm; Fluffy Trench and Kingsway. The position at Bolt Court was condemned and the Valley Position was occupied. We have completely taken over the new sector. Weather today, splendid	D.W.
	7th		The teams from the old part of the line reached this camp about 9.30 last night. About 10.30 p.m. an enemy aeroplane passed over & dropped bombs in the neighbourhood of Dranoutre. Enemy machine guns were not busy last night & ours did not fire. Snipers very active. In camp, we cleaned guns after work in the trenches & started to improve the camp. We find the location of the Transport Lines very inconvenient. Weather, fine.	D.W.
	8th		Machine Guns were quiet on both sides last night. In camp today, the men were all employed on fatigues. Weather fine.	D.W.
	9th		Very little machine gun fire last night. Only fatigue work in camp. Weather, fine.	D.W.

T2134. Wt. W708–776. 500000. 4/15. Sir J. C. & S.

Instructions regarding War Diaries and Intelligence Summaries are contained in F. S. Regs., Part II. and the Staff Manual respectively. Title pages will be prepared in manuscript.

WAR DIARY or INTELLIGENCE SUMMARY.

(Erase heading not required.)

No. 109 MACHINE GUN COMPANY.
No. Page 74.
Date.

Army Form C. 2118.

Place	Date	Hour	Summary of Events and Information	Remarks and references to Appendices
	1916. SEPT			
M^T KEMMEL	10th		Last night was quiet except for enemy snipers. Our guns did not fire. A Divine Service was held this morning by the Camp. A fine day.	D.W.
	11th		Reliefs carried out yesterday evening. Teams now in the line from 3 and 4 Sections. Last night was quiet. The gun at FRENCHMANS FARM fired on enemy communicating trenches. Teams in reserve examining guns after work in the trenches. A fine day.	D.W.
	12th		Enemy snipers busy last night but machine guns inactive. Our gun fired as on the night before. An enemy aeroplane was over our line yesterday evening. Fine weather.	D.W.
	13th		Conditions the same as usual in the line last night. Snipers busy: machine guns inactive. Some shells fell in the vicinity of the KINGSWAY emplacement this afternoon but no damage was done. Weather has changed. Showery day.	D.W.
	14th		Snipers were quieter than usual last night and machine guns again inactive. The men at QUADRANT GUN, front line, suspect the enemy uses explosive bullets.	

T2134. Wt. W708—776. 500000. 4/15. Sir J. C. & S.

Instructions regarding War Diaries and Intelligence Summaries are contained in F. S. Regs., Part II. and the Staff Manual respectively. Title pages will be prepared in manuscript.

WAR DIARY
or
~~INTELLIGENCE SUMMARY.~~

(*Erase heading not required.*)

No. 109 MACHINE GUN COMPANY. Page 75.

Army Form C. 2118.

Place	Date	Hour	Summary of Events and Information	Remarks and references to Appendices
	1916. SEPT.			
Mt KEMMEL	14th	(Contd)	At 10:30 this morning, the enemy shelled PICADILLY trench causing some six casualties not far from our gun position. A few shells fell near FRENCHMANS FARM. The enemy at odd times has scattered shells all over the valley behind the front line. The teams in reserve have worked according to programme. A showery day.	
	15th		Last night was quiet, enemy's snipers not so busy as usual. During the night an enemy machine gun occasionally played on the road running round FRENCHMANS FARM. Our artillery has been fairly busy all day. At mid-day a German aeroplane was over our line but he soon retreated, heavily shelled. A fine day.	
	16th		Yesterday evening was quiet up to 8:30 p.m. By that hour we had mounted two guns in the front line; one from CHIMNEY FARM on the left of the BULL RING and the QUADRANT gun, mounted to fire to its front. The SHELL FARM gun was moved earlier in the afternoon to CHIMNEY FARM, the old position being handed over to the 107th Brigade. Raiding parties left our trenches at 8:30 p.m. exactly. At 8:45 according to programme the artillery made a barrage round the raided area and the two Vickers swept the enemy parapet.	

T2134. Wt. W708–776. 500000. 4/15. Sir J. C. & S.

Instructions regarding War Diaries and Intelligence Summaries are contained in F. S. Regs., Part II. and the Staff Manual respectively. Title pages will be prepared in manuscript.

WAR DIARY
or
INTELLIGENCE SUMMARY.
(Erase heading not required.)

Army Form C. 2118.

Page 76.

Place	Date	Hour	Summary of Events and Information	Remarks and references to Appendices
	1916. SEPT.			
Mt KEMMEL.	16th	(Contd)	The guns from FRENCHMANS FARM and the VALLEY fired on enemy communicating trenches. The retaliation for the bombardment was negligable and the raid was successful. The remainder of the night was quiet: sniping entirely stopped. This morning our artillery concentrated on the enemy front line in our sector, firing heavily from 10.30 a.m. till 12.30 p.m. This bombardment was repeated from 2.30 p.m. till 5.0 p.m. During these bombardments, which were very successful, the front line was cleared & our gun withdrawn. Teams in reserve worked according to programme. A sunny day.	D.W.
	17th		Last night the gun from PICCADILLY took up a position in the front line on the left of the BULL RING to fire on expected parties of enemy repairing their wire after the shelling. The QUADRANT gun dispersed one of these parties. At midnight a large party of Canadians raided the enemy from our left and the gun near the BULL RING swept the enemy front line till all sniping ceased and then lifted fire on to the ground beyond raiding party. A heavy artillery bombardment lasted from 12.0 midnight to 12.30 a.m. Practically no reply. The amazing acquiescence of the enemy to the operations of the last two days leads us to suppose that in this sector at least he is a beaten man and very short of guns & ammunition. Teams in reserve prepared for tomorrow's relief. A fine day.	D.W.

T2134. Wt. W708—776. 500000. 4/15. Sir J. C. & S.

Instructions regarding War Diaries and Intelligence Summaries are contained in F. S. Regs., Part II. and the Staff Manual respectively. Title pages will be prepared in manuscript.

WAR DIARY or INTELLIGENCE SUMMARY.

(*Erase heading not required.*)

Page 77.

Army Form C. 2118.

Place	Date	Hour	Summary of Events and Information	Remarks and references to Appendices
	1916. SEPT.			
Mt KEMMEL.	18th		Last night, enemy machine guns were more active than usual but his snipers are very quiet. In co-operation with artillery, two of our guns fired heavily upon VALLEY position on trench at N30.c.2.6. The gun at FRENCHMANS FARM was also active during the night. Our artillery have shelled the enemy intermittently for the last 48 hours. Reliefs carried out yesterday. A very wet day.	D.W.
	19th		Last night was very quiet. Two of our guns fired on O31.a.2.5 and O31.b.0.1. Teams in reserve worked according to programme of training. Weather - fine.	D.W.
	20th		Two of our guns fired last night on enemy communication trenches about O31.a. and O25.c. also on the railway O31.a.6.2. The enemy was quiet. His snipers appear to be discouraged. This morning, several Minnenwerfer fell near our front line position & blew in two bays. Usual programme of training carried out in reserve. Weather - showery. Last night, for practice, the reserve guns were rushed up to the allotted reserve positions in satisfactory time.	D.W.
	21st		The enemy machine guns were more active last night: his snipers are still quiet. Our guns fired as on previous night. A few shells fell in DRANOUTRE yesterday evening. Four or five casualties. Work in camp according to syllabus. A fine day.	D.W.

T2134. Wt. W708-776. 500000. 4/15. Sir J. C. & S.

Instructions regarding War Diaries and Intelligence Summaries are contained in F. S. Regs., Part II. and the Staff Manual respectively. Title pages will be prepared in manuscript.

WAR DIARY ~~or~~ INTELLIGENCE SUMMARY.

(*Erase heading not required.*)

No. 109 MACHINE GUN COMPANY.

Page 78.

Army Form C. 2118.

Place	Date	Hour	Summary of Events and Information	Remarks and references to Appendices
	1916. SEPT.			
Mt KEMMEL.	22nd		Machine guns were active on both sides last night, ours firing at intervals throughout the night on enemy communication trenches and roads. Trench mortars co-operated with three of our guns this afternoon which fired 6,000 rounds on N36. b and N30. D. 8. 8. Usual training carried out in camp. Transport busy on horse standings. Fine weather.	D.W.
DRANOUTRE.	23rd		One of our guns fired last night on enemy trench railway. The night was quiet. This afternoon we left the camp at Mt KEMMEL and are now quartered at a large farm NE of DRANOUTRE (M36.a.9.3.) close by the transport lines, a great convenience. The billets do not require much alteration. The day was fine.	D.W.
	24th		Machine guns on both sides were quiet last night. No Church Parades this morning. Teams in reserve prepared guns etc. for work in the trenches. A hot day.	D.W.
	25th		Enemy machine guns fairly busy last night. We fired 2,500 rounds on his communication trenches. Several heavy T.M.s fell in the vicinity of QUADRANT gun this afternoon. No damage. Teams in reserve cleaned up after trench work. The weather is splendid.	D.W.

T2134. Wt. W708—776. 500000. 4/15. Sir J. C. & S.

Instructions regarding War Diaries and Intelligence Summaries are contained in F. S. Regs., Part II. and the Staff Manual respectively. Title pages will be prepared in manuscript.

WAR DIARY
or
INTELLIGENCE SUMMARY.
(Erase heading not required.)

Army Form C. 2118.

Place	Date	Hour	Summary of Events and Information	Remarks and references to Appendices
	1916. SEPT.			
DRANOUTRE.	26th		Machine guns were active on both sides last night. Three of our guns fired. Yesterday evening, fifteen of our battleplanes passed over the line flying east. We have a small party constantly at work on the advanced Bgy. H.Qtrs Dugouts being made off Kingsway about N.35.a.0.0. Weather is fine & seems settled.	D.H.
	27th		Enemy machine guns were quiet last night, ours fired 4,500 on enemy railways etc. At 6.30 a.m. today, T.M.s fell behind QUADRANT GUN & demolished the last wall of SNIPERS FARM. At our billets, there is an outbreak of Scabies caused probably by blankets just issued. A large number of men are affected. The remainder have today worked on horse standings. At 5.30 p.m. today a German observation balloon was seen drifting towards DRANOUTRE. We heard later, it had come from BAPAUME & had broken loose about 4 P.M. It was shelled by AA and finished off by our battleplanes which fired into it & finally ignited the gas. The balloon fell blazing at 5.45 p.m. close to our old camp on Mt KEMMEL. The observer, unhurt, was captured. One of our planes was slightly damaged landing near it. Splendid news last night from the SOMME district. Important advance. THIEPVAL and COMBLES taken. Weather splendid.	D.H.
	28th		Machine guns fairly busy last night on both sides. Two of our guns fired on enemy railways etc.	

Instructions regarding War Diaries and Intelligence Summaries are contained in F. S. Regs., Part II. and the Staff Manual respectively. Title pages will be prepared in manuscript.

WAR DIARY
or
INTELLIGENCE SUMMARY.
(Erase heading not required.)

No. 109 MACHINE GUN COMPANY.
No. Page 80.
Date.

Army Form C. 2118.

Place	Date	Hour	Summary of Events and Information	Remarks and references to Appendices
	1916. SEPT.			
DRANOUTRE.	28th	(Contd)	This morning our artillery and T.M.s heavily bombarded the enemy's 1st and 2nd lines from 9.30 a.m. to 11.0 a.m. During this period, four of our guns fired 12,000 rounds on enemy 2nd and 3rd lines & communicating trenches. The enemy made no reply. In reserve, all available men worked on horse standings. Weather holding fine.	D.W.
	29th		Last night our guns fired steadily on light railway at O31.a., cutting & road at O25.a.4.6 and the wood at O25.d. Enemy machine guns were quiet. His T.M.s were active this afternoon about 3.0 p.m. At 2.0 p.m. a small balloon was carried over our line going S.W. Probably the enemy was testing wind & preparatory to a gas attack. Available men in the Company at work on horse standings with which we are behind in point of time. It is very difficult to obtain material. Weather still excellent.	D.W.
	30th		Enemy machine guns were fairly active last night and ours fired at intervals on railway at O31.a.; on the road running NE of square N30.d. Enemy light artillery searched for our batteries round Daylight Corner about 4.0 p.m. The available men in reserve worked on the horse standings today. Weather splendid.	D.W.

Vol 7

Confidential.

War Diary

of

109th Machine Gun Company.

From 1st October 1916. To 31st October 1916.

(Volume I)

Instructions regarding War Diaries and Intelligence Summaries are contained in F. S. Regs., Part II. and the Staff Manual respectively. Title Pages will be prepared in manuscript.

WAR DIARY
or
INTELLIGENCE SUMMARY
(Erase heading not required.)

Army Form C. 2118.

Place	Date	Hour	Summary of Events and Information	Remarks and references to Appendices
	1916			
DRANOUTRE	Oct 1st		SUNDAY Teams in reserve attended divine service. At 10 P.M last night one of the Battalions of the Brigade carried out a raid on the Enemy trenches. The raiding party found the enemy front line vacated but they brought back one Machine Gun and a quantity of rifles and Equipment. Our Machine Guns co-operated – 2 of them being in the front line firing on the flanks and 3 others carried out a programme of Indirect fire against Enemy Communication Trenches and Strong points in the area behind the raiding party's objective. Weather to-day was fine	[initials]
	2nd		To-day further work was done to the Horse Standings. Teams in reserve carried out their training programme: 3 men from each Battalion in the Brigade (12 in all) were attached to the Company from to-day. They will undergo a course of Instruction before joining the Gun teams for duty. Nothing unusual was reported from the trenches last night. Our Machine Guns carried out Indirect Fire as usual against enemy Commn Trenches and Strong points. Weather very wet	[initials]
	3rd		Work on the Horse standings was proceeded with and all available gunners were engaged on drill & instruction under Section Officers. The Class of Instruction carried out its programme. In the trenches there was only the usual Sniping and Machine Gun fire on the part of the enemy but our M. Guns were active. To-day the enemy commenced a T.M. Strafe but was silenced by our Artillery. One of our Machine guns fired 250 rounds on the Light Railway running SE of O.31.a during the afternoon. Weather wet in the morning but dry later	[initials]

2449 Wt. W14957/M90 750,000 1/16 J.B.C. & A. Forms/C.2118/12.

Instructions regarding War Diaries and Intelligence Summaries are contained in F. S. Regs., Part II. and the Staff Manual respectively. Title Pages will be prepared in manuscript.

WAR DIARY
or
~~INTELLIGENCE SUMMARY~~
(Erase heading not required.)

No. 109 MACHINE GUN COMPANY.
No. Page 82

Army Form C. 2118.

Place	Date 1916	Hour	Summary of Events and Information	Remarks and references to Appendices
DRANOUTRE	OCTOBER 4th		Work on the Horse standings continued but difficulty in securing the necessary material is being experienced. Teams in Reserve & Class of Instruction carried out programme of training during the morning. In the evening relief of teams in the trenches was carried out. From the trenches nothing was reported as having taken place during last night except the usual enemy M. Gun activity. Our own guns were active also and fired 2000 rounds during last night on Enemy Trenches, Light Railway, Footpaths and Wood. Early this morning the Enemy Trench Mortars were active for about 15 minutes. Weather: Showery	[initials]
	5th		To-day again we worked at the Horse Standings and teams in reserve got Instruction on Machine Gunnery as did also the Class of Instruction. Late yesterday afternoon the enemy appeared to be registering on our trenches. KINGSWAY Trench was hit and our Machine Gun emplacement at S. MINESHAFT was also damaged. Later (About 7.30 PM) the enemy commenced to bombard our trenches with T. Mortars and H.E. His machine guns were also very active and traversed the road running thro FRENCHMANS FARM. During this bombardment which lasted for an hour and a half one of our Machine Gunners (18604 Priv J AICKEN) mounted his gun on the front parapet and steadily put a belt of fire across NO MAN'S LAND. Obviously the Enemy observed the flash of the gun and directed Artillery & M.G. fire onto it but AICKEN continued to fire and by his action greatly encouraged the Infantry in the front line and doubtless prevented the enemy attempting to raid our trenches. Priv AICKEN has been recommended for the Military Medal. During the remainder of last night there was nothing unusual but our guns carried out Indirect fire as usual. This morning our Artillery & T.M's bombarded Enemy trenches very heavily. We co-operated with five guns and fired 10.000 rounds on Trench Junctions, Communication Trenches and Strong Points. Weather to day was fine.	[initials]

Instructions regarding War Diaries and Intelligence Summaries are contained in F. S. Regs., Part II. and the Staff Manual respectively. Title Pages will be prepared in manuscript.

WAR DIARY
or
~~INTELLIGENCE~~ SUMMARY
(Erase heading not required.)

No. 109 MACHINE GUN COMPANY.

Page 83

Army Form C. 2118.

Place	Date 1916	Hour	Summary of Events and Information	Remarks and references to Appendices
DRANOUTRE	OCTOBER 6th		Work on Horse standings and improvement of Billets was continued. In addition all available men in reserve received instruction in Machine Gunnery. The Class of Instruction carried on as usual under the Sergt Instructors. Nothing unusual in the trenches last night has been reported. Arrangements had been made for our guns to co-operate with a Gas attack but the wind was unfavourable. During the night our guns were engaged in Indirect Fire against Enemy defences – about 2000 rounds were fired. Nothing of interest occurred during the day in the trenches. Five promotions in the ranks of the N.C.O's were made to-day	[illegible]
	7th		Further work was done on the Horse Standings and track leading thereto to-day. The usual instruction was given to all available men and the Class of Instruction. In the trenches nothing of importance is to be reported regarding the enemy's activity but our guns were active during last night against Enemy's Communication Trenches & Trench Tramway &c – about 3000 rounds were fired.	[illegible]
	8th		All available men paraded to-day for Divine Service but a party was kept at work on the standings. From the trenches it was reported that enemy Machine Guns were active last night and the enemy was observed to be sending up Very Lights from his second line. Two of his Shrapnel were also observed to burst just behind his front line and bombs were thrown from his second line. Our Machine Guns fired about 4000 rounds on Enemy Comm. Trenches, Trench Tramway and other defence works. Weather was showery.	[illegible]

2449 Wt. W14957/M90 750,000 1/16 J.B.C. & A. Forms/C.2118/12.

Instructions regarding War Diaries and Intelligence Summaries are contained in F. S. Regs., Part II. and the Staff Manual respectively. Title Pages will be prepared in manuscript.

WAR DIARY
or
~~INTELLIGENCE SUMMARY~~
(Erase heading not required.)

No. 109 MACHINE GUN COMPANY.
No. ...
Unit Page 84

Army Form C. 2118.

Place	Date 1916.	Hour	Summary of Events and Information	Remarks and references to Appendices
DRANOUTRE	OCTOBER 9th		Scarcity of the necessary materials permits only slow progress at our Horse Standings but no time is being lost in our efforts to complete them before winter sets in properly. The teams in reserve were given Instruction today and the Class of Instruction continued the usual programme. During last night there was great activity in the trenches. At 1.30 AM Gas was released from our front line and drifted rapidly towards the Enemy trenches. Two of our Machine Guns were in position in the front line and opened fire simultaneously with the release of the Gas but apparently the enemy was on the alert and immediately sent up a large number of Very lights. It was observed however that he sounded no Gongs or Hooters which would give the impression that some other means of giving a Gas alarm is used by him – probably Electric Bells in the dugouts. A few minutes after the release of gas our Artillery & T.M's opened fire and were replied to with Rifle Grenades and T.M's. At 1.45 AM the Enemy Artillery retaliated and were active until about 3.30 AM after which time everything was quiet. The enemy was obviously very nervous last night for when heavy bombing was heard on the right he commenced intense rifle fire all along our front. The usual indirect fire programme was carried out by our Machine Guns	[initials]
	10th		Today we again kept a party at work on the Horse Standings & other work. All other available men were engaged in M.G. training. Only the usual Enemy M.G. activity was reported as having taken place during last night. This morning about 10.30 AM the enemy shelled a working party in PICADILLY Trench with 5.9 shells. Our Machine Guns were as usual active last night & fired about 3000 rounds on Enemy defences and roads	[initials]

2449 Wt. W14957/M90 750,000 1/16 J.B.C. & A. Forms/C.2118/12.

Instructions regarding War Diaries and Intelligence Summaries are contained in F. S. Regs., Part II. and the Staff Manual respectively. Title Pages will be prepared in manuscript.

WAR DIARY
or
~~INTELLIGENCE SUMMARY~~
(Erase heading not required.)

No. 109 MACHINE GUN COMPANY.
Page 85

Army Form C. 2118.

Place	Date 1916	Hour	Summary of Events and Information	Remarks and references to Appendices
DRANOUTRE	OCTOBER 11th		In Reserve Billets work of improvement was gone on with and the building of Horse Standings was proceeded with. The report from the trenches deals only with the usual enemy M.G activity during last night and our own Indirect fire ~~—~~ we fired about 4000 rounds on the usual targets.	[initials]
	12th		Men were told off to assist the transport personnel with the Horse Standings and all other available gunners got the usual training as did also the Class of Instruction. The enemy was quiet last night except for Machine Gun fire. In the early hours of this morning a raid was carried out by One of the Battns in the line. Our Artillery opened fire at 2 AM and unfortunately were short in their range. We had two guns in the front line to Co-operate and the other guns fired during the night altogether about 15.000 rounds on the Enemy Trench Railway Communication Trenches and Strong points.	[initials]
	13th		The necessary men were detailed to work on the Horse Standings. A working party of 10 men was sent to the trenches and other work & fatigues used up all the available men. The Class of Instruction continued as usual at the programme of training. There was nothing unusual in the trenches during the night until 2 AM when the enemy commenced a Trench Mortar Bombardment which lasted 1¼ hours. We retaliated. Our Machine Guns carried out Indirect fire against the usual target — about 5,000 rounds being fired.	[initials]

2449 Wt. W14957/M90 750,000 1/16 J.B.C. & A. Forms/C.2118/12.

Instructions regarding War Diaries and Intelligence Summaries are contained in F. S. Regs., Part II. and the Staff Manual respectively. Title Pages will be prepared in manuscript.

WAR DIARY
or
~~INTELLIGENCE~~ SUMMARY
(Erase heading not required.)

No. 109. MACHINE GUN COMPANY. No. Page 86 Date.

Army Form C. 2118.

Place	Date 1916	Hour	Summary of Events and Information	Remarks and references to Appendices
DRANOUTRE	OCTOBER 14th		In addition to work on the Horse standings, a party of men were engaged to-day in building a Sandbag store for our Reserve ammunition. The Class carried on as usual In the trenches M.G. activity on the part of the enemy and ourselves during last night was all that was reported. We expended 4000 rounds in Indirect fire on Enemy defences. Weather was fair.	[illegible]
	15th		All available men paraded for Divine Service to-day. 2 Lieut D. WALKER and 2 N.C.O's proceeded to the Machine Gun School to-day for a Course of Instruction. Relief of teams in the trenches was carried out this evening. During last night nothing important occurred in the trenches. The enemy M.G's were active and our guns fired 4000 rounds on the Enemy's Trench Tramway & C.T's This morning about 11.30 AM. a few enemy shells came over near our Emplacement at S MINESHAFT. Weather was good.	[illegible]
	16th		Teams which were relieved yesterday spent to-day in cleaning up. We also got a good deal of work done on the Horse standings to-day From the trenches it was reported "about 6 PM yesterday the Enemy fired about 16 shells at DAYLIGHT CORNER Area". Last night was quiet in the line with the exception of Enemy Sniping fire. We got off about 3000 rounds during the night at the Enemy's Trench Tramway & Communication Trenches. We had a casualty to-day — 1 man wounded.	[illegible]

Instructions regarding War Diaries and Intelligence Summaries are contained in F. S. Regs., Part II. and the Staff Manual respectively. Title Pages will be prepared in manuscript.

WAR DIARY
or
~~INTELLIGENCE~~ SUMMARY
(Erase heading not required.)

No. 109 MACHINE GUN COMPANY. No. Page 87

Army Form C. 2118.

Place	Date	Hour	Summary of Events and Information	Remarks and references to Appendices
	1916 OCTOBER			
DRANOUTRE	17th		Our Horse standings are completed now except for Overhead Cover and shortage of Corr Iron prevents that being completed. The framework for the roof is being got ready. We have also made a track leading from the Road to the Horse standings.	
			All available men were given the usual training to-day but many were engaged on above work	
			The Class of Instruction carried on at the programme laid down	
			The Divisional Commander inspected our Billets and Transport lines to-day.	
			The report from the trenches was: "Nothing unusual last night except slight activity on part of Enemy M Guns and Snipers." Our own guns fired 3000 rounds at CROSS ROADS N30d 57.33, at strong point N30d 80.80 and the WOOD.	[initials]
			This afternoon our Artillery & T.M's carried out a Bombardment of the Enemy's line. Four of our Machine guns co-operated and fired 15.000 rounds at enemy communication trenches in N36B. The M Guns of the 49th Coy also co-operated. The Boche made little or no reply.	
	18th		A large number of the men of reserve teams were engaged to-day at the different jobs on hand. Those backward in Mechanism & stoppages were given special instruction. The Class continued its programme. In the trenches nothing of importance occurred. The Enemy M Guns were again active and our guns carried out Indirect Fire programme	[initials]
			We had one casualty to-day. One man wounding himself in the hand while cleaning his rifle	
	19th		The usual work was carried on in Billets. Available men received Training and the Class of Instruction carried out programme of training. On our own front last night was quiet in the trenches with the exception of Enemy Snipers & Machine Guns and some Rocket Bombs which the enemy sent over — 10 burst over the head of KINGSWAY. 4000 rounds were fired by us at Enemy Communication Trenches and other defences	[initials]

2449 Wt. W14957/M90 750,000 1/16 J.B.C. & A. Forms/C.2118/12.

Instructions regarding War Diaries and Intelligence Summaries are contained in F. S. Regs., Part II. and the Staff Manual respectively. Title Pages will be prepared in manuscript.

WAR DIARY
or
INTELLIGENCE SUMMARY
(Erase heading not required.)

Army Form C. 2118.

No. 109 MACHINE GUN COMPANY. No. Page 88

Place	Date 1916	Hour	Summary of Events and Information	Remarks and references to Appendices
DRANOUTRE	OCTOBER 20th		Work on Horse standings was proceeded with. All other men received training and the Class of Instruction carried out programme of training. Promotions were made with effect from 19th inst: 1 to Sergt and 8 to Cpl, 2 to L/Cpl. 36th Div Order ~~No~~ 1163 d/20.10.16 reads "The IX Corps Commander has awarded the Military Medal to 18604 Priv J. AICKEN 109th M.G. Coy." This is the man referred to on Page 82 as having been recommended. During last night the enemy M. Guns and Snipers were active. Our own guns fired 3.500 rounds on French Tramway & other enemy works. At 8.30 AM and 2.15 PM to-day the rather unusual sight (in this area) of a German Aeroplane over our lines was witnessed. Our Anti Air Craft guns drove them off. One of our Aeroplanes flew at a very low altitude over our own and Enemy lines several times during the afternoon. The enemy unsuccessfully fired rifles & machine guns at it. Weather good.	[illegible]
	21st		Horse Standings are now complete as far as standings and Head cover, a party of men were engaged at the Field Kitchen to-day - It is a new type and takes some time to build. Teams in reserve got some training to-day and the Class of Instruction carried on as usual. Capt McCONACHIE and Lieut CLOKEY journeyed to HAZEBROUCK to day with the Staff Captain and D.A.D.O.S for the purpose of inspecting a type of MG mounting in the II Army Workshops. On our front the night was quiet. Our Machine Guns were active against enemy defences. To day again a German Aeroplane crossed our lines at a high altitude at 9 AM and 11 AM. At 3 pm this afternoon our T.M's were active but the Boche didn't reply. The weather was beautifully fine to day but cold.	[illegible]

Instructions regarding War Diaries and Intelligence Summaries are contained in F. S. Regs., Part II. and the Staff Manual respectively. Title Pages will be prepared in manuscript.

WAR DIARY
or
~~INTELLIGENCE~~ SUMMARY
(Erase heading not required.)

No. Page 89

Army Form C. 2118.

Place	Date 1916	Hour	Summary of Events and Information	Remarks and references to Appendices
DRANOUTRE	OCTOBER 22nd		All available men in Billets paraded to-day for Divine Service In the evening the teams in the trenches were relieved. Report from the trenches says "Night quiet. Enemy M.Guns & Snipers active. We fired about 3000 rounds at Trench Tramway. Strong point & wood in the enemy lines" Weather: fine.	
	23rd		In Billets the teams which were relieved yesterday spent the day in cleaning guns equipment &c after duty in the trenches. The Class of Instruction carried out programme of training. Orders have been received that the establishment of a M.G Company is to be increased by 32 Privates 1 G.S. Limbered Wagon, 2 Spare Horses and 1 Driver. The 32 Privates are to be transferred from the Battalions of the Brigade. In our case we have, already attached to the Coy: 8 men for duty and 12 for Instruction. Arrangements were made for these 20 men to be retained and an additional 12 sent to us to complete the full number. The 12 additional men have reported and all will be transferred in course to the Machine Gun Corps for duty with this company. Only M.Gun activity & sniping activity on the part of the enemy was reported from the trenches. We fired 4000 rounds on the usual targets during the night. Weather to-day wet	
	24th		Teams in reserve received instruction – a number of them were engaged in waterproofing Billets and in building Field Kitchen. The new men also received instruction. Last night in the trenches was quiet. Boche working parties were out in front and our front line gun fired a belt at them. Our other guns were engaged in the usual indirect fire – 7000 rounds expended. We had a casualty amongst our animals last night. One of the mules of the ration limber was hit by an enemy bullet on returning from FRENCHMANS FARM. It was able to get back to the transport lines but died this morning. Weather to-day very wet	

2149 Wt. W14957/M90 750,000 1/16 J.B.C. & A. Forms/C.2118/12.

Instructions regarding War Diaries and Intelligence Summaries are contained in F. S. Regs., Part II. and the Staff Manual respectively. Title Pages will be prepared in manuscript.

WAR DIARY
or
~~INTELLIGENCE SUMMARY~~
(Erase heading not required.)

Army Form C. 2118.

Place	Date	Hour	Summary of Events and Information	Remarks and references to Appendices
DRANOUTRE	OCTOBER 25th		In Billets the teams in Reserve were given instruction. The 32 men attached for instruction with a view to transfer got further training. The Field Kitchen is still be worked at – It is nearing completion. In the trenches last night all was quiet except for intermittent Enemy M.G. fire and the Indirect fire of our own guns in which 6000 rounds were directed against enemy defences. Weather: Wet.	[illegible]
	26th		Training was carried on by all available M. Gunners and the attached men. A Party worked at building the Field Kitchen & other Billet Improvement work. In the trenches this afternoon things were lively. The enemy commenced to send "Minnies" over at 2.45 PM and was very active for a time. On one occasion 5 "Minnies" were in the air at the same time. In a small area about our front line gun the Enemy dropped five "Minnies" and within 5 yds of our MINESHAFT Emplacement he dropped 2. KINGSWAY TRENCH was somewhat knocked about also but fortunately we suffered no casualties in the Company. Indeed it appears that there were no casualties amongst the troops holding the line at all. During last night the only activity on the part of the Enemy was machine gun fire. We used Indirect fire as usual against his positions – firing about 4,000 rounds. Weather: Wet.	[illegible]
	27th		To-day the attached men fired a short course on the range. The other men were engaged at Training. The weather has been very bad – High wind & heavy showers. During last night the enemy was comparatively quiet altho his machine guns showed their usual activity. Our front line gun fired on Enemy front line and parapet and the guns used for Indirect fire were active against the Enemy C.T's and Trench Tramway to the extent of 4000 rounds.	[illegible]

Instructions regarding War Diaries and Intelligence Summaries are contained in F. S. Regs., Part II. and the Staff Manual respectively. Title Pages will be prepared in manuscript.

WAR DIARY
or
~~INTELLIGENCE~~ SUMMARY
(Erase heading not required.)

No. 109 MACHINE GUN COMPANY.
No. Page 91

Army Form C. 2118.

Place	Date 1916	Hour	Summary of Events and Information	Remarks and references to Appendices
DRANOUTRE	OCTOBER 28th		To day the usual instruction was given to all available gunners in Reserve. This included the men attached for transfer. In the afternoon the Coy played a Football match against the Anti Aircraft Battery: Result 2 goals each. From the trenches it is reported that last night was quiet with the exception of Enemy M.G. and Sniping activity early in the evening. Our own guns fired 11.000 rounds on Enemy Front line, French Tramway, Communication Trenches and Strong points during the night. Weather was wet	[initials]
	29th		Parades this morning were for Divine Service. Later the teams prepared for their tour of duty in the trenches and in the evening Reliefs were carried out. In the trenches last night the situation was normal. The Enemy M. Guns showed their usual activity only. We fired 10.000 rounds between 6 PM & 2 AM this morning at the Boche front line and other defences. Weather very wet & cold	[initials]
	30th		The attached men continued their studies to day and the teams which were relieved yesterday were engaged in cleaning their guns equipment &c On our own front there was nothing unusual on the part of the enemy, during last night. On our left the 16th Division carried out a raid accompanied by a heavy Bombardment. At about 10 PM last night an enemy M. G. was observed in his front line, and our front line gun immediately engaged it. There was a loud scream heard and the enemy fire ceased. We carried out our programme of night firing and directed 8.000 rounds against enemy defences. Weather Stormy wet & cold	[initials]

2449 Wt. W14957/M90 750,000 1/16 J.B.C. & A. Forms/C.2118/12.

Army Form C. 2118.

WAR DIARY
or
~~INTELLIGENCE SUMMARY~~

(Erase heading not required.)

Instructions regarding War Diaries and Intelligence Summaries are contained in F. S. Regs., Part II. and the Staff Manual respectively. Title Pages will be prepared in manuscript.

Place	Date	Hour	Summary of Events and Information	Remarks and references to Appendices
DRANOUTRE	1916 OCTOBER 31st		To-day the men attached for transfer received further instruction and all available Machine gunners were engaged on parade under the Section Officers. No activity on the part of the enemy during last night with the exception of the usual amount of M.G. and Sniping fire. Our own M. Guns fired 9.000 Rounds at Enemy front line. Communication Trenches and Trench Tramway during the night. Weather was much better today. There was only one shower but the high wind continues and in consequence there have been no aeroplanes aloft.	[illegible initials]

CONFIDENTIAL.

Vol 8

WAR DIARY

of

109TH BRIGADE MACHINE GUN COMPANY,

from 1st November 1916 to 30th November 1916.

Instructions regarding War Diaries and Intelligence Summaries are contained in F. S. Regs., Part II. and the Staff Manual respectively. Title Pages will be prepared in manuscript.

WAR DIARY
or
INTELLIGENCE SUMMARY
(Erase heading not required.)

No. 109 MACHINE GUN COMPANY. Page 93

Army Form C. 2118.

Place	Date 1916	Hour	Summary of Events and Information	Remarks and references to Appendices
DRANOUTRE	Nov 1st		To day the usual work of preparing Billets & Horse lines for the winter was continued. The necessary men having been detailed. All available gunners received instruction from the Section Officers. Five men of the Class of instruction after an examination were posted to teams for duty in the trenches. In the trenches last night the Enemy M. Guns and Snipers were active on our front. Our own Machine guns carried out their usual programme of Night Firing and in the early hours of this morning co-operated in a raid which was made by the 14th R.I.R. Unfortunately this raid was not a success as only an officer and Sgt were able to enter the Enemy trench. Weather was fair to-day.	[initials]
	2nd		In Billets to-day the gunners in reserve received instruction and the necessary men continued the work of improving Billets for the winter. A working party proceeded to the trenches to carry on the work of building emplacements & repairing trenches. Only the usual Enemy M.G. activity & sniping fire is reported as having taken place last night on the part of the enemy. Our own guns were busy and fired about 6,000 rounds. The weather to-day was showery.	[initials]
	3rd		A dry although cold day to-day allowed for more work to be carried on in Billets and in the trenches a good deal of work was got through. During last night our M. Guns fired 4000 rounds at enemy defenses and the enemy was inactive except for sniping and Machine Gun fire.	[initials]

2449 Wt. W14957/M90 750,000 1/16 J.B.C. & A. Forms/C.2118/12.

Instructions regarding War Diaries and Intelligence Summaries are contained in F. S. Regs., Part II. and the Staff Manual respectively. Title Pages will be prepared in manuscript.

WAR DIARY
or
INTELLIGENCE SUMMARY
(Erase heading not required.)

Army Form C. 2118.

Place	Date 1916	Hour	Summary of Events and Information	Remarks and references to Appendices
DRANOUTRE	Nov 4th		Gunners in reserve were engaged today in preparing for their tour of duty in the trenches. A number of men were engaged at the Drainage scheme of the Camp and a working party went to the trenches. Last night in the trenches was quiet except for Enemy Machine Gun fire which caused us one casualty. One of the ration party being wounded at FRENCHMANS FARM. The Enemy has been more active with his M.G.s of late. Our own guns fired about 4.000 rounds on Enemy road and Communication Trenches. Weather: Dry and Cold	[initials]
	5th		Divine services were attended this morning. In the afternoon relief of the teams in the trenches was carried out. During last night there was nothing unusual took place in the trenches. Our Machine Guns fired 8.000 on points of importance behind enemy lines. To day the Enemy Artillery was unusually active and in the afternoon he replied very vigorously to our Trench Mortar Bombardment. Our Machine Guns Co-operated with the Trench Mortars and fired about 3.000 rounds at selected targets in the enemy lines. The weather to day was ~~[illegible]~~ Fine	[initials]
	6th		The wet weather to-day prevented much outdoor work being done. In the trenches, last night was quiet so far as Enemy M Guns were concerned. Our own guns fired 4.000 rounds on Trench Tramway and Road in the enemy lines	[initials]

2449 Wt. W14957/M90 750,000 1/16 J.B.C. & A. Forms/C.2118/12.

Instructions regarding War Diaries and Intelligence Summaries are contained in F. S. Regs., Part II. and the Staff Manual respectively. Title Pages will be prepared in manuscript.

WAR DIARY
or
INTELLIGENCE SUMMARY
(Erase heading not required.)

No. 109 MACHINE GUN COMPANY. Dec 15

Army Form C. 2118.

Place	Date 1916	Hour	Summary of Events and Information	Remarks and references to Appendices
DRANOUTRE	Nov. 7th		A working party proceeded to the trenches to-day to carry on work for a couple of days. Other available gunners and the men attached for instruction carried on as usual with their drills but a number were engaged on work about the [illegible] & horse standings. During last night the enemy showed no activity but to-day his Trench Mortars were active and he also sent over a few whizz Bangs. In the afternoon a green & white flare were observed going up from the enemy lines and immediately his T.M. and artillery fire increased in violence. We carried out our usual programme of night firing last night and directed 6000 rounds on enemy Trench Railway C.7.b.7.c. Very heavy showers to-day	[illegible]
	8th		To-day we removed the Saddlery shed and reconstructed it in a more convenient place. Our camp is becoming more complete and compact each day. In Billets the reserve gunners received instruction in Machine Gunnery and the working party in the trenches carried on. During last night the enemy M. guns were quiet but ours were active to the extent of 6.000 rounds directed at points of importance. Weather: Showery	[illegible]
	9th		The working party mentioned above did not return last night but remained there to carry on the repair of KINGSWAY. An additional party of 20 OR. was sent to-day to assist and only the Class of Instruction remained in Billets; they carried out a programme of training. In the trenches last night the enemy machine guns were exceptionally quiet but we again fired 6.000 rounds during the hours of darkness at Trench Tramway Communication Trenches and Strong points. Weather to-day fine	[illegible]

2149 Wt. W14957/M90 750,000 1/16 J.B.C. & A. Forms/C.2118/12.

WAR DIARY
or
~~INTELLIGENCE SUMMARY~~
(Erase heading not required.)

Instructions regarding War Diaries and Intelligence Summaries are contained in F. S. Regs., Part II. and the Staff Manual respectively. Title Pages will be prepared in manuscript.

No. 109 MACHINE GUN COMPANY

Page 96

Army Form C. 2118.

Place	Date 1916	Hour	Summary of Events and Information	Remarks and references to Appendices
DRANOUTRE	NOV 10th		Most of the gunners in reserve are still in the trenches on a working party and the remainder were engaged to day in drainage and constructional work about billets. The class of Instruction carried on with the programme laid down. Last night and to-day were very quiet in the trenches but there was considerable aerial activity. Last night we got off about 6.000 rounds in night firing on enemy defences. Weather fine	[initials]
	11th		The teams in reserve were engaged to day in preparing their guns equipment etc for their tour of duty in the trenches. The class of Instruction continued its work. In the trenches our night firing programme I was carried out and during the night 6000 rounds were fired. In the early part of the night the enemy was inactive but towards dawn their Machine guns were busy. The weather to day was fine but in the afternoon a mist came up. We took advantage of the mist to fire 3000 rounds on enemy trench Tramway	[initials]
	12th		All available men paraded to day for Divine Service and in the evening relief of teams in the trenches was carried out. Only normal activity on the part of the enemy during last night is reported from the trenches. Our Machine guns were active between ~~dusk~~ and dawn and fired about 4000 rounds on points of importance in the enemy lines. Weather to-day was fine.	[initials]

2449 Wt. W14957/M90 750,000 1/16 J.B.C. & A. Forms/C.2118/12.

Instructions regarding War Diaries and Intelligence Summaries are contained in F. S. Regs., Part II. and the Staff Manual respectively. Title Pages will be prepared in manuscript.

WAR DIARY
or
INTELLIGENCE SUMMARY
(Erase heading not required.)

No. 109 MACHINE GUN COMPANY.
No. Page 97

Army Form C. 2118.

Place	Date 1916	Hour	Summary of Events and Information	Remarks and references to Appendices
DRANOUTRE	Nov 13th		The teams which were relieved yesterday spent to-day in cleaning up their guns equipment &c. The Class of Instruction carried on as usual. It is noticeable that enemy machine gun fire has decreased of late and his guns are active only at dusk and dawn. We find that he is now using a steel cased bullet instead of nickel. This steel bullet is dipped lightly cased with Brass or Copper apparently to allow for rifling. It is also interesting to note that only 4 "lands" are visible on these new bullets instead of the usual 8. At about 9 PM last night our front line gun got a chance at an enemy working party and quickly dispersed it. Our other guns engaged in night firing and directed 3000 rounds on enemy defences. 2 Lieut P N DINGLEY was accidently wounded this afternoon. Weather fine.	[illegible]
	14th		A working party proceeded to the trenches to-day and the remainder of the Gunners in reserve received the usual instruction. Last night in the trenches was more lively and enemy M guns & snipers were more active. Our own artillery was active and our Machine Guns fired 5000 rounds on enemy defences. Weather fine.	[illegible]
	15th		The usual work was carried on in Billets. During last night our Machine Guns in the line fired 6000 rounds on Enemy Trenches &c. To-day our Trench Mortars bombarded the enemy and in co-operation our Machine Guns fired 5000 rounds. The Enemy retaliated very feebly. Weather fine. Last night two enemy Aeroplanes were seen over our lines and our Anti Aircraft guns opened fire	[illegible]

Instructions regarding War Diaries and Intelligence Summaries are contained in F. S. Regs., Part II. and the Staff Manual respectively. Title Pages will be prepared in manuscript.

WAR DIARY
or
~~INTELLIGENCE~~ SUMMARY
(Erase heading not required.)

Army Form C. 2118.

No. 109 MACHINE GUN COMPANY. Page 98

Place	Date 1916	Hour	Summary of Events and Information	Remarks and references to Appendices
DRANOUTRE	Nov 16th		A working party proceeded to the trenches to day and in Billets work was carried on at the waggon lines. 30 O.R. were inoculated to day as per orders received In the trenches last night everything was quiet on the part of the enemy. We fired 3000 rounds during the night on points of importance in the enemy lines Weather: fine	[illegible]
	17th		All available men in reserve were engaged at work on Horsestandings &c. The 30 O.R. inoculated yesterday were of course free from duty to day. During the early part of last night the only activity in the trenches was on the part of our M Guns. At 10 PM we fired several guns in co-operation with a raid carried out by the 11th Innis Fus. This raid was very successful and four prisoners were taken. It was found that the enemy opposing us are Saxons. Weather fine	
	18th		Teams in reserve prepared for duty in the trenches Last night was quiet on the part of the enemy but we fired 6000 rounds on Enemy Light Railway Communication trenches & road. Weather Wet	[illegible]
	19th		Divine services were attended by all available men of the reserve teams to day In the trenches the early part of last night was quiet but at 1:30 AM this morning the enemy commenced a heavy Bombardment (T.M's & Artillery) and directed his fire chiefly against our left front. We had two casualties in our front line team (wounded) but the remaining members of the team remounted the gun, which had been upset, and stuck by it throughout the bombardment. Our gun at MINESHAFT Position was put temporarily out of action by getting a Bullet through the Barrel casing. The other guns fired upwards of 5000 rounds on Enemy Communication Trenches, Light Railways & roads during the Bombardment At 2:30PM to day the Stokes guns bombarded the Enemy trenches. Weather: Dry & cold	[illegible]

2449 Wt. W14957/M90 750,000 1/16 J.B.C. & A. Forms/C.2118/12.

Instructions regarding War Diaries and Intelligence Summaries are contained in F. S. Regs., Part II. and the Staff Manual respectively. Title Pages will be prepared in manuscript.

WAR DIARY
or
~~INTELLIGENCE SUMMARY~~
(Erase heading not required.)

Army Form C. 2118.

Place	Date 1916	Hour	Summary of Events and Information	Remarks and references to Appendices
DRANOUTRE	Nov 20th		All guns, equipment &c were thoroughly cleaned to day after the relief of teams which took place yesterday. There was also a feet inspection and Baths. In the afternoon 30 OR were inoculated. During last night we fired 2000 rounds on Enemy Trench Railway and C.T's. The enemy was very inactive, his Machine Guns were seldom heard. Weather: dry but some rain fell late this evening	[initials]
	21st		A working party proceeded to the trenches to day and other available men were engaged at waggon lines. Those requiring instruction on the gun joined on to the Class of Instruction. In the trenches last night there was nothing unusual happened the Enemy M.guns were inactive whilst ours fired 2000 rounds on the usual targets. Weather dry and very misty	[initials]
	22nd		2 Lieut R. WILLIAMS from M.G.T.C joined the Company to day for duty. The working party which proceeded to the trenches yesterday remained there overnight and continued their work to day. Teams in reserve carried out the usual programme of work & training. On our own front last night was comparatively quiet with enemy machine guns inactive. We fired 3000 rounds on Enemy defences. Weather: dry.	[initials]
	23rd		A working party proceeded to the trenches to day. The remaining men in reserve continued their training. Two officers of the Company proceeded to the sector of our line S.W of MESSINES on a reconnaissance to day. Orders were received to day for Lieut E.H. CLOKEY 2nd in command of the Company to proceed to take over command of the 118th M.G. Coy. In the early part of last night we fired 1600 rounds in co-operation with a "Dummy" Raid by the Brigade on our left. During the rest of the night we fired 2000 rounds on the usual targets in the enemy lines. This morning the enemy trenches were heavily bombarded by Light Medium & Heavy T.M's and Artillery. His reply was very feeble. During this bombardment our M guns fired 9.000 rounds on Communication trenches &c in Enemy lines. Weather: fine, dry.	[initials]

2449 Wt. W14957/M90 750,000 1/16 J.B.C. & A. Forms/C.2118/12.

Instructions regarding War Diaries and Intelligence Summaries are contained in F. S. Regs., Part II. and the Staff Manual respectively. Title pages will be prepared in manuscript.

WAR DIARY
or
~~INTELLIGENCE SUMMARY.~~
(Erase heading not required.)

Army Form C. 2118.

Place	Date 1916	Hour	Summary of Events and Information	Remarks and references to Appendices
DRANOUTRE	24th		Lieut. E H. CLOKEY left the Coy today to take charge of 118th Coy. We were all very sorry to lose him but are confident of his success. Brigadier General SHUTER saw all the young officers of the company and informed them that he didn't think they took their work seriously. He pointed out their failings and asked for a report in three weeks time. It was quiet in trenches all day but at 10.0 p.m. the enemy commenced a heavy bombardment of our line with artillery and trench mortars. He had evidently increased the number of his artillery and trench mortar guns. ~~At one time~~ Six heavy trench mortar shells were seen in the air at one time. The trenches of the left Battalion 11th R. Innis. Fus. got the most and they had heavy casualties 9. O.R. killed. 1 officer 13 O.R. wounded. His artillery fire was mostly shrapnel. Our Heavy How^s. silenced the enemy trench mortars in 30 minutes but his artillery kept going until 11.30 p.m. We heard an enemy machine gun which seemed much faster than usual and appeared to have had some arrangement for muffling the sound. Three of our machine Guns opened fire at once on Communication Trenches N36.B central and N30 central. We fire 9000 rounds. Had no casualties. Weather dry & dull.	MC

T2134. Wt. W708—776. 500000. 4/15. Sir J. C. & S.

Instructions regarding War Diaries and Intelligence Summaries are contained in F. S. Regs., Part II. and the Staff Manual respectively. Title pages will be prepared in manuscript.

WAR DIARY
or
~~INTELLIGENCE SUMMARY.~~
(Erase heading not required.)

Page 101

Army Form C. 2118.

Place	Date 1916	Hour	Summary of Events and Information	Remarks and references to Appendices
DRANOUTRE	Nov 25th		We had heavy rain all day and no work could be done in the trenches. Last night was quiet in the trenches. Our guns fired 2000 rounds on enemys communications. ~~The weath~~	MMC
	26th		Divine Services were attended by all available men. Teams in reserve prepared for duty in the trenches. weather was dull	MMC
	27th		The teams which were relieved yesterday spent the day cleaning guns equipment etc. Weather was fine. Our guns fire 4000 rounds on enemy communication trenches	MMC
	28th		~~A working party of 12 men and~~ A working party of 12 men and 1 N.C.O proceeded to the trenches. leaving billets at 12 o noon after they had their bath. 15 men were inoculated T.A.B. system. The drafts which joined us recently were found to have so little training in musketry etc that we found it necessary to put them through a course of training commencing today. The remainder of the company fit for duty received instruction in the use of the Anti Gas Box Respirator from Sergt Wilkes who had just returned from the Divisional School. Lieut J. BAXANDINE - REYPERT reported for duty today and was taken on the strength	MMC

T2134. Wt. W708—776. 500000. 4/15. Sir J. C. & S.

Instructions regarding War Diaries and Intelligence Summaries are contained in F. S. Regs., Part II. and the Staff Manual respectively. Title Pages will be prepared in manuscript.

WAR DIARY
or
INTELLIGENCE SUMMARY

(Erase heading not required.)

No. 109 MACHINE GUN COMPANY.
No. 102
Date.

Army Form C. 2118.

Place	Date 1916	Hour	Summary of Events and Information	Remarks and references to Appendices
DRANOUTRE	Nov. 29th		There was a very heavy mist all day. Our guns fired 4000 rounds on communication trenches in front of the 107th Brigade (our right) during the night. The enemy was quiet. Lieut. A.O. ROBINSON reported for duty as second in command today and was taken on the strength. Lieut J. BAXANDINE-REYPERT report sick and was sent to the F.A.	
	30th		The divisional Light and Medium Trench mortars and Artillery bombarded the enemy's trenches in front of the 107th Brigade commencing at 2.0 p.m. The Light Trench Mortars fired 3600 rounds and the Mediums 1000. The enemys retaliation was light. His trenches were badly knocked about and his duck boards were seen to go up in the air. Our guns fired 9000 rounds behind his first and second lines in the hope of catching a few when they were retiring. Weather still very misty	[illegible]

2449 Wt. W14957/M90 750,000 1/16 J.B.C. & A. Forms/C.2118/12.

CONFIDENTIAL

Vol 9

WAR DIARY

of

109TH BRIGADE MACHINE GUN COMPANY

from

1st December 1916

to

31st December 1916

Confidential

War Diary

of

109th Machine Gun Company

From 1st December 1916 To 31st December 1916.

Army Form C. 2118.

Instructions regarding War Diaries and Intelligence Summaries are contained in F. S. Regs., Part II. and the Staff Manual respectively. Title Pages will be prepared in manuscript.

WAR DIARY
or ~~INTELLIGENCE SUMMARY~~ 109th Machine Gun Coy

(Erase heading not required.)

No. 109 MACHINE GUN COMPANY. No. 103 Date.........

Place	Date 1916	Hour	Summary of Events and Information	Remarks and references to Appendices
DRANOUTRE	Dec 1st		The enemy was quiet during the night. He could be heard busy working in his front trenches repairing the damage done to them by our trench-mortar bombardments. Our Machine Guns fire 2000 rounds on the ~~to~~ enemy trench tramway and communication trenches O 31 central. The weather was misty with hard frost at night.	[initials]
	" 2nd		The enemy machine guns were active all night. Large working parties were again heard in his front line. We fire 3000 rounds on his communications O.31. central. Weather still misty.	[initials]
	" 3rd		The enemy machine guns were active all night. Working parties were again heard in enemy front trenches. Shouting and dropping of rails being heard frequently. We fired 3000 rounds on ~~[illegible]~~ enemy communications. Gas alarm was heard on our night at 9.45 p.m. Teams stood to for half an hour but no gas was seen. C.O visited the Billets of the 107th M.G. Coy which we are to take over in a few days and the trenches held by the 75th Machine Gun Coy. Hill 63. Ploegsteert. The weather was misty with hard frost in the morning	[initials]
	4th		The night was quiet. The C.O and two officers 47th Machine Gun Coy were shown over the trenches in the morning and took over from us that evening. The relief went smoothly and all our teams had returned to Headquarters at 8.30 p.m. We left one man with each team until next morning. The weather was misty	[initials]

2449 Wt. W14957/M90 750,000 1/16 J.B.C. & A. Forms/C.2118/12.

Instructions regarding War Diaries and Intelligence Summaries are contained in F. S. Regs., Part II. and the Staff Manual respectively. Title Pages will be prepared in manuscript.

WAR DIARY
of 109th Machine Gun Coy
~~INTELLIGENCE~~ SUMMARY
(Erase heading not required.)

Army Form C. 2118.

Place	Date 1916	Hour	Summary of Events and Information	Remarks and references to Appendices
DRANOUTRE	Decr 5th		No 1 & 2 Sections under 2nd Lts R. WALKER, 2nd Lt MONIE left DRANOUTRE to take over the trenches about Hill 63 north of PLOESTEERT. The relief was finished at 2.0 p.m. The emplacements were in very poor condition. The rest of the Company moved at 1.0 p.m and arrived their old camp KORTEPYP. The stable standings and huts for the men were ~~so~~ much better than those we had left. The Officers Mess is good and we hope to make it very comfortable. The weather is still misty but not so cold	
KORTEPYP	6th		Enemy machine guns were very quiet all the night. At 11.50 p.m a gas alarm was sounded on our right. The wind was due east. It was a false alarm. At 2.10 a.m an enemy aeroplane was heard flying very low over the trenches & our guns fired 2000 rounds SCHINTZEL FARM and Tramway 11.3c 80.20. The rest of the company were busy getting settled down in their new billets. Weather still misty	
	7th		The night was quiet. At 11.10 a.m our gun at ANTON'S FARM fired on an enemy working party which was seen, through the mist, working on their wire. They disappeared but no casualties were seen. Our guns fired 2000 rounds at last night's targets. The weather was still misty.	
	8th		The night was quiet but the enemy machine guns were fairly active. The C.O selected positions at DONNINGTON HALL U.8.C 4.9. ANTON'S FARM U 14 B 72.72 HASTED HOUSE U.14.C 77.83 ADVANCED EST U 14.A 68.47. MAC'S RUIN U 13 B 10.82 THATCHED COTTAGE T 18 B 85.77. ASH LANE U 13 D 75.72 and ordered work to be started at once. A few reserve positions were ~~[illegible]~~ selected in HEATH TR. Our guns fired 1000 rounds during the night. The weather was misty.	MAP PLOEGSTEERT 28.SW.4

2449 Wt. W14957/M90 750,000 1/16 J.B.C. & A. Forms/C.2118/12.

Instructions regarding War Diaries and Intelligence Summaries are contained in F. S. Regs., Part II. and the Staff Manual respectively. Title Pages will be prepared in manuscript.

WAR DIARY of 109th Machine Gun Coy
or
~~INTELLIGENCE SUMMARY~~

(Erase heading not required.)

Army Form C. 2118.

105

Place	Date	Hour	Summary of Events and Information	Remarks and references to Appendices
KORTEPYP	1916 Decr 9th		The enemy machine guns were active all night. Our guns fired 2000 rounds on the enemy's tramway MESSINES. PLOEGSTEERT ROAD and his communications. The Brigadier General visited the proposed sites for machine guns and approved of them. Work at the emplacements is getting on fast. The weather is misty. A Canteen for the men was started on the 8th inst and seems likely to prove a success. Lt WILGAR is taking a lot of interest in it and the men seem to appreciate it.	[initials]
	10th		The night was quiet. This is the first clear day we have had for about 10 days. The enemy artillery were fairly active registering. The Chateau getting some attention. At 5.40 pm a house was seen to be on fire in MESSINES. Our artillery gave it a few rounds to stir it up. All spare men are being sent up to the trenches to help the making of the emplacements.	[initials]
	11th		The night was quiet. Want of cement is hanging up the work at the emplacements in the trenches. Our guns fired 3500 rounds at enemy dump U 9 B 3 5. Heavy rain during the night and afternoon	
	12th		The night was fairly quiet. A terrible day of sleet. No work can be done in the trenches. Enemy artillery less active during last three days. Our guns fired 3500 rounds on - SCHNITZEL Fm U 3 C. 35 20 and DUMP U. 9. B. 30 50.	Ry. Map 28 S.W. 4 1/10,000 [initials]
	13th		About 4.15 pm while we were relieving gun guns. Our Trench Mortars opened on enemy who replied with heavy Trench mortars; no casualties were caused. At 5.0 pm enemy placed three shells near Le Rossignol emplacements at 10 pm. the enemy registered on the Chateau. The enemy appears to have a Trench Mortar	

2449 Wt. W14957/M90 750,000 1/16 J.B.C. & A. Forms/C.2118/12.

Instructions regarding War Diaries and Intelligence Summaries are contained in F. S. Regs., Part II. and the Staff Manual respectively. Title Pages will be prepared in manuscript.

WAR DIARY or INTELLIGENCE SUMMARY

of 109th Machine Gun Coy

(Erase heading not required.)

No. 109 MACHINE GUN COMPANY

No. page 106

Date.

Army Form C. 2118.

Place	Date	Hour	Summary of Events and Information	Remarks and references to Appendices
KORTEPYP	December 13th		at either U.2.d.32.78 or U.2.d.38.78 as smoke has often been seen rising from this spot on four separate occasions during the last two days. We have again noticed pigeons flying from Messines in the direction of Romarin and have reported the fact to the Brigade	AOR
	14th		Enemy Machine Guns fairly active. They also sent over an occasional Minnie on our left flank. The enemy artillery as usual registered on the Chateau and also dropped six shells of medium size on the Messines road. The weather still continues very misty	AOR
	15th		At 10.30 AM a combined Trench Mortar bombardment took place on the Salient in the enemys line south of La Petite Douve farm. U.8.a.99.40 – U.8.a.94.18. Twenty three Trench Mortars were in action assisted by one 4.5" Howitzer Battery and two 18-pdr Batteries. During the bombardment our Machine Guns kept up fire on the various trenches in the salient with the intention of catching the enemy if he attempted to leave the trenches. One of our Guns near Hasted House fired on road from La Petite Douve Farm to U.2.d.35.50 and on communication trench east of this road. One Gun at Chateau enfiladed enemys front line trench from La Petite Douve Farm to U.2.d.15.50. One gun east of HASTED HOUSE enfiladed 2ND LINE TRENCH U.8.b.6.2 to U.8.b.2.8. One gun from neighbourhood of LE ROSIGNOL enfiladed communication trenches U.8.b. central running east. Unfortunately the morning was very misty and good observation could not be obtained but great execution must have been caused as large masses of material were seen to be blown into the air.	Ref map 28 S.W 1/10,000 AOR

2449 Wt. W14957/M90 750,000 1/16 J.B.C. & A. Forms/C.2118/12.

Instructions regarding War Diaries and Intelligence Summaries are contained in F. S. Regs., Part II. and the Staff Manual respectively. Title Pages will be prepared in manuscript.

WAR DIARY or ~~INTELLIGENCE SUMMARY~~ of 109th Machine Gun Coy

(Erase heading not required.)

Army Form C. 2118.

No. Page 107

Date.........

Place	Date	Hour	Summary of Events and Information	Remarks and references to Appendices
KORTEPYP	DECEMBER 16th	7.30pm	Enemy artillery fired about ten heavy shells on lines between Chateau and Second Line	
		7.30	Searchlight played on our front line from Messines; our artillery caused it to cease operating. During the night enemy working parties were again heard opposite Antoni Farm and his transport also was clearly heard bringing up and dumping steel rails. During the night we fired 1500 rounds on Communication Trenches and Tramway U.8.d.19.70 to U.2.d.40.60	AOK
	17th		Enemy Searchlights again active from Messines & further away on the right. Le Rossignol again shelled. We fired 5000 rounds on following targets. Communication trenches and SCHNITZEL FM U.3.C Central running South East. Trench and Tramway on road U.8.b.30.95 to U.2.d.40.50. Work in the line proceeding in a very satisfactory manner. Since taking over this sector we have built Eight new emplacements and prepared up to date range charts for each position.	AOK
	18th		Early in the Evening one of our shells appeared to strike an enemy magazine to the NE of Institution Royal Messines, explosion being heard while smoke was observed rising from the spot early in the morning. Work is still being carried on opposite Antoni Farm. During the night we fired 1000 rounds on Communication trench and Tramway U.8.b.30.95 to U.2.d.40.50. Weather Wet & Stormy.	AOK

2449 Wt. W14957/M90 750,000 1/16 J.B.C. & A. Forms/C.2118/12.

Army Form C. 2118.

Instructions regarding War Diaries and Intelligence Summaries are contained in F. S. Regs., Part II. and the Staff Manual respectively. Title Pages will be prepared in manuscript.

WAR DIARY or ~~INTELLIGENCE SUMMARY~~

of 109th Machine Gun Coy

(Erase heading not required.)

Page No 108

Place	Date	Hour	Summary of Events and Information	Remarks and references to Appendices
KORTEPYP	DECEMBER 19th		Bright fine day. Unusual activity on the part of enemy Aircraft which came well behind our lines but kept very high. Our Anti Aircraft Guns were very busy; a few dud shells fell around the Camp. At night Enemy Machine Guns & Searchlights were active. It is increasingly evident that Institution Royal, Messines is being used as an Observation Post as with the aid of glasses much movement can be seen taking place there. We fired during the night 1000 rounds on Communication Trench and Tramway U.8.b.30.95 to U.2.d.40.50.	AOK
	20th		Weather again fine & bright and a few enemy Aeroplanes again crossed our line, but were soon driven back by our anti-aircraft guns. Two Germans, apparently Artillery observation Officers were seen passing through a hole in Institution Royal, Messines. Enemy fired a few shells in and about Messines Road; most of them did not explode.	AOK
	21	12-30	Light seen in the sky on the right Sector of our line; it remained stationary for about 15 minutes and then disappeared. At 6.0 AM enemy sent over a number of Trench Mortars on the left of our Sector. Our Aeroplanes were very active today and were heavily shelled by enemy Anti-Aircraft Guns. One of our planes descended very low and fired into enemy front line. Enemy replied with rifle and machine Gun fire without effect.	AOK

2449 Wt. W14957/M90 750,000 1/16 J.B.C. & A. Forms/C.2118/12.

Army Form C. 2118.

109

Instructions regarding War Diaries and Intelligence Summaries are contained in F. S. Regs., Part II. and the Staff Manual respectively. Title Pages will be prepared in manuscript.

WAR DIARY
or
INTELLIGENCE SUMMARY
109th Machine Gun Coy

(Erase heading not required.)

Place	Date	Hour	Summary of Events and Information	Remarks and references to Appendices
KORTEPYP	22/12/16		Weather very wet & stormy. The night was quiet with very little enemy machine gun fire. Quartermaster D. L. Patterson N° 16672 reported for duty with this Company. L/Cpl Harrison N° 42216 return to duty from the Base. Today we have drawn up a comprehensive scheme of defense showing the duties of each gun in the Sector in the event of the S.O.S signal being sent up on our front or on either right or left Sector. These instructions have been entered on the the back of the Standing Trench Orders at each gun position so that the Gun teams can see at a glance what the duties of each gun are in the above mentioned circumstances.	AOK
	23rd	5 0 pm	Gas was released by the Brigade on our left, the wind at this time was blowing at the rate of 15 miles per hour. Six minutes after release of gas the enemy sent up Orange Shower Flares, this brought prompt and effective retaliation from his Artillery which shelled our front line and its neighbourhood. At 5.20 pm Four Green lights were sent up on left and others were observed behind Messines; probably from the Salient. The Orange Shower was again seen on our right at 10-15 pm. Everything was again quiet at 10-45 pm. Aerial activity was great all day but on attempting to cross our lines enemy machines were driven back by our Anti Aircraft Guns. Weather Stormy.	AOK

Army Form C. 2118.

Instructions regarding War Diaries and Intelligence Summaries are contained in F. S. Regs., Part II. and the Staff Manual respectively. Title Pages will be prepared in manuscript.

WAR DIARY
of 109th Machine Gun Coy
or
INTELLIGENCE SUMMARY
(Erase heading not required.)

No. 109 MACHINE GUN COMPANY. Page 110

Place	Date	Hour	Summary of Events and Information	Remarks and references to Appendices
KORTEPYP.	24/12/16		Weather much more settled bright and clear. Our guns fired 2000 rounds on enemy Communication trenches U.16. Central	
		8.0 AM	A Lewis Gun opened fire from neighbourhood of SEAFORTH FARM. The enemy replied by firing a few heavies on our Front Line. One of our men Pte Shepherd A. No 30724 at DONNINGTON HALL gun position	
		11.0 AM	Enemy fired about 12 heavies round about HYDE PARK CORNER.	AOR
	25th		In the morning all ranks attended Church Service the latter part of the morning and early part of the forenoon were taken up by preparation for the Mens Christmas Dinner. Owing to the Generosity of Friends and Associations at home in Ireland our men had everything they could possibly desire in the way of Food and were amply supplied with Fruit Sweets and Cigarettes. The Ulster Women's Society and the Colraine Munition Workers contributed largely for the welfare of the men. The Enemy consistently shelled the Camp Round about from 4.0 pm to 10.0 pm. None of our men were hit.	AOR
	26th		The Enemy shelled Neuve Eglise with heavies last night. At 8.45 pm our artillery shelled the front of enemy trenches on our right for 35 minutes. Enemy seemed very nervous as he sent up an exceptionally large number Very Lights.	AOR

Army Form C. 2118.

Instructions regarding War Diaries and Intelligence Summaries are contained in F. S. Regs., Part II. and the Staff Manual respectively. Title Pages will be prepared in manuscript.

WAR DIARY
or
INTELLIGENCE SUMMARY
(Erase heading not required.)

Page 111

Place	Date	Hour	Summary of Events and Information	Remarks and references to Appendices
KORTEPYP	27/12/16		Weather fine and bright. Last night there was considerable sniping near ST IVES on our right otherwise the night was quiet.	
		1.0 AM	Two bombs were thrown into our wire on the right of our guns at ANTONS FARM. During the night we fired 2000 rounds on neighbourhood of FUSE COTTAGE U.10.D	
		7.0 AM	Our mortars and artillery were active for 20 minutes on the right of ANTONS FARM. Enemy retaliation slight	
		10.0 AM	Two enemy aeroplanes crossed our lines flying very low	
		2.0 pm	Enemy shelled front and Subsidiary Line	
			Exceptional aerial activity by the enemy has been noticed during the last week.	A.O.R.
	28th		The night was very quiet. Acting on information received re enemy wiring parties, our guns fired 2000 rounds on enemy wire U.2.d.1.1 to U.2.d.0.6 during the night. The enemy's artillery has been very active all day. Experimental bombardment by our 6" Trench Mortar at 2.25 p.m. drew heavy retaliation.	A.O.R.
	29th		Weather again wet & stormy. We fired from the CHATEAU position 2500 rounds early in the evening and again heavily at dawn on enemy wire and front Line. This fire was probably effective as the enemy searched CHATEAU grounds with about 12 heavies obtaining two direct hits on the Stables.	
			Our artillery was active during the afternoon. Several shells fell short of enemy's front Line.	A.O.R.

2449 Wt. W14957/M90 750,000 1/16 J.B.C. & A. Forms/C.2118/12.

Instructions regarding War Diaries and Intelligence Summaries are contained in F. S. Regs., Part II. and the Staff Manual respectively. Title Pages will be prepared in manuscript.

WAR DIARY
or
INTELLIGENCE SUMMARY

(Erase heading not required.)

Army Form C. 2118.

Place	Date	Hour	Summary of Events and Information	Remarks and references to Appendices
KORTEPYP	29/12/16		In addition to our old front we have today, taken over part of the front held by the 108th M.G. Coy. Two active gun positions WINTER TRENCH. U.7.b.95.10 and GABION FARM U.7.d.85.10 Reserve positions; – RATION FM (two guns) T.12.a.55.15, PLUS DOUVE FM T.12.a.45.35, STINKING FM U.7.a.63.90 FORT DUNHOLME T.12.b.45.60 VICARAGE T.12.a.99.02 and T.12.a.99.02. Open emplacements U.7.c.80.80. T.12.c.95.60. T.12.b.01.85. T.12.c.90.55 T.11.c.45.70. T.11.c.50.50. T.11.d.90.35. T.11.d.60.72. We have also taken over one Anti Aircraft position U.7.b.50.10	
	30th		Weather Misty. Our guns fired 2000 rounds at U.8.d.1.1 where working parties have previously been reported	ABR
		11.45 AM	The enemy shelled WINTER TRENCH. The dug-out attached to our Gun position at U.8.a.05.10 was destroyed. No casualties occurred here. The emplacement at DONNINGTON HALL U.8.c.40.90 was demolished one of our men: Private HUGHES E.R. No 35468 was wounded in the hand by shell fire and has gone to hospital Our artillery retaliated effectively	
		12.15 PM	Enemy again bombarded our front line from WINTER TRENCH to ANTONS FM. Enemy Aerial activity was again noticable from 3.0 pm. onwards	ABR

Instructions regarding War Diaries and Intelligence Summaries are contained in F. S. Regs., Part II. and the Staff Manual respectively. Title Pages will be prepared in manuscript.

WAR DIARY of 109th Machine Gun Coy
INTELLIGENCE SUMMARY

(Erase heading not required.)

Army Form C. 2118.

Page 113

Place	Date	Hour	Summary of Events and Information	Remarks and references to Appendices
KORTEPYP	31/12/16		Weather still very misty. We have today sent to each active Gun position a card shewing the target to be engaged in the event of the SOS signal being sent up on our front or on either the left or right Sectors. Enemy's artillery has been very active today registering on our lines. Last night enemy machine Gun were much more active. A direct hit on the Machine Gun emplacement at BAROSSA was obtained by enemy artillery, no damage done. A searchlight	
		5.0 AM	was observed about LA PETITE DOUVE FM U. 8. a. 90. 50	
		8.15 AM	Enemy sent up five Green lights, upon which their artillery opened and continued firing for 20 minutes	
		12.0 nn	Some heavy shells were fired on LA HUTTE CHATEAU. We had one casualty L/C HUME J. N° 18719. Direct hits were also obtained by enemy artillery on the ONLY WAY one of which was four yards to the north of our gun position at U. 14. a. 70. 50.	a.o.R

2449 Wt. W14957/M90 750,000 1/16 J.B.C. & A. Forms/C.2118/12.

CONFIDENTIAL

Vol 10

WAR DIARY

of

109TH BRIGADE MACHINE GUN COMPANY.

from

1st January 1917

to

31st January 1917.

Army Form C. 2118.

WAR DIARY
or
~~INTELLIGENCE SUMMARY~~

(Erase heading not required.)

Instructions regarding War Diaries and Intelligence Summaries are contained in F. S. Regs., Part II. and the Staff Manual respectively. Title Pages will be prepared in manuscript.

Place	Date	Hour	Summary of Events and Information	Remarks and references to Appendices
KORTEPYP	1.1.17		During the night enemy machine guns were active. Our machine guns fired 4000 rds during the night on SCHNITZEL FM U.3 c 80.20. and ROADSIDE REDOUBT U.2 d. 90.95. to U 3 a 27 21.	[initials]
		5.30pm } 6.30pm }	A heavy bombardment took place well away to the left. The enemy were observed to put up a number of red and green lights.	
	2.1.17	5 Am	Shortly after 5 a.m. this morning a searchlight was observed to the right of ANTON'S FM. U.14 B. Central.	
		10.30am	About 10.30 am. the enemy shelled the vicinity of ADVANCED ESTAMINET The enemy obtained another direct hit on BAROSSA U.8.c 10.60. today.	[initials]
			During the early part of the evening our machine guns fired 1000 rds on GREY FARM U.9 B 60.00.	
	3.1.17		During the night enemy machine guns were not so active as usual.	
		8.-Am } 8.40am }	The enemy put over 8 77mm shells in the vicinity of LE ROSSIGNOL - five of which failed to explode.	[initials]
		9.am } 10 am }	Between 9 am & 10 am the enemy put 14 "heavies" along HEATH TRENCH.	
			During the evening our machine guns fired 3500 rds on JUNCTION of ROADS U.32.c 65.10. ASH AVENUE U.9.D 80.10. to U.10 c.70 40.	

2449 Wt. W14957/M90 750,000 1/16 J.B.C. & A. Forms/C.2118/12.

Army Form C. 2118.

Page 115.

WAR DIARY
or
INTELLIGENCE SUMMARY
(Erase heading not required.)

Instructions regarding War Diaries and Intelligence Summaries are contained in F. S. Regs., Part II. and the Staff Manual respectively. Title Pages will be prepared in manuscript.

Place	Date	Hour	Summary of Events and Information	Remarks and references to Appendices
KORTEPYP.	4/1/17		The night passed quietly. At stand to this morning our machine guns fired 500 rds on enemy front line U. 2 d. 15.00. to U. 2 d. 10.50	
		7.45am	A gas horn was heard on the right sector but apparently it was a false alarm as nothing happened.	[initials]
		2. pm	The enemy's artillery put four heavies on MACS RUIN U. 13 B. 10 80.	
	5/1/17		Last night enemy machine guns were active. Our machine guns fired 4500 rounds on Trenches and Road O.32 d 20.20. Pathway U.2.B. 40.95. Ash Avenue U.9.D. 80.10. to Trench Tramway U. 9. A. 20.12. to U.9.A 70 50. Enemy searchlight was active just before dawn near U.10. c 40.30. La Petite Douve Fm U. 8. A. 90.50.	
		8.10am	At 8.10 am the enemy put up eight very lights to the right of Antons Fm. U 14 B Central	
		8.30am	The enemy shelled MACS RUIN U 13. B 15 70 with about 20. 4.2's.	[initials]
		10-am	About 10 A.M. IRISH FARM U. 7 D. 60.80. was shelled with "heavies".	
		10.30am	The enemy put twelve 77 mms. around LE ROSSIGNOL & vicinity U 13 A 90 80. There was considerable aerial activity on both sides.	
		6.30pm	At 6.30pm six brilliant lights were observed to our right over PLOEGSTEERT WOOD. These lights appeared to be star shells as they burst high & gave off a bright yellow light which lasted for a good time.	
		9.0pm	There was a heavy T.M. bombardment lasting half an hour. It was on our left	

2449 Wt. W14957/M90 750,000 1/16 J.B.C. & A. Forms/C.2118/12.

Army Form C. 2118.

WAR DIARY
or
INTELLIGENCE SUMMARY

(Erase heading not required.)

Page 11b.

Instructions regarding War Diaries and Intelligence Summaries are contained in F. S. Regs., Part II. and the Staff Manual respectively. Title Pages will be prepared in manuscript.

Place	Date	Hour	Summary of Events and Information	Remarks and references to Appendices
KORTEPYP	6/1/17		The night passed quietly. Enemy machine guns were fairly active at intervals during the night. Our machine guns fired at 3500 rounds on MESSINES R^D U.2.B.30.30 – U.2.B.50.35 Communication trench crossing road U.2.B.35.10. Tramway terminus U.9.A.15.10.	[illegible]
		6pm	at 6pm. two of our machine guns fired 1500 rounds in all on MESSINES O.32.D.60.00. – 1000 rounds were also fired on tracks at right edge of LA POTTERIE FM. U.10. Central.	
		6-7pm	Between 6-pm & 7pm. a large amount of traffic was heard moving about the MESSINES R^D from U.10.C Central. MESSINES – an engine was also heard running up the MESSINES R^D. This engine appeared to be hauling material into MESSINES and would then return running "light".	
	7/1/17		Enemy machine guns in our sector were fairly quiet during the night.	
		1-AM.	at 1 AM an aeroplane was heard flying over our right sector in the direction of PLOEGSTEERT. this plane was heard again at 1.45 am. flying in a N.E. direction over LE ROSSIGNOL.	
		3.45AM.	about 3.45 AM a heavy T.M. & artillery strafe took place in the vicinity of ONTARIO FM. U.1.A Central. The strafe finished at 4.55 A.M.	
		4.45am	at 4.45 am a red rocket was fired between GABION & ONTARIO FARMS when the bombardment abated in violence.	
		5-0am	Fencing working parties were heard at work about BARRICADE AVENUE at 5 AM. Considerable aerial activity took place on both sides today. One of our patrolling biplanes was attacked by a small Boche plane & caught fire. The machine planed towards DRANOUTRE under control – when near ground at about LINDENHOEK pilot apparently lost control & dashed to the ground.	

2449 Wt. W14957/M90 750,000 1/16 J.B.C. & A. Forms/C.2118/12.

Army Form C. 2118.

Instructions regarding War Diaries and Intelligence Summaries are contained in F. S. Regs., Part II. and the Staff Manual respectively. Title Pages will be prepared in manuscript.

WAR DIARY
or
INTELLIGENCE SUMMARY
(Erase heading not required.)

Page 117.

Place	Date	Hour	Summary of Events and Information	Remarks and references to Appendices
KORTEPYP	7/1/17	3.45pm	At 3.45pm. today our artillery heavily shelled the enemy's second line from U.3.c 10.90 to U.9 a.90.50. for ten minutes. His retaliation was with 77mm. shells. IRISH FARM U.7 D.60.80. being hit several times.	
	8/1/17		The enemy machine guns were fairly quiet during the night. Our machine guns fired 3500 rounds on Tramway U.9.d 70.90. to SCHNITZEL FM - tracks at right edge of LA POTTERIE FM. U.10. Central.	
			The Bosche artillery was fairly active throughout the morning.	
	9/1/17		During the night enemy machine guns were active at intervals. Our machine guns fired 2000 rds on GREY FM. U.9 d.70.90. - Enemy front trench U.2.d.15.00 to U.2 D.10 50.	
		6 am.	About 6 a.m. transport was heard moving behind enemy's lines. The traffic seemed to be on the road running from U 10 C Central to MESSINES.	
		8.15am	At 8.15 a.m. a red paper balloon was seen drifting from enemy's lines and fell near LE ROSSIGNOL U.13. The enemy shelled the balloon as soon as it landed. About the same time very lights were put up to the right of ANTONS FM. These lights appeared to come from ULSTER TRENCH. Artillery was active this morning on	
		9 30am	both sides. We started strafing at 9 30 am. The enemy retaliated on our front line to right of DONNINGTON HALL U 8 C. and shortly after 11 AM he shelled	
		11 am	between BAROSSA U 8 C and IRISH FM. U 7 D	
		11 30am	At 11 30 am enemy shelled LE ROSSIGNOL and our subsidiary line with 5.9's getting two direct hits on GAS TRENCH near THE CELLARS U 13 A. Our Reserve machine gun emplacement at LE ROSSIGNOL was shattered.	
		1.45pm 2.45pm	The Brigade on our right bombarded enemy's front line between 1 45 pm - 2.45 pm The retaliation was very slight	
		7.0pm	Transport was heard about 7 pm on the road running into MESSINES.	

Army Form C. 2118.

WAR DIARY
or
~~INTELLIGENCE SUMMARY~~

(*Erase heading not required.*)

Page 118

Instructions regarding War Diaries and Intelligence Summaries are contained in F. S. Regs., Part II. and the Staff Manual respectively. Title Pages will be prepared in manuscript.

Place	Date	Hour	Summary of Events and Information	Remarks and references to Appendices
KORTEPYP	10/1/17		During the night enemy machine guns were very quiet. We fired 3000 rounds on the following targets ASH AVENUE U 9 d 80.10. to U 10 c 70.40. path passing South end of POND U 2 B 40.95. ROAD in MESSINES U.2.B 30 30 to U 2 B 50.55. During the morning our Artillery was active.	
		6. AM	About 6 am this morning enemy transport was heard on the road running into MESSINES from U.10.C Central.	[initials]
		3.45pm.	About 3.45pm Boche aircraft appeared over the camp. They were heavily shelled and made towards their own lines but not until they set on fire one of our observation balloons in the neighbourhood of DRANOUTRE.	
		8-8.30pm	Transport was heard behind enemy lines between 8 – 8.30pm	
	11/1/17		Enemy machine guns were fairly active in the evening and towards dawn. During the night our machine guns fired 1500 rounds on Track at right edge LA POTTERIE FM. U.8 Central. Enemy FRONT LINE & WIRE U.2 d. 15.00 to U 2 d. 10 50. During the morning our machine guns fired 1000 rounds on SQUARE in MESSINES U.2.B. 80.95. Artillery very quiet on both sides during the day.	[initials]
	12/1/17		Enemy machine guns were active early in the evening and again between 5 AM & 7 AM this morning. During the night our machine guns fired 3500 rounds on – Tramway and Road U 2 A 90.02. to U.2 B. 20.20. Tramway near SCHNITZEL FARM U.3.C.90.20. Enemy Front Line U.2.d 15.00 to U.2 d. 10 50.	
		12 –	At noon today about a dozen "heavies" fell in a field S W of LOCALITY 3. U 7 c Central. The artillery on both sides after a quiet morning, were somewhat more active in the afternoon.	[initials]
		12. md.	During the evening our artillery was very active on the left. At midnight several red and green lights were observed away to the left. A short trench mortar bombardment followed	

2449 Wt. W14957/M90 750,000 1/16 J.B.C. & A. Forms/C.2118/12.

Instructions regarding War Diaries and Intelligence Summaries are contained in F. S. Regs., Part II. and the Staff Manual respectively. Title Pages will be prepared in manuscript.

WAR DIARY
or
INTELLIGENCE SUMMARY

(Erase heading not required.)

Page. 119

Army Form C. 2118.

Place	Date	Hour	Summary of Events and Information	Remarks and references to Appendices
KORTEPYP	13/1/17		Weather very wet with showers of sleet. During the night enemy machine guns were fairly active. Our machine guns fired 3000 rounds on the following targets - TRAMWAY + ROAD. U 2. A 90 02 to U 2 B. 20 20. Track near GREY FARM. U 9 D. 80. 95 to U 10 A 25 05. Artillery on both sides has been very quiet today	WTW
	14/1/17		Weather very wet. Enemy machine guns fairly active during the night. Our machine guns fired 4000 rounds on following targets Tramway, track round La Potterie Farm U 10 central. Tramway on Road U 2 D 43.71 to U 2 B 40.02. Artillery very quiet to-day	WTW.
	15/1/17		Weather extremely cold. Enemy machine guns were fairly active between 9 pm + 11 pm also between 4 am + 6 am this morning. Our machine guns fired 2000 rounds on TRAMWAY U 9 a 33.22 to 90.38.	WTW
		11 pm	S.O.S signals were observed from our own gun positions at 11 pm. Artillery very quiet on both sides	
	16/1/17		Slight fall of snow. Enemy machines guns very active at periods during the night. Our machine guns fired 1000 rounds on GREYS FARM U 9 during the night. Our artillery more active than usual	WTW.

2449 Wt. W14957/M90 750,000 1/16 J.B.C. & A. Forms/C.2118/12.

Instructions regarding War Diaries and Intelligence Summaries are contained in F. S. Regs., Part II. and the Staff Manual respectively. Title Pages will be prepared in manuscript.

WAR DIARY
or
~~INTELLIGENCE SUMMARY~~
(Erase heading not required.)

Page 120

Army Form C. 2118.

Place	Date	Hour	Summary of Events and Information	Remarks and references to Appendices
KORTEPYP	17/1/17		Weather very cold. Snow fell during night. Enemy Machine Guns quiet. Our Machine Guns fired 500 rounds on Enemy FRONT LINE U2D 15.00 to U8D 10.50 at Stand To this morning.	WW
	18/1/17		Enemy Machine Guns particularly quiet during night probably owing to the severity of the weather. Our Machine Guns fired 2000 rounds on the following target GREY FARM. U9B 60.09 SQUARE of MESSINES U2B. 82.74	WW
		3.45pm	Enemy shelled the ONLY WAY. & scored a direct hit on our Dug out at ADVANCED. ESTAMINET V14 A61.49. completely destroying it	
	19/1/17		Enemy Machine Guns were fairly active at dusk but not during the night	WW
		9AM	Enemy Artillery fairly active shells dropping on the left of ANTONS FARM. Our artillery retaliated	
			Our Machine Guns fired on target SQUARE of MESSINES U2B.82.74. and BETHLEHEM FARM U3D Central	WW
	20/1/17		Early in the morning Enemy Machine Guns were more active than	

2449 Wt. W14957/M90 750,000 1/16 J.B.C. & A. Forms/C.2118/12.

Army Form C. 2118.

Instructions regarding War Diaries and Intelligence Summaries are contained in F. S. Regs., Part II. and the Staff Manual respectively. Title Pages will be prepared in manuscript.

WAR DIARY
or
INTELLIGENCE SUMMARY

(Erase heading not required.)

PAGE.121

Place	Date	Hour	Summary of Events and Information	Remarks and references to Appendices
continued KORTEPYP	20/1/17		they have been of late, but their activity ceased about 8 pm	
			Our Machine Guns fired 5500 throughout the night on the following targets LA POTTERIE FARM + trenches in vicinity V.10. Central	
			GAEY FM U.9.D 60 95 + ULSTER. DRIVE U9 D to U10 A. SQUARE of MESSINES	WHW
		17.30 pm to 12 30 pm	Heavy artillery bombardment on our left	
	21/1/17		Enemy Machines Guns were quiet. Our Guns fired 5000 rounds	
			on Squares U3. U4. U9. U10. + SQUARE of MESSINES U.2.B	WHW
			Firing was carried out throughout the night at intervals	
	22/1/17		Extreme frost still prevails We again fired 5000 rounds	
			from our Guns on SQUARE of MESSINES + U3 U4 U9 U10.	WHW
		7 pm	Golden Spray was sent up in German lines also one Green	
			light Nothing happened	
		2 pm	An Extremely heavy Trench Motar bombardment started on our	
			right + spread to the ~~right~~ left of ANTONS. FARM. This bombardment	WHW
			continued till 4 pm. At this time relief of Infantry in the line was	
		4.15	taking place. The Enemy raided front line trenches of sector on our right.	

2449 Wt. W14957/M90 750,000 1/16 J.B.C. & A. Forms/C.2118/12.

Instructions regarding War Diaries and Intelligence Summaries are contained in F. S. Regs., Part II. and the Staff Manual respectively. Title Pages will be prepared in manuscript.

WAR DIARY
or
INTELLIGENCE SUMMARY
(Erase heading not required.)

Army Form C. 2118.

Page 122

Place	Date	Hour	Summary of Events and Information	Remarks and references to Appendices
KORTEPYP	22/1/17	4.15 pm	A few details of the enemy raiding party entered our trenches at ANTONS FARM. Our Gun team was forced to retire temporarily, but later again mounted the Gun in its old position. Our Guns from the CHATEAU & Subsidiary lines brought fire to bear on Enemy wire & front line trenches & it is thought caused many casualties amongst the raiding party on their return	[initials]
	23/1/17		Our guns fired throughout the night & also during the morning when the weather was very misty	
		10.am	Four Enemy aeroplanes were perceived crossing our line we brought Machine Gun Fire to bear upon them & succeeded in driving them back. During the night we fired 5000 rounds on the following target SQUARE of MESSINES La POTTERIE FARM & Trenches U D central. SCHNITZLE FM. U3c 80.20.	[initials]
	24/1/17		A Extremely heavy frost. Still prevails. 4000 were fired by our Guns during the night on SQUARE of MESSINES FARMS & Trenches in Square U3. U4 U10	[initials]

2449 Wt. W14957/M90 750,000 1/16 J.B.C. & A. Forms/C.2118/12.

Instructions regarding War Diaries and Intelligence Summaries are contained in F. S. Regs., Part II. and the Staff Manual respectively. Title Pages will be prepared in manuscript.

WAR DIARY
or
INTELLIGENCE SUMMARY
(Erase heading not required.)

Army Form C. 2118.

Page 123

Place	Date	Hour	Summary of Events and Information	Remarks and references to Appendices
KORTEPYP	25/1/17	4.15 pm	One of our Aeroplanes were brought down by the enemy & fell in their lines near MESSINES. Several enemy Aeroplanes crossed our lines. Enemy Machine Guns were again very quiet. We fired 2000 rounds on GREY. FM. U.9.B. 60.05. La POTTERIE. U.D central. SHNITZEL. FM. U.3.C 80.20.	WHW
	26/1/17		Weather still very severe. 2000 rounds fired on Farms in Squares U3. U4. U9. U10. The enemy shelled our Gun position in front of CHATEAU. putting over 4 large & 6 small Shells. No damage was caused	WHW
	27/1/17		The Night was unusually quiet on both sides. Enemy Aeroplanes again active. We fired 2000 rounds on SANITZEL. FM. U.3.C. 80.20 DUMP. O.32. D. 52. 40. Extremely hard to carry on work in the line owing to the intense frost.	WHW
	28/1/17		Rumour of an enemy offensive on this front. We have to-day sent in our 4 Reserve guns. The whole 16 Guns are now in the line. Reserves of Ammunition on all emplacements have been made up to 16000 rounds.	WHW

2449 Wt. W14957/M90 750,000 1/16 J.B.C. & A. Forms/C.2118/12.

Instructions regarding War Diaries and Intelligence Summaries are contained in F. S. Regs., Part II. and the Staff Manual respectively. Title Pages will be prepared in manuscript.

WAR DIARY
or
~~INTELLIGENCE~~ SUMMARY
(Erase heading not required.)

Army Form C. 2118.

Page 127

Place	Date	Hour	Summary of Events and Information	Remarks and references to Appendices
MORTEPYP	29/1/17	6pm to 8pm	Heavy bombardment took place on our right. Several red flares were observed. The rest of the night passed quietly. Our Machine ~~guns~~ fired 2500 rounds on MESSINES SQUARE & TRAMWAY U.2.A 42.70 Cross Roads MESSINES O.32.D.23.26. We have to-day provided all our Machine Gun emplacements with extra supplies of bombs & Very lights in view of the expected enemy attack.	
	30/1/17		Night was again very quiet. Enemy machine guns fairly active in the evening. At Stand-To 2 batteries Enemy Artillery opened fire on our front line.	
		1 am to 2 am	Heavy bombardment on our left. Three Red lights were observed to the right of ANTONS. FM U.14.B 80 75. About 7 am	
		9.30am	Enemy shelled the ONLY WAY around BACK ESTAMINET Position. We fired 6000 rounds on MESSINES Rd & TRAMWAY U.2.D 25.00. We have to-day completed our arrangements to withstand	

Instructions regarding War Diaries and Intelligence Summaries are contained in F. S. Regs., Part II. and the Staff Manual respectively. Title pages will be prepared in manuscript.

WAR DIARY
or
INTELLIGENCE SUMMARY.
(Erase heading not required.)

Army Form C. 2118.

Page 125

Place	Date	Hour	Summary of Events and Information	Remarks and references to Appendices
MORTEPYP	30/1/17		a prolonged Enemy attack & have provided Water, Rations, & Fuel, for all positions in the line. The weather is still extremely frosty. The Guns & Reserve water are kept near the braziers to ensure the Guns being available for instant use. All the teams are very confident of being able to beat back any Enemy attack.	WW
	31/1/17		The Night passed very Quietly. ~~[illegible]~~ Enemy Machine Guns shewed usual activity. Both enemy & our artillery were active. Enemy shelling the neighbourhoods of BACK ESTAMINET & FORT COGNAC	WW
		9 pm	Artillery bombardment took place on left of our Sector & lasted about one hour.	
			Our Machine Guns fired 4000 rounds on the following targets MESSINES SQUARE & Enemy FRONT LINE from U8a 90 70 to U8B 15-98	
			To day we withdrew from the line 4 Guns. (2 Guns from FORT COGNAC 1 Gun from FORT BRIGGS & 1 from HEATH TRENCH) & 50% of the personnel so that we can carry out a complete relief & rest the men.	

2353 Wt. W2544/1454 700,000 5/15 D. D. & L. A.D.S.S./Forms/C. 2118.

Vol XI

W A R D I A R Y

of

109th BRIGADE MACHINE GUN COMPANY,

From 1st February

To 28th February.

Instructions regarding War Diaries and Intelligence Summaries are contained in F. S. Regs., Part II. and the Staff Manual respectively. Title pages will be prepared in manuscript.

WAR DIARY
or
INTELLIGENCE SUMMARY.
(Erase heading not required.)

Page 126

No. 109 MACHINE GUN COMPANY.

Army Form C. 2118.

Place	Date	Hour	Summary of Events and Information	Remarks and references to Appendices
KORTEPYP	1/2/17		Weather very frosty. Enemy machine guns fairly active. Our Machine Guns fired 3000 rounds	
		6pm	Heavy bombardment to the right of ~~the~~ Division on our right lasting almost an hour.	
		7pm to 7/30pm	Lamp signalling was observed behind the enemy lines just to the left of Messines	
		9pm	There was 3 minutes rapid rifle fire by the Division on our right after two cream flares had been sent up in succession.	
	2/2/17		The Night on our front was quiet with enemy Machine Guns active early in the morning. Our Machine Guns fired 4000 rounds during the night on GREY FARM, vicinity U.9.B 65.08 TRAMWAY U.2.B 40.90 MESSINES SQUARE U.2.B .80.95	
		5 am	There was a heavy bombardment on our left. ~~[illegible]~~	
		5pm	Considerable aerial activity has taken place to-day on both sides.	
		8pm	Boche Aeroplane was heard flying over DEAD COW FARM U13 B 80.40 & dropped 2 flares & immediately enemy artillery fired 2 rounds in the neighbourhood	

Instructions regarding War Diaries and Intelligence Summaries are contained in F. S. Regs., Part II. and the Staff Manual respectively. Title pages will be prepared in manuscript.

WAR DIARY
or
INTELLIGENCE SUMMARY.
(Erase heading not required.)

Page 124

Army Form C. 2118.

Place	Date	Hour	Summary of Events and Information	Remarks and references to Appendices
KORTEPYP	3/2/17		The Night on our front was quiet, a marked increase in Enemy Machine Gun activity being noticeable. Our Machine Guns fired 4500 rounds on the following targets ENEMY FRONT line running North from U.8B 98.10. MESSINES Rd & TRAMWAY U2B 40 30. MESSINES SQUARE U2B 80 95.	
		10 pm	Enemy fired several tear shells in the Neighbourhood of BAROSSA FARM U8C 05 62.	
	4/2/17		Hard Frost still continues the Night passed quietly with enemy Machine Guns Normal.	
		2 Am	Red Flare sent up on left of our sector Nothing happened. During the Night our Machine Guns fired 3000 rounds on SCHNITZEL FARM U.3C.80.15 GREY FARM & vicinity of ASH AVENUE U.9D.60.95 and at Stand To 750 rounds on Enemy Front line running North from U.8B 98 10.	
	5/2/17		Enemy Machine Guns were fairly active at intervals during the night.	

2353 Wt. W2544/1454 700,000 5/15 D. D. & L. A.D.S.S./Forms/C. 2118.

Instructions regarding War Diaries and Intelligence Summaries are contained in F. S. Regs., Part II. and the Staff Manual respectively. Title pages will be prepared in manuscript.

WAR DIARY
or
INTELLIGENCE SUMMARY.
(Erase heading not required.)

Page 128

Army Form C. 2118.

Place	Date	Hour	Summary of Events and Information	Remarks and references to Appendices
KORTEPYP	5/7/17	2.30pm 3.30pm	Our Artillery & Trench Mortars bombarded the enemy lines. The Enemy's retaliation was very slight.	
			Our Machine Guns fired 4000 rounds during the night & at Stand To this morning on the following targets. SCHNITZEL FARM & TRAMWAY U3C 80.15 MESSINES ROAD U2B 40.30 & Enemy FRONT LINE running North from U8B 98.10.	
		8.15pm	Enemy dropped a shell immediately behind our Emplacement at DEAD COW FARM No Damage was done.	
	6/7/17		Enemy Machine Guns fairly active. During Night & at Stand To our Machine Guns fired 6000 rounds on MESSINES SQUARE Rdy running N.E from U2 Central. U3C 20.60. U3C 70.00. U9A 90.40. SCHNITZEL FARM & TRAMWAY U3C 80.15 & Enemy FRONT LINE running North from U8B 98.10.	
		9.30pm	Aeroplane was heard over our lines lights were dropped but no action followed from either side.	
	7/7/17		The Night was remarkably quiet. Our Machine Guns fired 1000 rounds on enemy ~~front~~ line at Stand To running North from U8B 10.90.	

Page 129

Army Form C. 2118.

Instructions regarding War Diaries and Intelligence Summaries are contained in F. S. Regs., Part II. and the Staff Manual respectively. Title pages will be prepared in manuscript.

WAR DIARY
or
INTELLIGENCE SUMMARY.
(*Erase heading not required.*)

Place	Date	Hour	Summary of Events and Information	Remarks and references to Appendices
KORTEPYP	8/7/17		The Night was very quiet.	
		1 pm	One of our planes in spite of very heavy shelling circled round several times over La Petit DOUVE FARM observing.	
		1 30pm	Our anti aircraft ~~guns~~ machine Guns fired on 2 Enemy Aeroplanes over NO MANS LAND & succeeded in turning them back. About 400 rounds being used.	
			During the Night our Guns fired 2000 rounds on the following targets MESSINES SQUARE SCHNITZEL FARM & TRAMWAY U3C 80 10	
	9/7/17		Night quiet. Machine Guns inactive on both sides.	
		11AM	Our artillery & Trench Mortars bombarded the Enemy lines on the front of the Division on our right. This fire was intense for 20 minutes & continued intermittently till 12 Noon.	
		12 NOON	Our artillery & Trench Mortars bombarded Enemy line on our front for half an hour. Enemy retaliation very weak. Our machine Guns co-operated & fired 6750 rounds on the following targets ULCER SUPPORT U2D 50.25 ULCER AVENUE TRENCHES at GREY FARM U9B 55.10	

2353 Wt. W2544/1454 700,000 5/15 D. D. & L. A.D.S.S./Forms/C. 2118.

Instructions regarding War Diaries and Intelligence Summaries are contained in F. S. Regs., Part II. and the Staff Manual respectively. Title pages will be prepared in manuscript.

WAR DIARY
or
INTELLIGENCE SUMMARY.
(Erase heading not required.)

Page 130

Army Form C. 2118.

Place	Date	Hour	Summary of Events and Information	Remarks and references to Appendices
KORTEPYP	9/7/17		TRENCHES V15A 90.85 to U9C 30.75 UNDER SUPPORT North from U2B 10.90	
		1 PM	Enemy dropped 8 "Heavies" in CHATEAU GARDINES 1 fell 20 yards from CHATEAU GATE position 1 being a direct hit on the CHATEAU.	
	10/7/17		Enemy appeared to be nervous during the night. Using a great number of Very lights also a considerable amount of rifle fire. His Machine Guns were more active than usual	
		4 am	Several Aeroplanes were heard over our line one of these dropped Red & Green light nothing happened.	
			Enemy Aeroplanes very active during the day. We fired 250 at an Enemy plane which was coming forward of our line It turned back immediately.	
	11/7/17		Weather warmer to-day snow slowly disappearing. The night was very quiet. Our Machine Guns fired 1500 rounds on the following target MESSINES ROAD U2B. 5.5	
		10.30 AM	Few shells fell North of LA HUTTE CHATEAU. No damage done	
		3 pm	Enemy trench Mortars active.	

2353 Wt. W2544/1454 700,000 5/15 D. D. & L. A.D.S.S./Forms/C. 2118.

Instructions regarding War Diaries and Intelligence Summaries are contained in F. S. Regs., Part II. and the Staff Manual respectively. Title Pages will be prepared in manuscript.

WAR DIARY
or
~~INTELLIGENCE SUMMARY~~
(Erase heading not required.)

Army Form C. 2118.

Place	Date	Hour	Summary of Events and Information	Remarks and references to Appendices
KORTEPYP	12/2/17	7-30 pm	Enemy machine Guns were more active than usual last night. One gun fired on road U.14.c.30.30 and another searched the ONLY WAY in the vicinity of U.14.a.70.20 from the direction of LA PETITE DOUVE FARM U.8.a.90.50. About 7-30 p.m. a huge fire was observed to the north, it was impossible to distinguish whether this fire was in our own or the enemys lines	
		8-30 pm	An intense bombardment began on right of our Sector and lasted for 30 minutes, during the bombardment the enemy put up many red lights. During the night our guns fired 2000 rounds on the dump at U.2.b.60.10	ADR
	13/2/17		Enemy machine Guns again fairly active during the night. We fired 1500 rounds during the early part of the evening on SCHNITZEL FARM U.3.c and 500 rounds at Stand to this morning on enemy front line U.2.d.10.00 to 15.30. Enemy artillery very quiet today. Thaw set in today. Captain P.D. Mulholland assumed command of the 109th M.G. Coy today.	
	14/2/17	6.30 to 7.00 pm	Enemy burst a number of Star Shells in front of the ONLY WAY between HASTED HOUSE and ADVANCED ESTAMINET	
		1-0 AM	Enemy commenced a heavy bombardment with artillery and trench mortars on Sector to the left of our brigade	
		1-10 AM	S.O.S signal was observed well to our left, too far off to allow our guns to give assistance	
		4-0 AM	Another bombardment on our right broke out. We fired 3000 rounds during the night on DUMP O.2.b.60.50 and GREY FARM U.9	ADR

Instructions regarding War Diaries and Intelligence Summaries are contained in F. S. Regs., Part II. and the Staff Manual respectively. Title Pages will be prepared in manuscript.

WAR DIARY
or
INTELLIGENCE SUMMARY
(Erase heading not required.)

Army Form C. 2118.

Place	Date	Hour	Summary of Events and Information	Remarks and references to Appendices
KORTEPYP	15/2/17	7.0 to 9.0 pm	Artillery and Trench Mortar activity on our left. Enemy machine Guns very active. More aerial activity than usual by both sides during the night we fired on the following targets GREY FARM U.9. SCHNITZEL FARM U.3.C. DUMP U.3.d.40.40. Weather mild and misty.	AOK
	16th	5.0pm	An enemy aeroplane damaged by shrapnel came over WINTER TRENCH flying very low. Owing to the barrage of fire put up by machine Guns the pilot could not get his machine over to his own lines and ultimately came to earth in a field north of LA HUTTE CHATEAU U.14.C.30.20. About an hour later enemy shelled the field with shrapnel, he also put his heavies on BAROSSA. U.8.C Our artillery was again very active on our right. During the night we fired 4000 rounds on DUMP U.3.d.40.40. MESSINES SQUARE and DUMP U.2.b.60.10. Our artillery carried out a large amount of registration today, assisted by our planes. Weather mild	AOK
	17th		Enemy seems very nervous on our front, using a great number of Very lights, especially on those parts of his line where the wire appears weak. During the night we fired 3000 rounds on the following targets DUMP U.3.d 40.40 MESSINES SQUARE and GREY FARM.	
		10.40am	Our Guns co-operated in a raid carried out by the 25th Division on our right. Enfilading left flank of area raided. The enemy retaliated with heavies & trench mortars and put a very effective barrage on no mans land, his shooting was bad, owing to weather being misty and observation difficult.	AOK

2449 Wt. W14957/Mgo 750,000 1/16 J.B.C. & A. Forms/C.2118/12.

Army Form C. 2118.

Instructions regarding War Diaries and Intelligence Summaries are contained in F. S. Regs., Part II. and the Staff Manual respectively. Title Pages will be prepared in manuscript.

WAR DIARY
or
INTELLIGENCE SUMMARY

(Erase heading not required.)

No. 109 MACHINE GUN COMPANY. No. Page 133 Date..........

Place	Date	Hour	Summary of Events and Information	Remarks and references to Appendices
KORTEPYP	17/2/17	7.0 pm	Enemy shelled HYDE PARK CORNE with Howitzers During the night our guns fired 3000 rounds on OKEY FARM U.9 and DUMP U.3.d. 40.40	
		2.0 pm	Our artillery opened on enemy trenches who immediately retaliated on SUBSIDIARY LINE. A few shells fell in the vicinity of our guns at BACK ESTAMINET and HASTER HOUSE. No damage done.	
		3.0 pm	The enemy again shelled LA HUTTE CHATEAU obtaining two direct hits. Weather still misty & bad for observation.	aok
	18th		Enemy machine Guns fairly active during the night	
		7 pm	Our artillery opened heavily on our right enemy retaliation was very weak a considerable number of coloured Very Lights & star shells were put up. Our artillery again opened at 11.0 pm on our right and continued for about an hour.	
		7.0 AM	An artillery and Trench Mortar bombardment broke out on our left. During the night our machine Guns fired 3000 rounds on the following targets. DUMP U.3.d. 40.40 SCHNITZEL FARM U.3.c Weather inclined to be rainy	aok
	19th		Enemy machine guns active during the night, otherwise quiet Our machine Guns fired 3000 rounds on enemy DUMP U.3.d 40.40 and SCHNITZEL FARM U.9	
		6.40 pm	A distinct earth tremor was was noticed probably a mine explosion	
		5.15 AM	Another explosion took place nothing could be seen from our line to account for these two explosions Weather again very wet	aok

2449 Wt. W14957/M90 750,000 1/16 J.B.C. & A. Forms/C.2118/12.

Instructions regarding War Diaries and Intelligence Summaries are contained in F. S. Regs., Part II. and the Staff Manual respectively. Title Pages will be prepared in manuscript.

WAR DIARY
or
INTELLIGENCE SUMMARY
(Erase heading not required.)

Army Form C. 2118.

Place	Date	Hour	Summary of Events and Information	Remarks and references to Appendices
KORTEPYP	20/2/17	9-30 AM	Nine teams under Lieut C.M LEA and 2nd/Lt D. WALKER proceeded to the trenches to relieve the team at present in the line, the relief was carried out without casualties. Except for activity on the part of enemy machine guns the night was very quiet. Our guns fired 2500 rounds on LA POTTERIE Fm U. 10 Central and GREY FARM	aok
	21/2/17		Operation Orders (attached) were issued today by Captain P.D Mulholland for Co-operation of the 109th M.G Coy in a raid to be carried out by the 109th Brigade on enemy's trenches at 7.30 pm tonight. Our machine Gun Officers in the line report that the night was exceptionally quiet until 7.30 pm when as ordered our guns co-operated with Infantry and Artillery and fired 7000 rounds on targets selected. Fire was opened on these targets at 7-33 pm and sustained till 8-15 pm. Enemy machine guns were very active during this period firing on DEAD COW FARM and LA HUTTE CHATEAU. Several gas shells dropped near DEAD COW FARM during this period. Previous to the raid we carried out the usual indirect fire the targets fired on being LA POTTERIE FARM U. 10 central and SCHNITZEL FARM. A bombardment broke out on our left about 9.30 pm in the direction of SUMMER TR The rest of the night passed quietly.	aok

Instructions regarding War Diaries and Intelligence Summaries are contained in F. S. Regs., Part II. and the Staff Manual respectively. Title Pages will be prepared in manuscript.

WAR DIARY
or
INTELLIGENCE SUMMARY
(Erase heading not required.)

Army Form C. 2118.

Place	Date	Hour	Summary of Events and Information	Remarks and references to Appendices
KORTEPYP	22/2/17		Operation Orders (attached) were issued by Captain P.D. MULHOLLAND for the movement of the Company to METERIN where we expect to put in a months rest and training. Our transport will stay at BULFORD CAMP. Teams in the line will remain till tomorrow 23rd when they will be relieved by the 107th M.G.Coy.	
			Our Machine Guns fired 2500 rounds on ULGER SUPPORT and MESSINES SQUARE.	U.2.b
			Reinforcements 2 OR Private Blackwell. C. 81670 + Private BARNES. H. 81303 reported for duty with this Coy.	
	23/2/17	9-30	The Company paraded under Lieut A.O. Robinson and proceeded to new billets at FONTAINE HOUCK. Our billets and Camp equipment were handed over in good condition to the 107th Machine Gun Coy. 2/Lt Idiens proceeded with a small advance party and took over billets from the 107th Machine Gun Coy. The Company arrived without accident at FONTAINE HOUCK at 10 pm. Transport less 7 Officers chargers 2 Gun limbers, 4 mules, mess Cart + 1 horse, remain at KORTEPYP CAMP.	
			Operation Orders by Capt P.D. MULHOLLAND were today issued to Officers in the line re relief of our 10 guns by the 107th Machine Gun Coy.	
			During the night our machine guns fired upon the following targets ULGER SUPPORT U.2.d. U.2.b 6.7 to 2.2. U 3 a 05.90 to 30.50. MESSINES SQUARE U.2.b and O.32.d.50 20 to B.25.05.	
	24/2/17		Today was spent in cleaning up the camp and preparing programmes of training and Sports during the coming months. Our Gun teams in the line were relieved by 107th M.G.Coy and stayed the night at KORTEPYP CAMP.	
	25/2/17		The Company attended Church Parade. At 2-30 pm CAPT MULHOLLAND inspected the Company. The team relieved ~~yesterday~~ arrived from KORTEPYP CAMP and took over their new billets.	

2449 Wt. W14957/M90 750,000 1/16 J.B.C. & A. Forms/C.2118/12.

Instructions regarding War Diaries and Intelligence Summaries are contained in F. S. Regs., Part II. and the Staff Manual respectively. Title pages will be prepared in manuscript.

WAR DIARY
or
INTELLIGENCE SUMMARY.
(Erase heading not required.)

Army Form C. 2118.

Place	Date	Hour	Summary of Events and Information	Remarks and references to Appendices
FONTAIN HOUCK	26/2/17		No parade held this morning as facilities to bath the men were granted to the company, the whole Company proceeded to BAILLEUL for this purpose and returned at noon. An afternoon kit inspection was held with the object of getting the Company thoroughly fitted out. Private HAWTHORN. J. No 18718 was today transferred to Transportation Services. Weather fine & sunny.	AOR
	27/2/17		Training commenced today. Early morning run at 7.0 A.M. in which the Officers took part, the men seem to be in fairly good condition. The morning was taken up by preliminary training – Squad drill, Guard mounting and Gas helmet drill.	AOR
	28/2/17		Training programme proceeded with on yesterdays lines with the exception that a greater variety was introduced, the morning run was carried out with much success and a perceptible smartening up is already to be noticed.	AOR

2353 Wt. W2544/1454 700,000 5/15 D. D. & L. A.D.S.S./Forms/C. 2118.

War Diary

SECRET.

OPERATION ORDERS

For co-operation of the 109TH MACHINE GUN COMPANY

on the night 2/5/1 Feby, '17.

GUN POSITION.	TARGET.	REMARKS.
1 Gun CHATEAU about Pt. U.13.d.60.50.	Enemy Support Line U.15.b.40.70 to U.16.a.00.20.	From dusk till ZERO the normal amount of night firing will be carried out.
1 Gun DEAD COW FARM Pt. U.13.c.60.60.	German Front Line U.15.b.15.85 to U.15.b.60.20.	At ZERO precisely all guns will open rapid fire on TARGETS as shown.
2 Guns CHATEAU.	German Front Line U.9.c.10.30 to U.8.b.50.10.	At ZERO plus 3 (three) minutes, concentrated fire on the inside limits of traverse will be maintained with occasional sudden traverses outwards and slow traverses inwards. Guns will maintain fire for at least 4 (four) minutes after the return of the raiding party. These guns will then assume their usual night firing positions.

P. L. B. Mulholland

Captain,
Commanding 109th Machine Gun Company.

In the Field.
20/2/1917.

Zero time. 7-30. P.M. 21.2.17.
Point of exit U. 14. b. 72.70.
Point of entry U. 15. a. 28. 88.
time in enemy's trenches 20 to 25 minutes.
2/Lt. GOLDMAN will synchronise his watch at PETITE MUNQUE FARM 2. hours before Zero. 10th R. Innis. Fus. and 109th T. M. B. will be present.

2nd in Command

OPERATION ORDERS.
by Capt. P. D. MULHOLLAND
COMMANDING 109th M. GUN COMPANY.

Map References.) Belgium & France. 27. S.E.
) Trench Map. Belgium & France 28. S.W. Ed. 3.

GENERAL.

1). The 107th M. GUN Coy will relieve the 109th M. GUN Coy between the 23rd and 25th. 2. 17.

2). COMPANY HdQrs and RESERVE GUN TEAMS will leave KORTEPYP CAMP at 9. A.M. 23rd inst. to proceed to FONTAINE HOUCK Map. BELGIUM & FRANCE 27. S.E. Squares X.8 [illegible] +.

3). The [illegible] GUNS in act[illegible] [illegible]ll be relieved on the 24th inst. and [illegible] [illegible] to KORTE[illegible] [illegible]AMP for the remainder of that day and the [illegible]/25th night.

4). The TRANSPORT will remain at KORTEPYP CAMP till the 26th inst. when it will take over the lines of the 107th M. Gun Coy.

DETAIL.

22nd 2. 17.

1). 2/Lieut IDIENS will be in command of the ADVANCED PARTY and will proceed to FONTAINE-HOUCK to take over REST BILLETS. He will make himself acquainted with the A.A. defences of BAILLEUL.

23rd 2. 17.

a). HEAD QUARTERS and 2. RESERVE GUNS and TEAMS will proceed to REST BILLETS starting from KORTEPYP CAMP at 9 A.M.

b). 2/Lt. ROOT will proceed with 4 (four) GUNS & TEAMS (team [illegible]) to FORKED ROAD at [illegible] 30. 70. TRENCH MAP 28. S.W. Ed. 3. where he will be met by 2/LIEUT IDIENS who will then direct relief of 4 guns of 107th M. GUN Coy under arrangements with O.C. 107th M. GUN Coy.

c). The Transport utilized for this purpose (1. G.S. Limbered Wagon) will return to KORTEPYP CAMP.

d). Detailed Orders for the 24th and 25th inst. will be issued later to those concerned.

22/2/17.

P. D. Mulholland Capt.
Commanding 109th M. GUN Coy

SECRET BURN.

2/Lt. GOLDMAN + Lt LEA + 2/Lt WALKER Copy

1. Please arrange to have one guide per position occupied by a gun, at the CHATEAU at 10.30. A.M. on 24/2/17. 2. men. No guide for STRAF....N. or CH^au need be found.

2/. Tripods will be handed over as TRENCH STORES also all gum boots.

3/. Three limbers will wait at H.P. Corner from 8. P.M. onwards tonight and will move back to K. Camp independently when loaded as per following para.

4/. Retain only the bare fighting kit in the line for Tomorrow. Send all surplus stores etc. down by tonight's 3. waggons.

5/. Retain Guns & 8.B. boxes per gun

6/. Only Breakfast rations will be sent up tonight.

7/. Dinners will be ready at K. Camp tomorrow.

1/. 24/2/17. The three forward positions will be relieved first. as soon as ~~they have~~ the relieving parties have moved off start the relief of your 4 guns.

1/. Let teams rendezvous at Ch^au

2) Transport 6. limbers will be at H.P. Corner at 12. NOON Tomorrow. and will return to K. Camp independently when packed.

1/. Be particularly careful about handing over T. stores.

2/. All Officers & teams remain at K Camp till 9.30. A.M. 25/2/17. LIEUT LEA will take command of the party and will march to REST BILLETS on the morning 25/2/17

23/2/17.

P.D. Mulholland Capt
O.C. 169th M.G. Coy.

C6ONFIDENTIAL.

Vol 12

W A R   D I A R Y

of

109th BRIGADE MACHINE GUN COMPANY,

from 1st March 1917,

to 31st March 1917.

Instructions regarding War Diaries and Intelligence Summaries are contained in F. S. Regs., Part II. and the Staff Manual respectively. Title pages will be prepared in manuscript.

WAR DIARY
or
INTELLIGENCE SUMMARY.
(Erase heading not required.)

No. 109 MACHINE GUN COMPANY. Page 137

Army Form C. 2118.

Place	Date	Hour	Summary of Events and Information	Remarks and references to Appendices
MOOLENACKER	1/3/17		Programme of training was suspended today, the morning being passed in cleaning up the camp and packing limbers preparatory to moving off to new billets at MOOLENACKER. At 2-0 pm the company moved off the order of march being - Column of Route - when fighting is imminent this affording practise for possible open fighting coming in. The march passed off very well the company arriving at the new billets in good order	AOK
	2/3/17		Training continued today. Physical exercise & running at 7-0 AM Gun drill, Squad drill & lectures took up the morning while Sports were carried on during the afternoon	AOK
	3/3/17		A great increase in the smartness of the mens appearance and in their drill is already noticable and the programme of training is undoubtedly turning the Company up to its old Standard	AOK
	4/3/17		Church Parades were held and the mens were conducted to METEREN to attend Services. 2ND Lt A. S. CREW reported for duty with this Company today	AOK
	5/3/17		The baths being available for use of this unit - All the Company were marched to BAILLEUL and bathed, arriving back at camp at 11-30 AM. The remainder of the morning was taken up by Gun cleaning. In the afternoon an inter-section football match took place.	AOK

2353 Wt. W2544/1454 700,000 5/15 D. D. & L. A.D.S.S./Forms/C. 2118.

Instructions regarding War Diaries and Intelligence Summaries are contained in F. S. Regs., Part II. and the Staff Manual respectively. Title pages will be prepared in manuscript.

WAR DIARY
or
INTELLIGENCE SUMMARY.
(*Erase heading not required.*)

Army Form C. 2118.

Place	Date	Hour	Summary of Events and Information	Remarks and references to Appendices
MOOLENACKER	6/3/17		The morning programme included Company drill under Capt P.D. MULHOLLAND, Immediate Action and mechanism. The rest of the morning and Afternoon was taken up with cleaning guns and the mens equipment in readiness for an inspection tomorrow under the GOC.	AOR
	7/3/17		The Company paraded at 9.0 AM the men being in full marching order and the Company drawn up in line under their respective Section Officers. All the guns with spare parts were placed in line in front of the Company. Brigadier General Ricardo inspected the Company and complimented the Commanding Officer upon the exceedingly smart turnout and appearance of the men. The afternoon was passed in games - Football and Tug of War	AOR
	8/3/17		The morning was very Cold & Stormy, snow falling heavily and putting a stop to all outside drill. The morning was therefore given up to lectures by the C.O & Orderly Officer. In the afternoon the whole of the Company indulged in a snowball fight which afforded plenty of strenuous exercise and amusement combined.	AOR

2353 Wt. W2544/1454 700,000 5/15 D. D. & L. A.D.S.S./Forms/C. 2118.

Instructions regarding War Diaries and Intelligence Summaries are contained in F. S. Regs., Part II. and the Staff Manual respectively. Title pages will be prepared in manuscript.

WAR DIARY
or
INTELLIGENCE SUMMARY.
(Erase heading not required.)

Army Form C. 2118.

Place	Date	Hour	Summary of Events and Information	Remarks and references to Appendices
MOOLENACKER	9/3/17		The Company were taken on a route march this morning and were all in very good spirits, part of the Company stayed behind to construct a miniature range so that we can get some practice with the guns. The afternoon was again given over to Football	ADR
	10/3/17		A very varied programme was carried out today. In the morning a lot of work was put in to complete the miniature range and the afternoon was devoted to rifle competitions and Football The weather has now got much warmer and the men are getting very fit.	ADR
	11/3/17		Church Parades were held for C of England, Presbyterians and Roman Catholics. Services were held at METEREN	ADR
	12/3/17		Range taking, Practice Part 1 and Points before, during & after firing took up the whole of the morning. Sports were again carried on during the afternoon. We have today been notified by the Brigade that we shall be taking over part of the line in a few days time. CAPTAIN P.D. MULHOLLAND has gone down to inspect the Sector to be taken over. Weather rainy.	ADR

2353 Wt. W2544/1454 700,000 5/15 D. D. & L. A.D.S.S./Forms/C. 2118.

Instructions regarding War Diaries and Intelligence Summaries are contained in F. S. Regs., Part II. and the Staff Manual respectively. Title pages will be prepared in manuscript.

WAR DIARY
or
INTELLIGENCE SUMMARY.
(Erase heading not required.)

Army Form C. 2118.

Place	Date	Hour	Summary of Events and Information	Remarks and references to Appendices
MOOLENACKER	13/3/17		Company paraded at 8.45 AM ready to move off to KEMMEL. Limbers with fighting Kit & Guns of A. C & D Sections departed from here at 7.0 AM the men being taken by motor-bus leaving at 9.0 AM. Transport left at 1-45 pm and arrived at KEMMEL at 6.0 pm. Relief was completed by 2.0 pm	a.o.k.
KEMMEL	14/3/17		Everything very quiet last night on this sector. A heavy bombardment broke out about 2.0 AM on our right. The weather is fine & sunny	a.o.k.
	15/3/17		No 12999 Pte WEBB. G.S and No 42371 Pte MARTIN. T reported for duty with this Company from base. No 73237. Pte DELANY. W evacuated to base as under age. About 5.15 pm enemy sent over about 20 small shells on junction of SUICIDE Rd and YOUNG St one direct hit being obtained about N.29.A.52.75. 10-45 to 12.0 midnight an artillery bombardment broke out on left of our Sector, red Very lights were observed but unable to say whether they were ours or the enemys. Enemy machine guns were active during the night. Our M Gs fired 2000 rounds on OCCASION ALLEY O.19.C.d.	a.o.k.
	16/3/17		The night was remarkably quiet in the Sector very little rifle & machine gun fire. The enemy seemed nervous as he put up a very large number of Very lights. Our M Gs fired 2000 rounds on OCEAN ALLEY - O.25.a and O.19.C. The weather is very fine & sunny	a.o.k.

Instructions regarding War Diaries and Intelligence Summaries are contained in F. S. Regs., Part II. and the Staff Manual respectively. Title pages will be prepared in manuscript.

WAR DIARY
or
INTELLIGENCE SUMMARY.
(Erase heading not required.)

Army Form C. 2118.

Place	Date	Hour	Summary of Events and Information	Remarks and references to Appendices
KEMMEL	17/3/17		Information received this morning that this Company will be relieved tomorrow by the 108th M.G. Coy. We shall then return to MOOLENACKER on 18th instant to complete our period of training. Machine Gun Officers of the 108th M.G. Coy were today shewn over the sector. The weather is again very fine.	[initials]
	18/3/17		Our guns in the line were relieved by the 108th M.G. Coy relief being complete by 3.0 pm. This Company then moved off to MOOLENACKER arriving at 7.0 pm	[initials]
MOOLENACKER	19/3/17		The day was spent in cleaning guns, gun kit and limbers preparatory to moving off tomorrow destination HAZEBROUCK. All gun limbers were ready packed by 6.0 pm.	[initials]
HAZEBROUCK	20/3/17		Moved off at 9.30 AM and arrived at HAZEBROUCK about 2.0 pm all the men in good condition. Good billets for the men were obtained, they were well fed and rested and fit for tomorrows long march to WIZERNES	[initials]
	21/3/17		Company paraded at 9.0 AM and moved off at 9.30 AM billeting parties were sent ahead to WIZERNES and arranged good billets for the whole of the Company. A hot meal was ready for the men on arrival. The Company arrived about 4.0 pm after a long trying march of 25 Kilometres. We have a few cases of blistered feet. Weather bad. Wet snow falling	[initials]

2353 Wt. W2544/1454 700,000 5/15 D. D. & L. A.D.S.S./Forms/C. 2118.

Instructions regarding War Diaries and Intelligence Summaries are contained in F. S. Regs., Part II. and the Staff Manual respectively. Title pages will be prepared in manuscript.

WAR DIARY
or
INTELLIGENCE SUMMARY.
(Erase heading not required.)

Army Form C. 2118.

Place	Date	Hour	Summary of Events and Information	Remarks and references to Appendices
WIZERNES	22/3/17		The Company marched off at 9-30 AM destination QUERCAMP where Brigade training will be carried out. Extreme difficulty was experienced in finding sufficient billets to accomodate the transport but ultimately managed to get all the animals & men under cover. We shall probably be here for the next twelve days. The mens billets are quite good. The weather is again very cold, with snow falling	AOK
QUERCAMP	23/3/17		Recommenced training today the first part of the morning being taking up with getting all guns kit cleaned up after the last three days march. We have only 4 men reporting sick with sore feet, a very satisfactory condition of things under the existing circumstances.	AOK
	24/3/17		The weather is still very cold with snow lying on the ground. Preliminary stage of training was finished off today. tomorrow the more advanced stages will be commenced. All the men are keeping very fit.	AOK
	25/3/17		The whole Company attended Church parade at Acquin where a church Service under Brigade arrangements was held.	AOK

2353 Wt. W2544/1454 700,000 5/15 D. D. & L. A.D.S.S./Forms/C. 2118.

Instructions regarding War Diaries and Intelligence Summaries are contained in F. S. Regs., Part II. and the Staff Manual respectively. Title pages will be prepared in manuscript.

WAR DIARY
or
INTELLIGENCE SUMMARY.
(*Erase heading not required.*)

No. 109 MACHINE GUN COMPANY.

Army Form C. 2118.

Page 143

Place	Date	Hour	Summary of Events and Information	Remarks and references to Appendices
ZUERCAMP	26/3/17		Weather again extremely cold & wet, very little opportunity of carrying on outdoor training. Under these circumstances the programme of training underwent alteration. Mechanism, Stoppages and Immediate action took up most of the morning the remainder being spent in Belt filling & cleaning. During the afternoon wet snow fell continuously and put a stop to all sports. At 3.0 pm the C.O and six officers of the Company attended a demonstration of "The Attack" held at WISQUES.	aoK
	27/3/17		The weather still being very wet, most of the training had to be carried out under cover. The afternoon was given over to Sports in which the whole of the Company took part	aoK
	28/3/17		Today the weather has much improved, enabling the Sections to carry out advanced gun drill, taking up positions and indication and recognition.	
	29/3/17		Weather again very wet. Lectures were given to the men by Section Officers on "The Offensive" Mechanism, Stoppages and immediate action were also carried on.	aoK

2353 Wt. W2544/1454 700,000 5/15 D. D. & L. A.D.S.S./Forms/C. 2118.

Instructions regarding War Diaries and Intelligence Summaries are contained in F. S. Regs., Part II. and the Staff Manual respectively. Title pages will be prepared in manuscript.

WAR DIARY
or
INTELLIGENCE SUMMARY.
(Erase heading not required.)

Army Form C. 2118.

Place	Date	Hour	Summary of Events and Information	Remarks and references to Appendices
QUERCAMP	30th		The weather again was very inclement, heavy showers were encountered all day: owing to this the programme of training was carried out with slight alteration: Lt. D.C. Cayley 1st Bn K.O.S. Borderers takes over 2nd in command of the Coy vice Lt. A.O. Robinson under the W.O. exchange of Officers scheme	DLC
QUERCAMP	31st		The weather again was extremely showery; there was no training carried out to day owing to the Brigade Sports the Company marched down to the sports at 9.15 AM.	DLC

2353 Wt. W2544/1454 700,000 5/15 D. D. & L. A.D.S.S./Forms/C. 2118.

CONFIDENTIAL.

Vol 13

W A R   D I A R Y

of

109th Brigade Machine Gun Company,

from 1st April 1917

till 30th April 1917.

Instructions regarding War Diaries and Intelligence Summaries are contained in F. S. Regs., Part II. and the Staff Manual respectively. Title pages will be prepared in manuscript.

WAR DIARY
or
INTELLIGENCE SUMMARY.
(Erase heading not required.)

Army Form C. 2118.

No. 108 MACHINE GUN COMPANY. PAGE 145

Place	Date	Hour	Summary of Events and Information	Remarks and references to Appendices
C QUERCAMP	1/4/17		There were no church parades today except for Roman Catholics but company sports were held on the village green. The competitions between sections in tests of elementary training were well contested, the company showed great evenness in training all through. A section won the aggregate points competition.	DLC.
QUERCAMP	2/4/17		A+C section paraded under C.O and marched to ACQUIN to give demonstration to Brigade. B section attached to 10th Royal Inniskillens for practice in Battalion in attack. D section attached to 14th Royal Irish Rifles for Battalion training in attack	DLC
QUERCAMP	3/4/17		A+C sections were to have paraded with the 9th 11th Royal Inniskillings, but owing to a very heavy fall of snow during the night it was decided not to hold any manoeuvres. The company were occupied in preparing to quit their billets and overhauling equipment	DLC
On the march. WIZERNES	4/4/17		The coy started off at 9 AM on its march to WIZERNES a distance of 15 Kilometres. Wizernes was reached soon after two PM there were no men who had to fall out which was good considering that seventy two pairs of boots had been issued the day before the march	DLC.

Instructions regarding War Diaries and Intelligence Summaries are contained in F. S. Regs., Part II. and the Staff Manual respectively. Title pages will be prepared in manuscript.

WAR DIARY
or
INTELLIGENCE SUMMARY.
(Erase heading not required.)

Army Form C. 2118.

Place	Date	Hour	Summary of Events and Information	Remarks and references to Appendices
HAZEBROUCH	5/4/17		The company today had to march the distance of eighteen kilometers from WIZERNES to HAZEBROUCH. a start was made at 8-30 at 12 the Brigade halted and the battalions had dinners cooked in the "cookers" owing to the lack of any means of cooking lunch the Coy did not wait a full hour but came on reaching HAZEBROUCH at 2.45 PM and Billets outside at 3 PM. The billets were scattered farms about one mile out.	DCC
KEMMEL	6/4/17		Today permission had been given by the GOC to march in fighting order Reveille went at 5 AM and the company were on the road to Kemmel at 7 AM. we were second in the line of march behind the 9th RIF. Thirty men of the Coy who were suffering from bad feet* were taken in the lorry which had been provided. No men fell out today and the Coy arrived at Kemmel into the billets vacated by the 108 Coy at 4 30 PM. The long march / the distance was 24 Kilometers had told on the men who were very tired but beyond a few blisters allright.	* See "Boots" 4/4/17

2353 Wt. W2544/1454 700,000 5/15 D. D. & L. A.D.S.S./Forms/C. 2118.

Instructions regarding War Diaries and Intelligence Summaries are contained in F. S. Regs., Part II. and the Staff Manual respectively. Title pages will be prepared in manuscript.

WAR DIARY
or
INTELLIGENCE SUMMARY.
(Erase heading not required.)

Army Form C. 2118.

Place	Date	Hour	Summary of Events and Information	Remarks and references to Appendices
KEMMEL 7/4/17			At ten thirty eleven guns and three officers left headquarters to take over from the 108 Machine gun company, machine gun belt boxes were handed over to avoid porterage: The coy are now half in the trenches and half out, B & C in A D out	[illegible]
KEMMEL	8/4/16		Today being Easter Sunday was spent fairly quietly; ~~the company~~ B & D section paraded from 9AM – 11AM under Section Officers; and there was a voluntary church parade in the afternoon; at 6 PM the Canteen was opened for the men of the Company. There was very little activity today, except for a few German planes who flew about over KEMMEL at odd intervals during the day	[illegible]
KEMMEL	10th 4-16		Today the company were issued out with a full equipment of revolvers, which before had only been carried by No 1 & 2 also NCOs. There was little activity in the line but one of our guns engaged with indirect over head fire two of the enemies cookhouses in WYCHAETE from which smoke had been seen issuing on the previous day	

2353 Wt. W2544/1454 700,000 5/15 D. D. & L. A.D.S.S./Forms/C. 2118.

Instructions regarding War Diaries and Intelligence Summaries are contained in F. S. Regs., Part II. and the Staff Manual respectively. Title pages will be prepared in manuscript.

WAR DIARY
or
INTELLIGENCE SUMMARY.
(Erase heading not required.)

No. 100 MACHINE GUN COMPANY

Page 148

Army Form C. 2118.

Place	Date	Hour	Summary of Events and Information	Remarks and references to Appendices
KEMMEL	10/4/17		The morning was spent in instruction on our new weapon the Revolver which was issued to the company yesterday. Also a range was commenced as it had been decided to give practice to the two sections now living in KEMMEL. In the line was was not much activity we engaged three targets with indirect fire. No results were observed but it is hoped the fire took effect	DCC
KEMMEL	11/4/16		B.C. A.D. Sections (the sections at present not in the line) spent the morning practising revolver shooting on an extemporised range, in the afternoon went to baths at DRANOUTRE. The sections in the line carried on against several targets in WHYTSCHAETE, namely one cookhouse and two dumps which had been reported in the Corps intelligence. The Corps Machine Gun officer Lt Col Wylie and the 36th Div G.S.O. one Lt Col Place had a conference with Capt Mulholland at Company Headquarters.	
KEMMEL	12/4/17		Today has been an extremely quiet day, all thoughts being turned to our advance at ARRAS: A few targets were engaged by indirect fire: two thousand rounds were expended by two guns.	

Instructions regarding War Diaries and Intelligence Summaries are contained in F. S. Regs., Part II. and the Staff Manual respectively. Title pages will be prepared in manuscript.

WAR DIARY
or
INTELLIGENCE SUMMARY.
(Erase heading not required.)

Army Form C. 2118.

Place	Date	Hour	Summary of Events and Information	Remarks and references to Appendices
KEMMEL	13th		The enemy still are showing very little desire to court retribution by any unfriendly action on us: no reports come in of the Germans doing any indirect MG fire on important junctions in our trench system, inspite of the fact that this Company alone expends nearly 8000 rounds every twenty four hours on indirect fire. Targets reported by Airmen in their reconnaissance flights are fired on within twenty four hours. This system may seem wastefull as no results are ever vouched for; but the writer for one can testify from experience + that with proper care very great inconvenience can be caused by MG firing bursts at intervals on roads, villages etc.	DLL + On the Somme 1916 Germans used indirect fire on roads and ration when the [illegible] and the transport coming up
KEMMEL	14th		Today the village of KEMMEL WAS SLIGHLY SHELLED BY THE GERMANS using 77 MM shrapnel; as the shelling was about fifty yards from the Chateau; the order was given to evacuate the place: The order was carried out with great coolness, no Casualties were inflicted; though some other units suffered. The two sections in rest carried on training as usual, the two section in the line indulged in indirect night firing as usual.	DLL

2353 Wt. W2544/1454 700,000 5/15 D. D. & L. A.D.S.S./Forms/C. 2118.

Instructions regarding War Diaries and Intelligence Summaries are contained in F. S. Regs., Part II. and the Staff Manual respectively. Title pages will be prepared in manuscript.

WAR DIARY
or
INTELLIGENCE SUMMARY.
(Erase heading not required.)

NO. 109 MACHINE GUN COMPANY.
Page 150

Army Form C. 2118.

Place	Date	Hour	Summary of Events and Information	Remarks and references to Appendices
KEMMEL	15th		The sections B & C who have been in the trenches for eight days are now relieved by A D sections; for further particulars of the relief see Operation order* in the Appendix: otherwise the day was fairly quiet	Operation order dated 14/4/15 for 15/4/15
KEMMEL	16th		Today most of the company have been engaged: B C sections have to find a guard; 20 men for baths and two fatigue parties each of eleven other ranks. We now have to find twenty other ranks daily to do unloading: a fatigue which has nothing to do with the company and which is preventing us sending working parties up to the line to do construction work	
KEMMEL.	17th		The company is still finding two fatigues daily for unloading and also parties for work in the trenches; while this is happening no improvements of billets are going on.	
KEMMEL.	18th		The issue of revolvers to the company is nearly complete: Tonight no less than 7 limbers of material went up to the line for building emplacements. Three limbers went up Suicide Road to YONGE St and the remaining four went to Bully Beef farm.	

2353 Wt. W2544/1454 700,000 5/15 D. D. & L. A.D.S.S./Forms/C. 2118.

Instructions regarding War Diaries and Intelligence Summaries are contained in F. S. Regs., Part II. and the Staff Manual respectively. Title pages will be prepared in manuscript.

WAR DIARY
or
INTELLIGENCE SUMMARY.
(Erase heading not required.)

No. 1?? MACHINE GUN COMPANY. Page 151

Army Form C. 2118.

Place	Date	Hour	Summary of Events and Information	Remarks and references to Appendices
KEMMEL	19th		Today the sections not in the line were engaged all day. Strong parties were sent up to the line to work on the positions. The forward Headquarters of the Company BULLY BEEF Farm is having its dugout strengthened. Also yonge Street the headquarters of the left subsection are being improved.	acc
"	20th		Work went on in the line as before. The whole company working during the night there was a lot of artillery fire but besides this the usual night firing went on. BOGAERT FARM the new target was fired on.	acc
"	21st		A heavy bombardment was today given the Germans, during most of the morning and also during the night. orders had been received from Brigade that no indirect fire was to be done, so no ammunition was expended tonight.	
	22nd		Work is proceeding in the line ~~the~~ satisfactorily. A new concrete emplacement of the open type to accomodate a No. IV Tripod has been erected. The new dugouts in BULLY BEEF are waiting for some material which has been hard to get. Four hundred rounds were expended on a german airplane today by two AA guns.	

2353 Wt. W2544/1454 700,000 5/15 D. D. & L. A.D.S.S./Forms/C. 2118.

Instructions regarding War Diaries and Intelligence Summaries are contained in F. S. Regs., Part II. and the Staff Manual respectively. Title pages will be prepared in manuscript.

WAR DIARY
or
INTELLIGENCE SUMMARY.
(Erase heading not required.)

Army Form C. 2118.

Place	Date	Hour	Summary of Events and Information	Remarks and references to Appendices
KEMMEL	23rd		Today Monday the sections in the line A-D are relieved by C+B who have had eight days: For further particulars see operation orders which are appended. The relief was without incident. During the night of the 22nd 23rd 8500 were fired by the guns in the line on various targets.	* Operation orders are appended
KEMMEL	24th		This day proved without incident at all: the weather was very good, 205000 of special ammunition for machine guns was added to the regimental reserve at headquarters. This ammunition externally does not differ from any other 303 SAA, and is packed in bandoliers.	
	25th		Nothing of note happened today, the only change being that our B echelon transport has come up and occupies TYRONE Farm along with the A echelon, 20000 rounds of SAA goes up to Bully beef Farm.	
	26th		The Coy has fired 80000 rounds during the last twenty four hours with its ten guns in the line; The 36th Division has approved of the MG defence scheme of MG barrages, brought out by Capt Mulholland, it is attached.	

Instructions regarding War Diaries and Intelligence Summaries are contained in F. S. Regs., Part II. and the Staff Manual respectively. Title pages will be prepared in manuscript.

WAR DIARY
or
INTELLIGENCE SUMMARY.
(*Erase heading not required.*)

Army Form C. 2118.

Place	Date	Hour	Summary of Events and Information	Remarks and references to Appendices
KEMMEL	29th		General Ricardo the GOC Brigade having decided for various reasons to put the whole 109 Company in the line; also to move the Company headquarters out of KEMMEL and put them up closer to the line the following alterations were made, seven guns in the right of the Brigade sector held by the 108 Company were relieved by the 109 Company, A D section taking over. the Company headquarters were also moved up; the headquarters and signals were at BULLY BEEF FARM the orderly room at SPY FARM. Minor changes were carried out by gun teams in the left sector held by B C section. The Quarter-master stores were moved by to TYRONE FARM with the transport. The headquarters in KEMMEL were taken over by the 108 Light Trench Mortar Battery. The artificers shop is at the BAKERY; A D Section headquarters at BEEHIVE DUGOUTS, C Section YONGE Street, D Section FORT REGINA	

2353 Wt. W2544/1454 700,000 5/15 D. D. & L. A.D.S.S./Forms/C. 2118.

Instructions regarding War Diaries and Intelligence Summaries are contained in F. S. Regs., Part II. and the Staff Manual respectively. Title pages will be prepared in manuscript.

WAR DIARY
or
INTELLIGENCE SUMMARY.
(Erase heading not required.)

Army Form C. 2118.

Place	Date	Hour	Summary of Events and Information	Remarks and references to Appendices
SPANBROKE SECTOR	28th		The day was spent by A-D Sections in overhauling the positions lately taken over in the 108 MG Company, working out the barrages and deciding alterations in the emplacements to suit our requirements. The night was spent in the usual indirect fire about 13-15 thousand rounds were fired	[illegible]
	29		The day being very hot and bright no day firing was done and the usual work was carried on all day, during the night about 14000 rounds were fired off	
	30th		Fourteen thousand rounds were fired off in indirect fire which is rather a risky business in these days, when the S.A.A is very bad; only four days ago C Section killed two of the 16th R.I.R who were working in front with on paper a 100 foot clearance.	

2353 Wt. W2544/1454 700,000 5/15 D. D. & L. A.D.S.S./Forms/C. 2118.

SECRET. Copy No. 10

U.E.G. OPERATION ORDER NO.

14th APRIL 1917

1. THE FOLLOWING RELIEFS WILL BE CARRIED OUT ON THE 15th APRIL 17

RIGHT M.G. COMMAND

'A' SECTION WILL RELIEVE 'B' SECTION

LEFT M.G. COMMAND

'D' SECTION WILL RELIEVE 'C' SECTION.

2.

	GUN POSITIONS R.M.G. COMMAND.		GUNS.	TEAMS	
*	S.P. 9.	"	A.	1. N.C.O.	5. MEN.
	S.P. 10.	"	A.	"	5 "
*	"	"	A.	"	5 "
	BULLY BEEF Fm.	"	A.	"	5 "
*	FORT VICTORIA (1).	"	B.	"	6 "
	(2).	"	B.		
*	FORT REGINA (1).	"	D.	"	6 "
	(2).	"	D.		
	L.M.G. COMMAND.				
*	YONGE ST (S)	"	D.	1. N.C.O.	5. MEN
	YONGE ST (N)	"	D.	"	5 "

3. THE SPARE MEN OF 'D' SECTION WILL BE ACCOMMODATED IN THE DUGOUT AT R.1. POSITION. FOR WORK.

THE RELIEVING TEAMS WILL LEAVE COY H.Q. AT INTERVALS OF 5 MINUTES STARTING AT 1.30. P.M. GUIDES FROM * TO BE AT C.H.Q. AT 1 P.M.

TRIPODS AND AMMUNITION ONLY WILL BE LEFT AS TRENCH STORES. HANDING AND TAKING OVER CERTIFICATES WILL BE RENDERED TO ORDERLY ROOM BY 6 P.M 15th INST.

ACKNOWLEDGE.

[illegible] Capt.

COMMANDING "U.E.G."

S E C R E T. Copy No. 72

MACHINE GUN DEFENCE SCHEME.

-----------oOo-----------

LEFT SUB-SECTOR.

1. FRONTAGE.

The BRIGADE FRONT extends from the WULVERGHEM - WYTSCHAETE Road (inclusive) to KETCHEN AVENUE (inclusive).

2. DISPOSITIONS.

The RIGHT SUB-SECTOR will extend from the Right limit of the BRIGADE FRONT to 1. bay North of PICCADILLY. The LEFT SUB-SECTOR extends from the Right limit of the RIGHT SUB-SECTOR to the Left limit of the BRIGADE FRONT.
INFANTRY FRONT COMPANY H.Q. of the two SUB-SECTORS are situated as follows :-

RIGHT SUB-SECTOR.	RIGHT.	N.35.b.80.30.
	LEFT	N.29.d.89.10.
LEFT SUB-SECTOR.	RIGHT.	N.29.b.65.20.
	LEFT.	N.23.d.43.40.
BATTALION H.Q.	RIGHT	NEWPORT DUGOUTS.
	LEFT	FORT VICTORIA.

3. CONCENTRATION LINES.

For purposes of concentrating the fire of the MACHINE GUNS of the LEFT SUB-SECTOR on any Company frontage of the BRIGADE FRONT, the two SUB-SECTORS will be sub-dividedequally. Pickets being laid in the parapet of every gun position by map and compass delineating the direction of the Company fronts.

4. NIGHT LINES.

All guns on the "GENERAL LINE" at "STAND TO" as laid down on the "BARRAGE CARDS" existing at each position. These cards provide for five eventualities, i.e. should there be a raid or an attack on either of the following fronts the MACHINE GUNS will come into action according to the particular front threatened.

RIGHT, RIGHT CENTRE, LEFT CENTRE, LEFT and GENERAL (i.e. BRIGADE FRONT).

5. ALARMS.

MACHINE GUN DETACHMENTS will not wait for the S.O.S. rocket to be sent up before getting into action. When any bombardment takes place, that, in the opinion of the N.C.O. i/c DETACHMENT, denotes - "Preliminary to RAID", he will, having decided which of the four Company fronts is affected, get his gun into action with bursts of fire; in this way the guns are certain of anticipating any minor attacks instead of being late. Should a "Lift" indicate that the anticipated raid is taking place the guns will fire rapid and continue to do so while the raid is still in progress. When the raid is obviously over, the back areas will be searched with a view to harassing any parties of the enemy that may be withdrawing. At this stage however care must be taken to ensure that the positions are not discovered by any observation that the enemy may get.

6. TELEPHONE COMMUNICATIONS.

The M.G. Coy. H.Q. situated at N.21.c.40.30 is connected with BRIGADE H.Q. and with each of the M.G. Officers dugouts situated at N.29.a.50.90 and BULLY BEEF FARM direct. Arrangements are being made by the BRIGADE SIGNAL SECTION for direct communication between both the BATTALION H.Q. in the LINE and the two M.G. Officers' dugouts

7. INDIRECT FIRE.

It has been established that this night firing has a very harassing effect on the enemy, therefore indirect fire will be carried out at intervals throughout the night, particularly so between midnight and 'STAND DOWN'.

Targets will be forwarded to the M.G. Officer in the line daily as they appear in BRIGADE, DIVISIONAL and CORPS Intelligence Summaries. A log book of night firing will be kept at each Officer's dugout.

8. STANDING ORDERS.

The N.C.O. i/c DETACHMENT is responsible for the following :-

(a) Every man in his Detachment is to know the smallest details of the surrounding country and the ACTION to be taken should the enemy break through the front system of trenches.

(b) Every man in his Detachment is to know exactly what action to take in assisting in repelling raids as laid down in para. 4.

(c) If the immediate vicinity of the position is heavily bombarded, the Detachment and Gun will not retire but may move a short distance laterally or forward to escape the intentions of the bombardment. On the cessation of the bombardment the DETACHMENT will immediately return to its original position and will 'STAND TO' until ordered to do otherwise by an Officer.

(d) In the above case every man must put on his equipment with revolver loaded at the first sign of shelling.

(e) The good sanitary condition of dugouts and latrines utilized by his men and the cleanliness of the position in his charge.

[signature]

Captain,
Commanding 109th Machine Gun Company.

SECRET. C. No. 10.

U. G. G. OPERATION ORDERS No. 6 (a)

26th April 1917

1. Reference Bde. Operation Order No. 2... the guns in action of the 108th M.G.C. will be relieved by the 109th M.G. Coy on the 27th inst.

2. The following positions will be taken over by the Sections indicated below.

Position		Section	Position		Section
YONGE St. N. 1.		"C"	Fort Regina	1	"B"
" " S. 1.			Fort Victoria	1	
Reserve Trench Gun	1	4 Teams	Bully Beef Fm	1	3. Teams.
S. P. 10 Gun	1				

Position		Section	Position		Section
S. P. 9	1	"D"	Chimney Fm		"A"
S. P. 8	1		Fluffy Post. L.	1	
Piccadilly	1	4 Teams	Snipers Post	1	4 Teams. A.
Kingsway	1		Frenchmans Fm	1	1 Team. B.

3. (a) The Gun and Team of "B" at present at S. P. 9 will be relieved by the Gun and Team of "C" from Fort Regina, the first mentioned Gun team to occupy Fort Regina.

(b) One Gun of "B" at present at Fort Victoria with a Team of "D" from Billets will relieve the Gun and Team of "B" at S. P. 9, the last mentioned Gun is to be carried back to Fort Victoria, and the last mentioned team (i.e. of "B") to carry the remaining Gun of "D" out to Billets.

(c) The remaining Gun of "C" at Fort Regina will be exchanged with the Gun of "B" in the Reserve Trench.

4. Para. 3 (a) will be completed by 10-0 am.
Para. 3 (b) " " " " 11-0 am
" 3 (c) " " " " 12 0 noon.

5. Completion of reliefs to be reported at earliest.

6. Operation Orders No. 6 (b) will be issued later.

[signature] Capt.
Commanding U. G. G.

SECRET

OPERATION ORDERS. No. 6. (b)

27th April 1917

HEADQUARTERS

1 HEADQUARTERS WILL [illegible] AT KEMMEL AT 8 p.m. AND WILL OPEN AT BULLY BEEF FARM AT 8-0 p.m.

ORDERLY ROOM

2 COMPANY ORDERLY ROOM WILL ACCOMODATED IN SPY FARM DUGOUT [illegible]

TELEPHONE EXCHANGE

3 [illegible] TELEPHONE EXCHANGE WILL BE IN BULLY BEEF F^m.

OFFICERS ACCOMODATION

4 ACCOMODATION OF OFFICERS WILL BE AS FOLLOWS:-

A SECTION 2 OFFICERS AT CORNER F^m 1 TELEPHONE

B SECTION 1 OFFICER 2ND LIEUT [illegible]

C SECTION 2 OFFICERS 2ND LT. ROOT + 2ND LT GEAR, YONGE [illegible] "

D SECTION 2 OFFICERS [illegible] DUGOUTS "

AFTERNOON RELIEFS

5 [illegible] ORDERS No. 6(a) PARA. 3.

D SECTION WILL [illegible] F^m

B " " " " KINGSWAY

[illegible] OFF FROM KEMMEL AT TWO MINUTES INTERVALS BETWEEN TEAMS, STARTING AT 3-0 p.m. BULLY BEEF [illegible] WILL MOVE TO S.P. 10 AT 4-0 p.m. [illegible]. THE TELEPHONE EXCHANGE WILL BE IN THE TEAMS DUGOUT AT BULLY BEEF F^m.

6 [illegible]

[illegible] REGENT S^t, NEWPORT DUGOUTS [illegible]

[illegible] REGENT S^t [illegible] St PICCADILLY

7 AMMUNITION

[illegible] WILL BE TAKEN OVER FROM THE 108th M. Gun Coy AND SIGNED FOR ON THE [illegible], WHICH WILL BE FORWARDED TO H^D QRS BY 10 a.m. [illegible] 28th INST.

8 RATIONS + FUEL

[illegible] WILL BE CARRIED BY THE TEAMS [illegible] FOR THE FOLLOWING DAY

9 GUNS, TRIPODS AND ACCESSORIES

[illegible] WILL BE CARRIED BY THE TEAMS TO THEIR POSITIONS.

CONT'D:-

10.

[illegible]ION ORDERS No. 6 (B).

CONTD.

[illegible] RATION ROUTES

SUICIDE ROAD FOR "C" SECTION, HD. QRS, 4 TEAMS "B" SECTION HD QRS 2 TEAMS

LINDENHOEK ROAD " COMPANY " " AND " SECTION 1 TEAM

SPOIL ROAD " "D" SECTION " " [illegible] TEAMS " "B" SECTION HD QRS, 3 TEAMS

[illegible] POST

LETTER POST WILL BE DRAWN AT HD QRS DAILY, [illegible] FOR DRAWING WILL BE NOTIFIED DAILY.

PARCEL POST WILL GO DIRECT TO TEAMS WITH THEIR RATIONS.

D C Kayley Lt for Captain

COMMANDING K.E.G.

C O N F I D E N T I A L.

Vol 14

W A R D I A R Y

OF

109TH. MACHINE GUN COMPANY.

FROM 1ST. MAY, 1917.

TILL 31ST. MAY, 1917.

Instructions regarding War Diaries and Intelligence Summaries are contained in F. S. Regs., Part II. and the Staff Manual respectively. Title pages will be prepared in manuscript.

WAR DIARY
or
INTELLIGENCE SUMMARY.
(Erase heading not required.)

Army Form C. 2118.

Place	Date	Hour	Summary of Events and Information	Remarks and references to Appendices
SPANBROEKE SALIENT	1 MAY.		The weather remains glorious and the work proceeds well. At 12 midday, 40 men of the 9th R Innis Fus made a daylight raid, but captured no prisoners and had no casualties. They had not informed the Machine Gun company, as a result of which they might easily have been fired on by some of detachment who were laid ready to fire on the (enemy) unknowing in noman's land. This is a poor example of cooperation between different units. The Company fired 14000 rounds on lines of communication to the enemies line.	
	2nd		During the night we had one casualty the sentry at BLIGHTY Fm gun being hit by two bullets. At about 10.30 Frenchman's Farm was shelled and the dugout where the team of the gun there lived was blown in. The[y] were excavated later by a party of Machine Gunners under Lt Lea with three other officers under very heavy shell fire. The whole team were got out but two men died from suffocation and fumes. The casualties of this affair was 2 men killed, 2 badly suffocated, 2 shellshock, one officer who displayed great heroism 2Lt Walker shellshock. The two men were buried at POND Fm Cemetery REF WYTSCHAETE 28 SW2 N34 D 50 90. (Pte Wally & Pte Bentley	

2353 Wt. W2544/1454 700,000 5/15 D. D. & L. A.D.S.S./Forms/C. 2118.

Instructions regarding War Diaries and Intelligence Summaries are contained in F. S. Regs., Part II. and the Staff Manual respectively. Title pages will be prepared in manuscript.

WAR DIARY
or
INTELLIGENCE SUMMARY.
(Erase heading not required.)

Army Form C. 2118.

Place	Date	Hour	Summary of Events and Information	Remarks and references to Appendices
SPANBROEKE SALIENT.				
May	4		Shelling on both sides was frequent during the day, the SP 10 position (C Section) was shelled as usual, the emplacement being hit but no damage done.	HC
"	5th		During the early morning at about 3.45 the enemy raided to the Right of the Brigade sector, however 11 of the 16 Machine guns opened fire on the ~~Left~~ Right Barrage with success. During the day the Coy were relieved by the 108 Coy. The Coy goes back to TYRONE Fm with the exception of C section who are in the KEMMEL DEFENCES (opperation orders attached)	HC
TYRONE Fm	6th		The morning was spent overhauling equipment and guns. The Company are sending 25 men daily on fatigues.	HC
"	7th		The company parade at 8.30 this morning for Commanding Officers inspection, the idea was to see how the Clothing was. It was found that it was all servicable, though rather oily in some cases. After this most of the Company went to the Divisional horse Show which took place near DRANOUTRE	HC

2353 Wt. W2544/1454 700,000 5/15 D. D. & L. A.D.S.S./Forms/C. 2118.

Instructions regarding War Diaries and Intelligence Summaries are contained in F. S. Regs., Part II. and the Staff Manual respectively. Title pages will be prepared in manuscript.

WAR DIARY
or
INTELLIGENCE SUMMARY.
(Erase heading not required.)

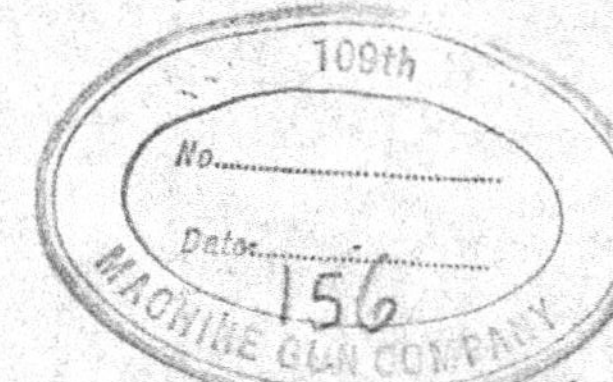

Army Form C. 2118.

Place	Date	Hour	Summary of Events and Information	Remarks and references to Appendices
TYRONE Fm	8th		The day was spent by overhauling belts and guns, and painting tripods.	V
"	9th		The day was spent cleaning limbers, a lecture was given by the C.O to Officers and NCO's on Machine gun barrage. The range finders were receiving instruction on range finding from Sergeant Smith.	
"	10th		Company baths at DRANOUTRE. A Section relieves B section in KEMMEL HILL DEFENCES	
"	11th		B Sections Bath. C+D Tactical scheme under Lt. Cayley in the afternoon washing limbers	
TYRONE Fm TO WAKEFIELD LINES.	13th		The company is relieved by the 108 Company and moves back to WAKEFIELD LINES on the DRANOUTRE - LOCRE ROAD in Divisional reserve. A Section in KEMMEL DEFENCES are relieved by the 108 Company. D Section relieve the 107 Company to man the two AA guns at HAGEDORNE: The Company less one section spend the night in Bivouacs.	vide Coy op order No 8

2353 Wt. W2544/1454 700,000 5/15 D. D. & L. A.D.S.S./Forms/C. 2118.

Instructions regarding War Diaries and Intelligence Summaries are contained in F. S. Regs., Part II. and the Staff Manual respectively. Title pages will be prepared in manuscript.

WAR DIARY
or
INTELLIGENCE SUMMARY.
(Erase heading not required.)

Army Form C. 2118.

Place	Date	Hour	Summary of Events and Information	Remarks and references to Appendices
~~WAKEFIELD~~ WAKEFIELD LINES Nr LOCRE BELGIUM	May 14th		The company at 2PM moved into huts in WAKEFIELD Camp vacated by the 9th Royal Irish Fusiliers. The transport under Lt Bulgar are working very hard in painting the waggons: as it has been decided to use the SAA limbers and headquarter limbers as much as possible and to keep the gun limbers in smart condition.	
"	15th		The whole company less the section at HAGEDORNE and a few men to guard the camp are now necessary to form the working parties asked for by the Brigade ie 75 OR (~~4~~ Sergeants) one officer. Of these 50 work under the 173 Bde Artillery at DAYLIGHT CORNER and 25 at LITTLE KEMMEL. This means that no work can be done in the company.	
" "	16-17		The company are all working from 9PM – 4A under the Artillery.	
	18th		Working parties for the Artillery are now stopped as a certain amount of work has to be done for the Advance, this means digging emplacements in the line [illegible].	

2353 Wt. W2544/1454 700,000 5/15 D. D. & L. A.D.S.S./Forms/C. 2118.

Army Form C. 2118.

Instructions regarding War Diaries and Intelligence Summaries are contained in F. S. Regs., Part II. and the Staff Manual respectively. Title pages will be prepared in manuscript.

WAR DIARY
or
INTELLIGENCE SUMMARY.
(Erase heading not required.)

Place	Date	Hour	Summary of Events and Information	Remarks and references to Appendices
19th WAKEFIELD CAMP			At 11 AM two guns from C section with 8 OR and one officer relieved D section at the AA guns at HOOGEDRAE. The remainder spent the morning at Gun drill. The signal section practised visual signalling. At 4 30 PM	
20 "			The work was commenced today in building 10 Gun positions and trench system necessary for it between BOARDMAN Pt 1 RESERVE trench. The trench has to be built in a stream, so a lot of work will have to be done, putting duck boards down.	
21			~~So~~ Eight men were up working at the Gun positions today; parties going up at 10 AM 2 PM and 4 PM. The positions for 4 of the guns are nearly finished	
22			Work continues today as yesterday. 4 reinforcements arrived tonight from the Base	

2353 Wt. W2544/1454 700,000 5/15 D. D. & L. A.D.S.S./Forms/C. 2118.

Instructions regarding War Diaries and Intelligence Summaries are contained in F. S. Regs., Part II. and the Staff Manual respectively. Title pages will be prepared in manuscript.

WAR DIARY
or
INTELLIGENCE SUMMARY.
(Erase heading not required.)

Army Form C. 2118.

Place	Date	Hour	Summary of Events and Information	Remarks and references to Appendices
WAKEFIELD CAMP N^B LOCRE BELGIUM	23rd		The company is doing no training at present except two classes for attached men in the morning; the working parties provided daily are about 80 strong.	
	24th		Working parties as usual, at 10 AM, 2 PM, 7 PM. The company are now full strength	
	25th		Working parties as usual. 2/Lt [illegible] reports for duty from the base.	
	26th		Working parties 40 strong at 2 PM and 10 AM. 80 of the company have baths at DRANOUTRE	
	27th		Parties working at Machine Gun emplacements in the line at 10 PM WAKEFIELD HUTS WERE SHELLED in evacuating the lines we had two casualties one being an attached man	
	28		Working Parties as usual during the day. The Company has now taken 113 000 rounds of SAA up to the line. Camp was shelled as usual at 10 12 2 AM and 4. No Casualties	

2353 Wt. W2544/1454 700,000 5/15 D. D. & L. A.D.S.S./Forms/C. 2118.

Instructions regarding War Diaries and Intelligence Summaries are contained in F. S. Regs., Part II. and the Staff Manual respectively. Title pages will be prepared in manuscript.

WAR DIARY
or
INTELLIGENCE SUMMARY.
(Erase heading not required.)

Army Form C. 2118.

MAY

Page 160

Place	Date	Hour	Summary of Events and Information	Remarks and references to Appendices
WAKEFIELD CAMP Nr LOCRE BELGIUM	29th		In the morning the training programme was not carried out according to the programme as most of the Company had spent the night away from the camp owing to the shelling. The usual working parties went up the line at 10 AM and 2 PM. At 10 PM the camp was shelled by a 5.9 German naval gun as per German programme, however the Company were all [illegible] outside and the transport had been evacuated earlier so no damage was done.	[illegible]
"	30th		Fatigue party as usual during the day working in the line. Camp shelled at night.	
	31st		Company parade at 9 AM to practice the YUKON pack, a new kind of pack with which it is claimed a man can carry two to five belt boxes of Ammunition. Eight have been allotted to the Company for the advance. WAKEFIELD Camp shelled as usual during the night, no casualties.	

SECRET.

COPY NO.....12.

109TH MACHINE GUN COY.

OPERATION ORDERS NO. 8.

12TH MAY. 1917.

1. THE 109TH BRIGADE WILL BE RELEIVED IN THE SPANBROEK SECTOR ON THE 14TH MAY 1917, BY 108TH BRIGADE

2. LIEUT CAYLEY WILL REPORT TO THE STAFF CAPTAIN AT 109TH BRIGADE HD. QRS. BY 11. AM. 13TH [illegible] AS BILLETING OFFICER.

3. ONE ½ SECTION OF "D" SECTION WILL RELEIVE THE ½ SECTION OF THE 107TH M.G. COY AT HAEGEDOORNE BY 4-30 AM. 13TH INST. RATIONS FOR THAT DAY WILL BE CARRIED [illegible] TRANSPORT WILL BE PACK TRANSPORT.

4. "A" SECTION IN [illegible] DEFENCES WILL BE RELEIVED BY ONE SECTION OF THE 108TH M.G. COY. AT ABOUT [illegible] 13TH INST.

5. THE GUNS AND ACCESSORIES OF "B" "C" AND ½ "D" SECTIONS WILL BE PACKED IN THE BATTLE WAGGONS BY 9-30 AM, IT MUST BE UNDERSTOOD THAT THESE WAGGONS CONTAIN <u>ONLY</u> BATTLE STORES.

6. "B" ECHELON WAGGONS WILL BE PACKED BY 10. AM.

7. SECTION. "B" ECHELON STORES (WHICH INCLUDES [illegible]) WILL BE MOVED ON THE FIRST JOURNEY.

8. THE HD. QRS. WAGGON WILL CARRY THE ARTIFICERS AND SADDLERS STORES ON THE FIRST JOURNEY

9. A. GUARD CONSISTING OF 1. N.C.O AND THREE MEN WILL ACCOMPANY "A" ECHELON TO THE NEW PARK. WITH DAY'S RATIONS WHERE IT WILL REMAIN UNTIL FURTHER ORDERS. 2ND LIEUT IDIENS WILL ACCOMPANY "A" ECHELON AND WILL ATTEND TO THE ARRIVAL AND DISTRIBUTION OF STORES, THE PARKING OF THE WAGGONS, AND THE CARE OF ANIMALS.

10. THE COOKS CART WILL CARRY THE COMPANY COOK'S STORES IN COMPANY WITH "B" ECHELON. DINNERS WILL BE PREPARED IN THE WAGGON LINES BY [illegible] P.M. FOR THE COMPANY

11. ON RETURN "B" ECHELON WILL BE LOADED UP WITH THE C.Q.M.S. STORES.

12. LOADING PARTIES. "C" AND ½ "D" SECTION UNDER 2ND LIEUT WALKER, WILL BE THE LOADING PARTY. "B" SECTION UNDER LIEUT GEARD THE UNLOADING PARTY. THE LATTER PARTY WILL BE MARCHED TO THE WAGGON LINES WITH "A" ECHELON.

[signature] Capt.

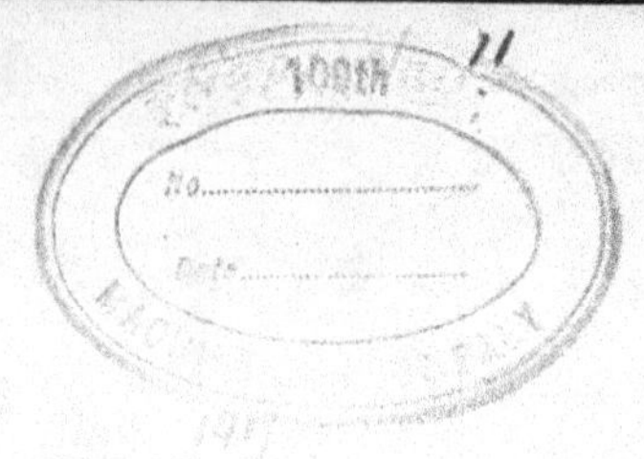

SECRET.

109th Mac[illegible] Gun Coy.

OPERATION ORDERS No [illegible]

[illegible] No M.G 1725 [illegible] 1917

1\. The 109th Machine Gun Coy will be relieved by [illegible] Gun Coy on the 3.5.17. All reliefs [illegible] from the [illegible] [illegible] at 10.0 am at 5 mins interval between detachments.

2\. One section of the 108th Coy will relieve Guns [illegible] 9. 11 12 14, all movement via Queens Gate starting at [illegible] of Queens Gate at [illegible]. On relief from the trenches "B" Section will relieve the Section of the 108th Coy in Kemmel Defences. O.C "B" [illegible] will report to O.C Kemmel Defences on completion of relief.

3\. The Se[illegible] of the 108 M.G Coy from Kemmel Defences will relieve Guns No's 10 11, 12, 13. On completion of relief "C" Section [illegible] No 10 Gun Detachment under Lieut Geard will move to Rest Billets making use of the limbered waggon of the 108th M.G Coy. No's. 11. 12. 13 Guns will be relieved via Virgellia. No. 10 Gun via Queens Gate.

4\. The reliefs of the detachments for Guns No's 6. 7 8. will move via Queens Gate, these will move to Lindenhoek Cross Rds. and meet the No. 10 Gun detachment. These four detachments will move to Rest Billets under Lieut [illegible], making use of the limbered waggon of the 108th M.G Coy.

5\. No's 1 to 5 Gun Detachments' Reliefs will be via Kingsway. There will [illegible] a limbered waggon [illegible] 108th M.G Coy waiting at the head of [illegible] way for these five detachments, who will move to Rest Billets under 2nd Lieut. Goldman.

6\. (a) The Belt S.A.A from the Forts will be collected at Fort Victoria.
(b) " " " Guns in Yonge St and Reserve Trench will be collected on Suicide Road.
(c) The Belted S.A.A from Guns No's [illegible] & 10. will be collected at Bully Beef Fm.
(d) Two sentries for each of A & B, will remain at the Dumps for the limbers which will arrive in the evening.

7\. Headquarters will close at Bully Beef Fm at 11 0 pm, and will open in [illegible] [illegible] pm 3.5.17.

[signature] Capt
Commanding
109th Machine Gun Coy

SECRET

Copy No. 12.

No. 109
MACHINE GUN
COMPANY.
No. MG. 1725
Date 3-5-17

RE NUMBERING OF EMPLACEMENTS [illegible] BY THE

109TH MACHINE GUN COMPANY

1. THE MACHINE GUNS OF 109 BRIGADE (FRONT) WILL BE RE NUMBERED FROM RIGHT TO LEFT.

THE FOLLOWING ARE THE NUMBERS ALLOTTED TO THE EMPLACEMENTS:-

No. 1.	AT	N 35.c [illegible]	No. 9	AT	[illegible] FARM
" 2.	"	N 35.c [illegible]	" 10	"	S.P. 10.
" 3.	"	N 34.[illegible]	" 11.	"	RESERVE TRENCH
" 4.	"	N 35.a. 26. 13	" 12	"	YONGE ST SOUTH
" 5.	"	N 34.[illegible]	" 13	"	YONGE ST NORTH
" 6.	"	N 35.a. 98. 89	" 14	"	FORT REGINA
" 7.	"	S.P. 8	" 15	"	" "
" 8.	"	S.P. 9	" 16	"	FORT VICTORIA

THE ABOVE POSITIONS WILL ALWAYS BE REFERRED TO BY THEIR NUMBERS ONLY

2. THE FOLLOWING ARE THE NUMBERS ALLOTTED TO THE INDIRECT FIRE EMPLACEMENTS

No. 1	AT	N [illegible]	No. 5	AT	N 29 a. 53. 62
" 2	"	N 35 a. [illegible]	" 6.	"	N 29 a. 63. 78
" 3	"	N 34 [illegible]	" 7	"	FORT REGINA
" 4	"	N 29. a. [illegible] 05	" 8	"	FORT REGINA

3. THE ATTACHED PROFORMA COMPLETED WILL BE FORWARDED DAILY TO O.C. SUB SECTORS FOR INFORMATION AND REMARKS, AND WILL BE RETURNED BY BEARER TO COMPANY HD. QRS. AT SPY FARM.

[illegible] CAPT:
COMMANDING
109TH MACHINE GUN COY.

Vol 15

W A R   D I A R Y   FOR   THE   MONTH   OF   J U N E, 1917.

o-o-o-o-o-o-o-o-o-o-o-o-o-o-o-o-o-o-o-o-o-o-o-o

109TH   M A C H I N E   G U N   C O M P A N Y.

o-o-o-o-o-o-o-o-o-o-o-o-o-o-o-o-o-o-o

Instructions regarding War Diaries and Intelligence Summaries are contained in F. S. Regs., Part II. and the Staff Manual respectively. Title pages will be prepared in manuscript.

WAR DIARY
or
INTELLIGENCE SUMMARY.
(Erase heading not required.)

JUNE

Army Form C. 2118.

Place	Date	Hour	Summary of Events and Information	Remarks and references to Appendices
	JUNE			
WAKEFIELD HUTS Nr LOCRE BELGIUM	1st		During the day the following moves were carried out: A subsection of B section and the same from D section went up to the line to take part in the five days bombardment preliminary to the offensive. Subsections of A D B sections with most of the transport went to WESTOUTRE: 'C' section remains at WAKEFIELD HUTS with headquarters. A subsection of A section also at HAGEDORNE on Anti Aircraft duty	HC
" "	2nd		Nothing of importance happened today. our 6 guns in the line (VICKERS ROW) fired under the orders of the Divisional M.G.O. C section ~~at~~ WAKEFIELD CAMP received instruction from the C.O. on their duties in the coming advance	
" "	3rd		A general relief was carried out today between sections; see Company Operation Orders in the Appendix of this date. The six guns in VICKERS ROW are manned by the 4 gun teams of 'C' section	

2353 Wt. W2544/1454 700,000 5/15 D. D. & L. A.D.S.S./Forms/C. 2118.

Instructions regarding War Diaries and Intelligence Summaries are contained in F. S. Regs., Part II. and the Staff Manual respectively. Title pages will be prepared in manuscript.

WAR DIARY
or
~~INTELLIGENCE SUMMARY.~~
(Erase heading not required.)

Army Form C. 2118.

JUNE

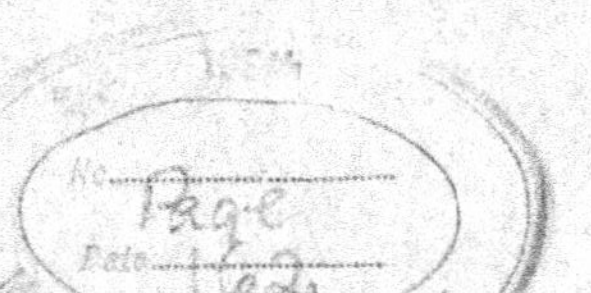

Place	Date	Hour	Summary of Events and Information	Remarks and references to Appendices
WAKEFIELD CAMP	4		The eight guns in the line fired during artillery bombardments under the direct orders of the Divisional Machine Gun Officer.	
Nr LOCRE BELGIUM			At about 5 P.M. the two gun teams of D section at the Anti Aircraft position at HAGEDORNE were relieved by the 218th Machine Gun Company.	
"	5th		During the morning C section in the line were relieved by B section, C section returning to WAKEFIELD CAMP. The following preparations were made for the offensive. All cap badges and numerals were withdrawn to the QM Stores, all ~~[illegible]~~ packs were collected. The surplus stores and various things such as [illegible] biscuits etc and some ammunition were sent up the line the former commodities to be stored at Company rallying post. Five reinforcements arrived during the morning.	

2353 Wt. W2544/1454 700,000 5/15 D. D. & L. A.D.S.S./Forms/C. 2118.

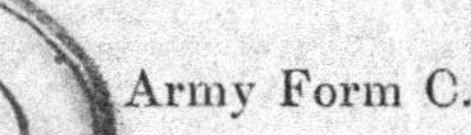

Army Form C. 2118.

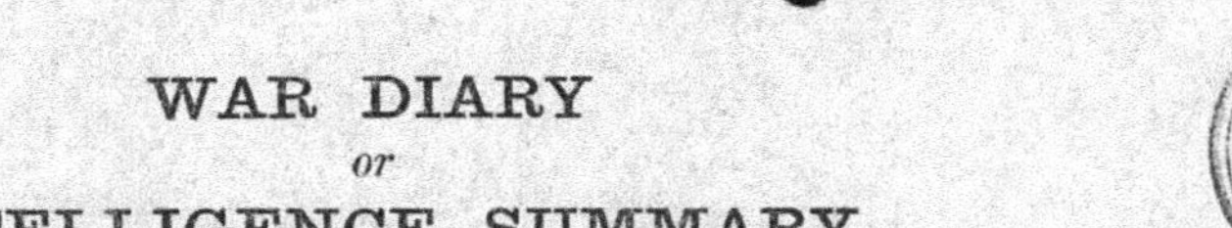

Instructions regarding War Diaries and Intelligence Summaries are contained in F. S. Regs., Part II. and the Staff Manual respectively. Title pages will be prepared in manuscript.

WAR DIARY
or
~~INTELLIGENCE SUMMARY.~~

(Erase heading not required.)

JUNE

Place	Date	Hour	Summary of Events and Information	Remarks and references to Appendices
WAKEFIELD CAMP	6th		Today is "Y" day for the offencive:	See
NR LOCRE		AM 8.45	A section reaches WAKEFIELD CAMP FROM WESTOUTRE:	
BELGIUM		10AM	Inspection of kit of A section; ½ C and D sections Vide (Operation orders attached)	
		3PM	Service & holy Communion	
		4PM	Dinners	
		4.30	PM D section moves off with headquarters and two limbers	
		6.PM	½ C & A " " with two limbers	
			The following officers are remaining with the 25% in WAKEFIELD CAMP	
			Lt Cayley (2nd in C) Lt Wilgar (transport duties) 2/Lt Stevens in	
			Charge of the mules who are fetching up SAA on Z day.	

2353 Wt. W2544/1454 700,000 5/15 D. D. & L. A.D.S.S./Forms/C. 2118.

Instructions regarding War Diaries and Intelligence Summaries are contained in F. S. Regs., Part II. and the Staff Manual respectively. Title pages will be prepared in manuscript.

WAR DIARY
or
~~INTELLIGENCE SUMMARY.~~
(Erase heading not required.)

Army Form C. 2118.

JUNE

Place	Date	Hour	Summary of Events and Information	Remarks and references to Appendices
WAKEFIELD HUTS N^R LOCRE BELGIUM	9th		At 10 AM The company left their bivouacs near "FORT REGINA" and marched back to WAKEFIELD HUTS WITH the exception of B section who followed later. The company arrived at 1 PM. The transport and "B" section arrived at 2.30 PM. As every one was very tired and exhausted no further parades were held to day.	OCC
	10th		At 10.30 the Company fell in for Church parade, 16 of the Transport men were on parade; The Company were marched on parade by Captain Mulholland at 1PM forty men of the company went to Baths at DRANOUTRE 3PM all guns were cleaned and stores packed away Ammunition overhauled.	
	11th		The day was spent overhauling kit and making list of all deficiencies The loss in materiel was found to be exceedingly small one tripod was lost and one gun was so injured by shell fire that another was issued in lieu	

2353 Wt. W2544/1454 700,000 5/15 D. D. & L. A.D.S.S./Forms/C. 2118.

Instructions regarding War Diaries and Intelligence Summaries are contained in F. S. Regs., Part II. and the Staff Manual respectively. Title pages will be prepared in manuscript.

Army Form C. 2118.

WAR DIARY
or
~~INTELLIGENCE~~ SUMMARY.
(Erase heading not required.)

JUNE

Place	Date	Hour	Summary of Events and Information	Remarks and references to Appendices
"RUDDIGORE LINES" Nr LOCRE BELGIUM	12th	9.45	To make room in WAKEFIELD CAMP for a battalion the company had orders to shift to RUDDIGORE LINES	
			The company with all transport ~~arrives~~ left W. Camp at 9.45 reached RUDDIGORE lines at 10.15. ½ B section ½ A Section remained for loading parties. All Gun limbers were parked but the SAA limbers made four journeys back to Camp for Stores etc. Dinners were at 1.30 PM.	
		6pm 6P	At 6 pm orders were received that the Brigade would be moving west tomorrow. So Limbers were packed again.	
NR WESTOUTRE	13		~~All~~ Orders were received to march to new Camp near WESTOUTRE on the slopes of Montnoir.	
			The company started at 2.30 and arrived at the new Camp at 4PM. Waggons were parked in the same field as the unit the animals were accomodated in lines which were shared with the 14th R.I.R. (1st YCV)	
	14		The day was spent getting our Camp "shipshape". Cleaning limbers. C Section who are doing working parties at FORT VICTORIA are absent. Also 8 men of B section were sent of to WHITE CHATEAU	

2353 Wt. W2544/1454 700,000 5/15 D. D. & L. A.D.S.S./Forms/C. 2118.

Instructions regarding War Diaries and Intelligence Summaries are contained in F. S. Regs., Part II. and the Staff Manual respectively. Title pages will be prepared in manuscript.

WAR DIARY
or
INTELLIGENCE SUMMARY.
(Erase heading not required.)

Army Form C. 2118.

JUNE

Place	Date	Hour	Summary of Events and Information	Remarks and references to Appendices
Nr. WESTOUTRE	15th		The company paraded 9 AM for elementary training fourhours work was put in the morning. it was too hot to work during the afternoon	
"	16th		Company training was carried out as usual during the morning D section relieves B section in the working party at FORT VICTORIA	
"	17th		The whole of the 2½ sections in Camp were away on a working party till 2 PM under Lt Bowerbank. 2/Lt Braxton reports for duty from the base.	
DONCASTER HUTS Nr. LOCRE	18th		At 2 PM the coy minus D section leaves the Camp and marches with all the transport to new accomodation at DONCASTER HUTS near LOCRE. Arriving 7 PM.	
	19th		The company was paid out at 9. AM: "D" section arrived from working parties at LITTLE KEMMEL at 9.30 AM: The CO and section officers to reconnoitre the line rode up to OSTERVERNE.	

Instructions regarding War Diaries and Intelligence Summaries are contained in F. S. Regs., Part II. and the Staff Manual respectively. Title pages will be prepared in manuscript.

WAR DIARY
or
INTELLIGENCE SUMMARY.
(Erase heading not required.)

JUNE

No. 109 MACHINE GUN COMPANY
No. 164

Army Form C. 2118.

Place	Date	Hour	Summary of Events and Information	Remarks and references to Appendices
WYCHAETE 28 SW 5A.				See
OYD 41	20		At 230 PM The company left NEWMARKET HUTS preceded by the transport, the water cart had an accident and broke in two.	
GRANDBOIS			The company arrived near GRANDBOIS at 10.30 they were met by guides of the 57 + 58 Companys ABC sections took over positions about 600 yards from the front line and D Section on AA work in reserve some 800 yards back Headquarters being in GRAND BOIS. The relief was complete by 2AM the 21st.	
	21		At 4 AM The OC A Section reported that he had been shelled all night and has altered his position slightly. The situation at present is very difficult to Cater with as the German is occupying no visible lines but holding an outpost in shell holes: Concealment is very difficult; any movement over the Ridge in daylight brings on violent shelling; the enemy keeps up a lot of balloons and movement even behind the ridge is difficult & precarious. Water is taken up at night with the rations at the rate of 14* tins of water a day	*28 gallons
	22nd		During the preceding night work was done on all the positions, work being impossible by day. During the afternoon headquarters moved to O13 A 35 90. the late Bde HdQrs	

2353 Wt. W2544/1454 700,000 5/15 D. D. & L. A.D.S.S./Forms/C. 2118.

Instructions regarding War Diaries and Intelligence Summaries are contained in F. S. Regs., Part II. and the Staff Manual respectively. Title pages will be prepared in manuscript.

WAR DIARY
or
INTELLIGENCE SUMMARY.
(Erase heading not required.)

Army Form C. 2118.

JUNE

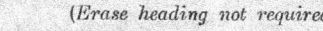

Place	Date	Hour	Summary of Events and Information	Remarks and references to Appendices
GRANDBOIS 013A3590	23rd		German artillery very active all day heavy shells fell round most of the positions but caused no casualties no firing was done owing to the uncertainty of the enemies position.	
	24th		It was decided by the OC company and DMGO Major Miller DSO to place two guns to the left of OOSTAVERNE village this was done by putting two of "D" section guns into those positions. Lt Lea OC D section evacuated with bad nerves	
	25th		Enemy shelled company headquarters for a bit only one casualty in the Company: one of "B" section tripods hit and put out of action.	
			1500 rounds expended on GREEN WOOD suspected of holding enemy.	
			Enemy inspite of captured documents shewing scarcity of Ammunition continues to throw heavy shells recklessly away most of the day & night	
	26th		Enemy artillery very active all day paying most of his attention to roads and places where he can see people moving about with his balloons four of five of which are up opposite this sector.	
			enemies aeroplanes also are very active compared with this time a month ago, they seem to do whatever they want. on the 24th they brought down 3 balloons on this sector	

2353 Wt. W2544/1454 700,000 5/15 D. D. & L. A.D.S.S./Forms/C. 2118.

MAP REF
REF WYTCHAETE 28 SW 2

Instructions regarding War Diaries and Intelligence Summaries are contained in F. S. Regs., Part II. and the Staff Manual respectively. Title pages will be prepared in manuscript.

JUNE

WAR DIARY
or
INTELLIGENCE SUMMARY.
(Erase heading not required.)

Army Form C. 2118.

Place	Date	Hour	Summary of Events and Information	Remarks and references to Appendices
O13B 15 90	27th		Shelling as usual was bad during the days night: work was done during the night only no movement being possible by day. Hot soup and cocoa is sent up from the horselines with rations at night; captured German food containers being used for this purpose.	DC
	28th		At 10.30 PM the 63rd Company in the 57th Division came into the line to release 109 Company as per attached operation orders.	
KLONDYKE Fm	29th		The Company spent the night of the 28/29 at the horselines. At 11.30 AM The company marched to their new billets at KLONDYKE Fm. The afternoon was spent cleaning gun equipment which was in very dirty condition.	DC
	30th		At to 8.25 AM the company left KLONDYKE Fm at 9 AM LOCRE was passed 11.20 BAILLEUL STRAZEELE was reached at 2.15 PM. The farm were the company was billeted was reached at 2.35 No men fell out the march was about 18 Kilometres	

2353 Wt. W2544/1454 700,000 5/15 D. D. & L. A.D.S.S./Forms/C. 2118.

[illegible] the Action of the Machine Guns of the 109th Machine Gun Company [illegible]

From 3.10 am 7th [illegible] to midnight [illegible] June 1917.

The distribution of the guns [illegible] Company [illegible] as follows:-

"C" Section. 4 guns were attached to the 11th (S) Bn [illegible] Fus. and assembled in the "Sutton" trench west [illegible] at about 11 pm on "Y" night.

"A" Section. [illegible] guns were [illegible]

[illegible] six guns advanced first in rear of the [illegible] infantry, reached the enemy front line without [illegible] casualty though not without [illegible]

[illegible] No man's land [illegible] resulted in [illegible]

The four guns advanced on the left and took up their positions [illegible]

S.P. [illegible]

[illegible] the field of fire [illegible] in all directions and [illegible] the construction of [illegible]

[illegible]

S.P. [illegible] the western and southern edges of the Bois de Wytschaete.

[illegible]

(No) Two guns under 2nd Lieut Carew attached to the [illegible] Fus. [illegible] into action on [illegible] the advance of the first line.

These two guns reached [illegible] Point very shortly after the [illegible] of the infantry and got into position on the left flank [illegible]

Later on the enemy starting to shell [illegible] Point [illegible] Lieut Carew had to withdraw his guns still further [illegible] a better position [illegible] Lieut Carew [illegible] his right [illegible] moving his guns and had to return to the Dressing Station [illegible]

[illegible]

[illegible]

The exact amount of ammunition expended during this time is not known but a rough and low estimate is about [illegible] rounds.

The [illegible] were a great saving of time, as [illegible] not [illegible] CHECK THE [illegible] so frequently as would have been necessary had they not been [illegible].

Only one [illegible] was [illegible] it is inconceivable [illegible] was fairly heavy in the vicinity.

At about zero [illegible] the [illegible] guns of "A" Section under 2/Lieut. D. Walker moved out of Vickers Farm and [illegible] the 10th (S) Bn R. Innis: Fus:

It was intended that this officer should report his readiness to move off to the Officer Commanding the 10th R. Innis: Fus: before crossing "No Man's Land" but this was found to be impossible owing to the distance from Vickers Farm to the Hd. Qrs of the Battalion and also to the short time left between the time of leaving [illegible] and the time the leading companies of the battalions were to move off to the Blue Line.

2/Lieut Walker reached the Black Line at about Z + 5-30 and placed his guns in Torreken Farm. He however moved these away as there were four Lewis and [illegible] Vickers Guns (the latter of the 16th Division) in the vicinity of this farm.

The two guns of "A" Section were eventually placed at O. 20. c. 10. 2. and O. 26. a. [illegible].

The 4 guns of "D" Section [illegible] out of Vickers Farm at about Z + 3 [illegible] and arrived in the vicinity of Stanyzer Cabt at about Z + 6.15. – Two guns being held in reserve at O. 30. b. 4. 6. and two guns in action at O. 20. c. 5. 0. and O. 20. c. 6. 6.

Company Hd. Qrs. with a reserve of one section of guns were established at Scott Farm at Z + 5. at about Z + 5. 20 and very shortly afterwards a reserve of 96 belt boxes and 32 gallons of drinking water were BROUGHT UP on pack mules by 2/Lieut [illegible] to Scott Farm.

The fact that my headquarters were established at Scott Farm, was a great piece of luck as a cable head was in position here by Z + 9, and I was in [illegible] telephone communication with Brigade Hd. Qrs in [illegible] Dugouts.

One or two detachments required some S.A.A. and water after [illegible] and these were despatched without any trouble.

<u>Observations</u>

1\. The [illegible] were not as close [illegible] as they could have been. It would have been better to have one [illegible] only. There were so many [illegible] flags in use that it was confusing.

[illegible] (Contd)

The units should now have their own guns such as the [illegible] [illegible]. It was impossible for the gunners to locate [illegible] of enemy [illegible].

RUMOUR

3 The construction of [illegible] and light railways might have been carried [illegible] the case [illegible] very late in arriving [illegible] instructions owing to the lack of [illegible] and direction [illegible].

4 The consolidation of the Black Line could have been carried out with even less casualties than those sustained.

I would suggest that the outpost line should have moved out of the Black Line, almost as soon as this line was [illegible] about 600 to 800 yds. in front, with [illegible] Lewis and Vickers Guns.

A smoke cloud should also have been put up about 300 yards in front of the Black Line.

All the work of consolidation, the movement of [illegible], the carrying of material and [illegible], and the work of the [illegible] etc. gave the enemy to understand at once that this was to be a strong line of defence consequently he did not use his shrapnel sparingly.

In regard [illegible] Y [illegible] were rarely used at all. [illegible] Posts full is too heavy a [illegible] to carry [illegible] boxes, one in each hand.

The loss in material of the Company was very light. One machine gun was damaged by a shrapnel bullet passing through the [illegible] casing.

Two tripods were lost but eventually one was found in "No Man's Land".

Cleaning [illegible] many were lost or broken.

There should be a leather cap to fit tight over the muzzle attachment to keep out the dust etc. I am having [illegible] [illegible].

[illegible] Capt

109th COMMANDING
MACHINE GUN COY.

No. 8.

[illegible] MACHINE GUN COY

OPERATION ORDERS FOR RELEIF OF 8 GUNS UNDER LIEUT LEA

3RD JUNE 1917.

1. LIEUT ROOT WITH "C" SECTION WILL RELEIVE LIEUT LEA WITH 6 GUNS ON THE 3RD JUNE
THE TWO GUNS NOT OF "C" SECTION WILL BE SUPPLIED BY 2ND LIEUT GREW.

THE O.C. 8 GUNS IN VICKERS ROW COMES DIRECTLY UNDER THE D.M.G.O. WHOSE HD. QRS ARE IN M.G. ALLEY NEAR 105TH BRIGADE HD QRS. ON KEMMEL HILL.

THE TWO GUNS OF "B" SECTION WILL REMAIN UNDER LIEUT ROOT UNTIL RELEIVED BY 2 GUNS OF "A" SECTION FROM HAEGEDOORNE

THE MEN OF "A" SECTION WHO BRING UP THESE TWO LATTER GUNS WILL RETURN TO WAKEFIELD CAMP WITH THE TWO GUNS OF "B" SECTION.

<u>MOVEMENT OF GUNS</u>

ON THE FOUR GUNS OF "D" SECTION BEING RELEIVED BY 4 GUNS OF "C" SECTION, TWO OF THE FORMER WILL PROCEED STRAIGHT TO HAEGEDOORNE AND RELEIVE TWO GUNS OF "A" SECTION IN A.A.

THEN THE TWO A.A GUNS WILL PROCEED STRAIGHT TO VICKERS ROW AND RELEIVE THE REMAINING TWO GUNS OF "B" SECTION.

THE TWO REMAINING GUNS OF "D" SECTION WILL REPORT AT WAKEFIELD CAMP, PRIOR TO PROCEEDING TO WESTOUTRE.

THE FINAL DISPOSITION OF THE GUNS ON THE 3RD JUNE WILL BE:-

4 GUNS OF "A" SECTION — VICKERS ROW
4 GUNS OF "C" " — " "
4 GUNS OF "B" " — WAKEFIELD CAMP.
2 GUNS OF "D" " — HAEGEDOORNE A.A.
2 GUNS OF "D" " — WESTOUTRE CAMP.

THE FINAL DISPOSITION OF THE PERSONELL OF SECTIONS WILL BE:-

"A" SECTION — WESTOUTRE CAMP
"B" " — WAKEFIELD "
"C" " — VICKERS ROW
½ "D" " — HAEGEDOORNE A.A.
½ "D" " — WESTOUTRE CAMP

OPERATION ORDERS (CONT'D)

(a) "C" SECTION WILL PARADE AT 7-30 AM. 3RD JUNE TO HAND IN TO
THE Q.M. STORES ALL BLANKETS AND PACKS AND WATERPROOF SHEETS.

(b) PARADE READY TO MARCH OFF AT 9-0 AM.

(C) FIVE PACK MULES WILL BE REQUIRED TO CARRY:-
6 MACHINE GUNS
6 SPARE PARTS
1 TRIPOD
RATION FOR "C" SECTION
2 OFFICERS KITS.

ALL MULES MUST CARRY A FEED AS THEY WILL BE REQUIRED ALL DAY.
ALSO OFFICERS CHARGERS.

(D) "C" SECTION WILL CARRY THE UNEXPENDED PORTION OF RATIONS OF 3RD JUNE
WITH THEM. THE SAME THING APPLIES TO ALL PERSONELL ON THE MOVE.

(E) THE PERSONELL OF "B" SECTION AT WESTOUTRE WILL ARRIVE IN WAKEFIELD CAMP
BEFORE 12 PM TOMORROW. 3RD JUNE.

(F) ONE LIMBER WILL BE DETAILED TO CALL AT HAEGEDOORNE FOR THE PACKS
AND OFFICERS KIT OF "A" SECTION. THIS LIMBER WILL BE PROVIDED FROM
HEADQUARTERS TRANSPORT.

(G) THE TWO MULES WILL PROCEED TO HAEGEDOORNE WITH LIEUT LEA'S KIT
AND TWO GUNS.

ONE OF THESE MULES WILL RETURN TO THE LINE WITH A SMALL PARTY OF
"A" SECTION AND 2. M. GUNS OF "A" SECTION. THIS MULE WILL WAIT AT
KINDENHOEK CROSS ROADS FOR THE RETURN OF THIS PARTY OF "A" SECTION
BRINGING OUT THE TWO REMAINING GUNS OF "B" SECTION TO WAKEFIELD CAMP.

THE SMALL PARTY OF "A" SECTION WILL PROCEED TO WESTOUTRE THE
FOLLOWING DAY. 4TH. JUNE

[illegible] Mulholland Capt.
O.C. 109TH MACHINE GUN COY.

SECRET

COPY Nº 9

COMPANY OPERATION ORDERS
109TH MACHINE GUN COY.
4TH JUNE 1916

1 "B" SECTION WILL RELIEVE "C" SECTION ON THE 5TH - 6 - 17. MARCHING FROM CAMP AT 9 AM. "C" SECTION WILL RETURN TO WAKEFIELD CAMP.

2 THE DETACHMENT OF "D" SECTION AT THE BRIGADE CAMP AT WESTOUTRE WILL MARCH OFF FROM THAT CAMP IN TIME TO REPORT ARRIVAL AT WAKEFIELD CAMP AT 8-30 AM. THE GUNS MUST BE CLEAN BY THIS TIME AS THEY ARE REQUIRED FOR DUTY IN THE TRENCHES.

3 O.C. "C" SECTION WILL ASCERTAIN IF THE GUNS BEARING THE FOLLOWING NUMBERS ARE UNDER HIS COMMAND IN VICKERS ROW. 4456, 4468. IF THIS IS THE CASE HE MUST MAKE SURE THAT THEY ARE WITHDRAWN FROM THE LINE BY HIS SECTION.

4 FINAL DISPOSITION OF MACHINE GUNS WILL BE:-

VICKERS ROW	"B" SECTION	4. GUNS
	"A" "	2 GUNS (NOT OF THE ABOVE NUMBERS)
	"D" "	2 GUNS
WAKEFIELD CAMP	"C" "	4 GUNS
	"D" "	2 GUNS
	"A" "	2 GUNS.

5 RATIONS FOR THE 6TH INST.; WILL BE CARRIED BY "B" SECTION.

6 EQUIPMENT OF "B" SECTION WILL BE FULL FIGHTING ORDER. IRON RATIONS WILL BE CARRIED.

7 THE FOLLOWING ARTICLES WILL BE HANDED INTO STORES BY 7-30 AM TO-MORROW BY "B" SECTION. ALL BLANKETS IN BUNDLES OF TEN. ALL PACKS. EACH MAN WILL TIE HIS GREATCOAT UP IN HIS WATERPROOF SHEET IN A NEAT SMALL BUNDLE, AND WILL MARK HIS NAME ON OUTSIDE OF THE SHEET.

8 THE BLANKETS OF "A" SECTION AT WESTOUTRE WILL FORWARDED TO HD. QRS IN BUNDLES OF 10; BY 10-AM 5TH INST.;.
THE BLANKETS OF "D" SECTION WILL BE HANDED TO STORE PUNCTUALLY AT 11-30 AM 5TH INST. THE UNEXPENDED PORTION OF THE RATIONS OF "D" SECTION DETACHMENT MUST BE BROUGHT WITH THE DETACHMENT TO HD. QRS.

9 TRANSPORT 9 PACK MULES WILL BE REQUIRED AT HD. QRS 8. AM. LIEUT. WILSAR WILL FORWARD 6 PACK MULES FROM HIS DETACHMENT.

[illegible signature] Capt.
O.C. 109TH MACHINE GUN COY

W. D

SECRET COMPANY OPERATION ORDERS (No 11) COPY No. 15.

109 MACHINE GUN COY.

5th JUNE 1917.

1. 'A' SECTION AND TRANSPORT UNDER LIEUT WILCOX WILL MOVE FROM THE BRIGADE CAMP IN TIME TO REPORT ARRIVAL AT WAKEFIELD CAMP AT 9.30 AM 6th INST.

2. EXTRACT FROM 109th BRIGADE. S.C. 24/469.
THE BIVOUACS AND TARPAULINS WILL BE STRUCK AND HANDED IN TO THE BDE Q.M.S. BEFORE DEPARTURE ON THE 6th INST. IT MUST BE UNDERSTOOD THAT THE BIVOUACS ISSUED BY THE BRIGADE AT WESTOUTRE ARE THOSE REFERRED TO. THE REMAINDER WILL ACCOMPANY THE DETACHMENT TO WAKEFIELD CAMP.

3. ON ARRIVAL IN WAKEFIELD CAMP. "A" SECTION WILL REST TILL 9.45 AM AT WHICH TIME IT WILL FALL IN ON THE PARADE GROUND WITH FULL COMPLEMENT OF EQUIPMENT LESS GUNS, SPARE PARTS AND TRIPODS. O.C. "A" SECTION WILL INSPECT THE FOLLOWING ARTICLES IN THE ORDER ENUMERATED BELOW:-

(1) GAS APPLIANCES
(2) REVOLVER AMMUNITION
(3) FIELD DRESSINGS AND IODINE AMPOULES
(4) IDENTITY DISCS.
(5) IRON RATIONS.

4. C.S.M. [illegible] WILL [illegible] DETAIL THE ARTICLES AND EQUIPMENT REQUIRED BY THE TEAMS FOR FIGHTING ORDER.

5. C+D SECTIONS WILL PLACE ALL THEIR GUN EQUIPMENT, BELTED S.A.A. AND YUKON PACKS THAT ARE REQUIRED ON ZERO DAY ON THE PARADE GROUND READY FOR INSPECTION BY 10-30 AM.

6. AT A TIME TO BE NOTIFIED LATER ALL N.C.O.s AND MEN WHO HAVE NOT ALREADY DONE SO WILL COMPLY WITH COMPANY OPERATIONS ORDERS OF THE 4th INST: PARA. 7. IN ADDITION TO THIS ALL RANKS WILL PACK ANY ARTICLES OF PERSONAL OR PRIVATE VALUE IN A SANDBAG WITH A LIST OF CONTENTS INSIDE THE SANDBAG. THE OUTSIDE OF THE SANDBAG WILL BE MARKED WITH THE OWNERS NAME IN INDELIBLE PENCIL.

7. ALL OFFICERS KIT WILL BE PACKED BY 2.30 PM, AND WILL BE HANDED INTO STORES AT 3. PM.

8. LIEUT CAYLEY WILL SUPERVISE THE WORK DETAILED IN PARA'S 6 AND 7.

9. ALL RANKS MUST BE PREPARED TO MARCH FROM WAKEFIELD CAMP IN FULL FIGHTING ORDER AT 11 PM.

10. DETAILED OPERATION ORDERS FOR THE 6th INST WILL BE ISSUED LATER TO ALL CONCERNED.

[illegible signature] Capt.
O.C.
109th MACHINE GUN COY

Vol 16

109TH MACHINE GUN COMPANY.

WAR DAIRY

for

MONTH of JULY, 1917.

Instructions regarding War Diaries and Intelligence Summaries are contained in F. S. Regs., Part II. and the Staff Manual respectively. Title pages will be prepared in manuscript.

WAR DIARY
or
INTELLIGENCE SUMMARY.
(Erase heading not required.)

Army Form C. 2118.

JULY 1

Place	Date	Hour	Summary of Events and Information	Remarks and references to Appendices
STRAZEELE	1st	1917	The company fell in at 8.50 AM and moved off from [illegible] farm with full transport at 8.55. rain fell the whole way the company passed through LOCRE BAILLEUL near Meteren and arrived at STRAZEELE at 1.30 dinners were at 2.50. Guns were cleaned before tea.	
	2nd		Guns kit and limbers were thoroughly cleaned, a list of clothing deficiencies were taken, deficiencies were chiefly entrenching tools, [illegible] tins and other pieces of [illegible] equipment.	
	3rd		Physical drill at 9 AM: The rest of the morning cleaning limbers	
	4th		At 12.30 General Ricardo inspected the company drawn up in inspection order with transport in a farm near the billeting farm. The appearance of the company was very good. The only fault being the packs which might have been better. The turnout of the transport was especially marked and commended by the General. The afternoon was spent preparing for the morrows move.	

2353 Wt. W2544/1454 700,000 5/15 D. D. & L. A.D.S.S./Forms/C. 2118.

Instructions regarding War Diaries and Intelligence Summaries are contained in F. S. Regs., Part II. and the Staff Manual respectively. Title pages will be prepared in manuscript.

WAR DIARY
or
INTELLIGENCE SUMMARY.

(Erase heading not required.)

Army Form C. 2118.

Place	Date	Hour	Summary of Events and Information	Remarks and references to Appendices
HON[D]EGHEM	5th		The company left STRAZEELE at 7.30 AM and reached HONDEGHEM at 10.15 AM The march was only about 12 Kilometers. The transport was brigaded and arrived shortly afterwards The whole company and transport were living in one big estaminet. The weather was good for marching	
ARQUES.	6th		The company left HONDEGHEM at 6.30 Breakfasts were issued before leaving: The march was about 15 Kilometers. The march was a brigade one; the whole brigade halted at 9.0 [illegible] for one hour. Battalion had breakfast from their cookers. Transport went ahead after the ½ an hours halt. Arques was reached at 11.15 AM. Towards the end it was very hot for marching: At 2.0 the company had bathing in the lake at Arques. Three men were admitted to Ambulance from bad feet etc	

2353 Wt. W2544/1454 700,000 5/15 D. D. & L. A.D.S.S./Forms/C. 2118.

Instructions regarding War Diaries and Intelligence Summaries are contained in F. S. Regs., Part II. and the Staff Manual respectively. Title pages will be prepared in manuscript.

WAR DIARY
or
INTELLIGENCE SUMMARY.

(*Erase heading not required.*)

Army Form C. 2118.

Place	Date	Hour	Summary of Events and Information	Remarks and references to Appendices
PETIT QUERCAMP				
7th June		AM 2.40	At 1.30 AM Reveille was sounded at 2AM the company were issued with hot coffee at 2.45 sections fell in and the company moved off being joined by the transport in Arques. The route was leaving out 1st Army at 8 AM the brigade halted and the mules were watered & fed, the men got their breakfast 10 kilometers had been covered. The going was good at 8.30 The march proceeded at 9.15 the company reached QUERCAMP where the were billeted last March April. PETIT Quercamp was reached at ~~9.30~~ 10.10 AM where the company were billeted in several farms. The transport being ~~carried~~ parked on the green.	
8th			Today being sunday no training was carried out. Guns and equipment were unloaded & cleaned, and then packed again in the limbers. There were no church parades	
9th			Training was carried out as per attached training programme. the afternoon being given over to recreation & football.	

2353 Wt. W2544/1454 700,000 5/15 D. D. & L. A.D.S.S./Forms/C. 2118.

Instructions regarding War Diaries and Intelligence Summaries are contained in F. S. Regs., Part II. and the Staff Manual respectively. Title pages will be prepared in manuscript.

WAR DIARY
or
INTELLIGENCE SUMMARY.
(Erase heading not required.)

Army Form C. 2118.

Place	Date	Hour	Summary of Events and Information	Remarks and references to Appendices
Petit Quercamp	10th		Training carried out as per programme: a very fine manœuvres field being quite close to the billets also a drill field. The transport are getting trained for open fighting and practised at putting on packsaddles in a hurry.	
	11th		A section on the range fired about 50 rounds per man at the following ranges: 30 rounds per man at range of about 350 yards at a khaki target 6ft by 4ft on green background: one point for each shot on the target, after that at 25 yards range 10 rounds grouping: points as follows 30 points for a two inch group, 20 for a 4" group, 10 for an 8" group. The average for the section was about 40 points out of 60	
	12th		To day had been allotted to units for sports, so no training was carried out however in the morning each section cleaned its limbers. The sports started at 2.30 Pm on the drill field. There were foot races, mule races, and a competition for action from pack mules won by C Section	

2353 Wt. W2544/1454 700,000 5/15 D. D. & L. A.D.S.S./Forms/C. 2118.

Instructions regarding War Diaries and Intelligence Summaries are contained in F. S. Regs., Part II. and the Staff Manual respectively. Title pages will be prepared in manuscript.

WAR DIARY
or
INTELLIGENCE SUMMARY.
(*Erase heading not required.*)

Army Form C. 2118.

Place	Date	Hour	Summary of Events and Information	Remarks and references to Appendices
PETIT QUERCAMP 15 K from St OMER	13th		During the morning "D" section went on the range and fired the same practices as A section on the previous day. No further training was carried out during the daytime but after tea each section marched off to the battalion it was attached to for night manoeuvres, a brigade outpost scheme with a relief, the last section was back by 2 AM.	
	14		No physical training owing to the rain "C" section who were to have been on the range were unable to fire.	
	15th		Sunday: Massed church parade for the Brigade at ALQUINES: one hundred and fifty three men on parade. Medal ribbon for Military Medal presented to L/Cpl Walker by G.O.C.	
	16th		Training carried out as per training programme. B section fired on the range: remainder combined drill.	
	17th		A Company scheme defence of a locality and attack one half company on each side.	

2353 Wt. W2544/1454 700,000 5/15 D. D. & L. A.D.S.S./Forms/C. 2118.

Instructions regarding War Diaries and Intelligence Summaries are contained in F. S. Regs., Part II. and the Staff Manual respectively. Title pages will be prepared in manuscript.

WAR DIARY
or
INTELLIGENCE SUMMARY.
(Erase heading not required.)

Army Form C. 2118.

Place	Date	Hour	Summary of Events and Information	Remarks and references to Appendices
PETIT QUERCAMP	18th		B section were attached to the 10th Innis Fusiliers but owing to rain they	
BOUVELINGHEM			were returned: The Company did in door training.	
	19th		The whole company were attached to the Brigade for training	
			one section to each battalion, all spare parts were examined	
			and all kit inspected by the C.O. deficiencies were taken and indented	
			for.	
	20th		C section fired on range; remainder were attached to battalion	
	21st		B section did field firing scheme before General Ricardo which	
			was not a great success latter D section did a scheme which	
			was better done.	
	22nd		Divisional Gymkhana held at ~~Ac~~ Acquin the Company had an	
			entrant in the Driving. Lt Welgar rode in the 3 furlongs pony	
			race, also other events.	
	23rd		Brigade field firing scheme; all sixteen guns were employed and	
			fired on average 1000 rounds per gun at range of about 300	
			yards;	

A6945 Wt. W11422/M1160 350,000 12/16 D. D. & L. Forms/C./2118/14.

Instructions regarding War Diaries and Intelligence Summaries are contained in F. S. Regs., Part II. and the Staff Manual respectively. Title pages will be prepared in manuscript.

WAR DIARY
or
INTELLIGENCE SUMMARY.
(*Erase heading not required.*)

Army Form C. 2118.

Place	Date	Hour	Summary of Events and Information	Remarks and references to Appendices
Petit QUERCAMP				
[illegible]VELINGHEM	24th		In preparation for the move all surplus kit was sent off to BAILLEUL the	
			Divisional dump in a motor lorry.	
			The Watercart accompanied by the Watercarts of the rest of the brigade	
			marched off with three days rations to the new billeting area	
			behind POPERINGE; training carried out during the morning	
	25th		The four sections were to have taken part in a brigade field day	
			but owing to rain it was put off and	
			The advance party of Lt Geard and 3 others left by Lorry to	
			reconnoitre the new positions	
	26th		~~Training was carried out, rough ground drill, gas inspections by~~	
			~~[illegible]~~ At 12.15 PM the Company marched to QUERCAMP where	
			the brigade embussed and reached the new billeting area WINNEZELEA	
			at 7. PM with a 4 mile march to billets.	
			The transport left Petit QUERCAMP at 8 AM and reached NORD PENNA	
			at 3 PM having covered about 26 kilometers; and were	
			billeted there for the night	

A6945 Wt. W11422/M1160 350,000 12/16 D. D. & L. Forms/C./2118/14.

Instructions regarding War Diaries and Intelligence Summaries are contained in F. S. Regs., Part II. and the Staff Manual respectively. Title pages will be prepared in manuscript.

WAR DIARY
or
INTELLIGENCE SUMMARY.
(*Erase heading not required.*)

Army Form C. 2118.

Place	Date	Hour	Summary of Events and Information	Remarks and references to Appendices
[illegible]NEZEELE A	July 27th		The transport arrived in billets at 9.45 PM having marched fifteen	
Nr Lawe			Kilometers. In the morning the company were lectured in gas. In	
5 mile from			the afternoon Guns were cleaned and overhauled	
Belgian	28th		Field day. Brigade field day to day in training area Nr WINNEZEELE	
Boundary			AB sections with 3 battalions attacking CD with one battalion	
			defending. AB left Camp at 6.15 mule transport, CD later	
			The attack lasted till 12 PM the country was too thick for m[illegible]	
			work proper, the company had dinners out in a field	
			and marched off at 3 PM reaching Camp 4.15 having covered	
			47 Kilometers.	
	29th		Church parades in the morning interfered with by rain.	
	30th		Training carried out in the morning in the afternoon packed limbers and at	
			8 PM left billets and marched to a Camp 3 Kilo S of POPERINGHE	
Nr POPERINGHE	31st		Camp was reached at 3.15 PM. The 2nd in command went up to look	
			at the [illegible] ground in front of Ypres captured that morning in the advance	
			The Company overhauled ammunition etc	

A6945 Wt. W11422/M1160 350,000 12/16 D. D. & L. Forms/C./2118/14.

109th Machine Gun Coy

Programme of Training for Week Commencing Monday 9th July 1917

Date	Time	Subject	Remarks
Monday 9th	7.30 to 8.15 am	Physical Training	Whole Co.
	8.30 to 9.30 am	A Section – Paras. 8 to 15. I.M.G.T. B C + D Sections. Allocation of Duties + Characteristics	
	9.30 to 10.30 am	A Section – Allocation of Duties + Characteristics. B. Sectn Paras 8 to 15 I.M.G.T. (C + D) Squad + Saluting Drill.	
	10.30 to 11.30 am	(A + B) Squad and Saluting Drill. (C) P 8 to 15 I.M.G.T. (D) Lecture on Maps + Compass with Demonstrations.	
	11.30 to 12.30 pm	(A. B + C) Map + Compass Lecture + Demonstration. (D) Paras 8 to 15 I.M.G.T.	
	1.30 to 2.30 pm	Specialists.	Remainder of Coy Lecture by C.O.
Tuesday 10th	7.30 to 8.15 am	Physical Training	
	8.30 to 9.30 am	(A + B) Action from Limbers + Pack Transport. (C + D) Gun Drill.	
	9.30 to 10.30 am	(A + B) Action from Limbers + Pack Transport (C + D) Points Before, During + After Firing + Cleaning Guns	
	10.30 to 11.30 am	(A + B) Gun Drill. (C + D) Action from Limbers + Pack Transport.	
	11.30 to 12.30 pm	(A + B) Points B. D + A Firing, Cleaning Guns. (C + D) Action from Limbers + Pack Transport	
	1.30 to 2.30 pm	Specialists	Remainder of Coy Lecture by C.O.
Wednesday 11th	7.30 to 8.30 am	(A) Range. (B.C + D) Physical Training	
	8.30 to 9.30 am	(A) Range (B C + D) Combined Drill by Sections.	
	9.30 to 10.30 am	(A) Range. (B. C + D) Mechanism + Stoppages	
	10.30 to 11.30 am	(A) Range (B C + D) Rough Ground Drill.	
	11.30 to 12.30 pm	(A) Range. (B.C + D) Care + Cleaning, Packing Limbers.	
	1.30 to 2.30 pm	Specialists	Remainder of Coy Lecture by C.O.
Thursday 12th	7.30 to 8.15 am	(B) Range (A C + D) Physical Training.	
	8.30 to 9.30 am	(B) Range. (A) Combined Drill. (C + D) Concealment + Use of Ground, + Cover	
	9.30 to 10.30 am	(B) Range (A) Mechanism + Stoppages (C + D) Rough Ground Drill.	
	10.30 to 11.30 am	(B) Range (A) Rough Ground Drill (C + D) Clean Guns + Limbers	
	11.30 to 12.30 pm	(B) Range (A) Care + Cleaning, Packing Limbers (C + D) Indication + Recognition of Targets	
	1.30 to 2.30 pm	Specialists	Remainder of Coy Lecture by C.O.
Friday 13th	Whole Day.	Brigade Field Day.	
Saturday 14th	7.30 to 8.15 am	(A. B + D) Physical Training. (C) Range	
	8.30 to 9.30 am	(A + B) Use of Ground + Cover (C) Range (D) Overhead Fire *	* Pack Mules for Transport to Ground
	9.30 to 10.30 am	(A + B) Use of Ground + Cover (C) Range (D) Overhead Fire *	*
	10.30 to 11.30 am	(A + B) Clean Guns + Mechanism. (C) Range (D) Action from Pack Transport.	
	11.30 to 12.30 pm	(A + B) Indication + Recognition of Targets. (C) Range. (D) Action from Pack Transport. ⓐ	ⓐ Afterwards Clean Guns
	1.30 to 2.30 pm	Specialists	Remainder of Coy. Lecture by C.O.

S. D. Mulholland Capt.
O.C. 109th M. Gun. Coy.

2nd Command

CONFIDENTIAL.

36 Vol 17

W A R   D I A R Y

109th MACHINE GUN COMPANY.

For Month of AUGUST '17.

Army Form C. 2118.

Instructions regarding War Diaries and Intelligence Summaries are contained in F. S. Regs., Part II. and the Staff Manual respectively. Title pages will be prepared in manuscript.

AUGUST WAR DIARY or INTELLIGENCE SUMMARY.

(Erase heading not required.)

Page 1

Place	Date	Hour	Summary of Events and Information	Remarks and references to Appendices
			REF BELGIUM 28 NW 6A	
WATOU AREA N^S^ POPERINGHE	1		The weather was very bad; no exercise was possible. The ~~CO and two~~ party of one officer and one sergeant who were proceeding to the line was put off owing to weather.	
	2nd		No change in the weather three officers went up to the line; no training was carried out.	
	3rd		Lt Geard went ahead to the new area. At 2.20 PM the company moved off with full transport; the road being very bad. In the rain the Company reached the new camp on the YPRES POPERINGHE road: G5C44. All animals & men are accommodated under cover. The Camp was reached at 4.30 PM.	
G5C44	4th		At 5.20 AM D C Section went up to the line to relieve 8 guns of the 166 Comp during the relief three men were killed and ~~four~~ 3 wounded in ~~WIELTJE~~ St JEAN. The killed were Ptes 18658 MOORE J 4826 SILLS, H 14/42573 NICHOLLS J H (attached from 14th RIR). WOUNDED Ptes 81303 BAINES H — 10187 BENNIONS — 36514 WEAR. The two sections come under the command of the 104th Company.	
	5th		The eight guns came under heavy fire but no further casualties except Sergeant 10690 BLUMIRE the transport Sergeant who was slightly wounded getting up rations at WIELTJE; two riding horses were lost. Sergeant BLUMIRE remains at duty.	

2353 Wt. W2544/1454 700,000 5/15 D. D. & L. A.D.S.S./Forms/C. 2118.

Instructions regarding War Diaries and Intelligence Summaries are contained in F. S. Regs., Part II. and the Staff Manual respectively. Title pages will be prepared in manuscript.

WAR DIARY
or
~~INTELLIGENCE~~ SUMMARY.
(*Erase heading not required.*)

Army Form C. 2118.

2

Place	Date	Hour	Summary of Events and Information	Remarks and references to Appendices
G5C44 NR POPERINGHE	6th		The guns reported heavy ~~casualtie~~ shelling most of the day. Pte Jones E 10437 was wounded. Rations were sent up at 2PM arriving 4.30 PM consisting of cooked meat and tea in petrol cans. No food can be cooked in the line. 4 guns put out of action through shell fire.	
	7th		No rations were sent up today and consequently no news was received from the line.	
	8th		At 2AM Captain Mulholland Lt Cayley (2nd in C) accompanied by A section went up to the line. ~~to take~~ Captain Mulholland takes over the command of the Divisional guns from Capt Grissel OC 104 MG Coy. The guns in the line consist of, 8 of 104 Coy in the front (Black line), 12 of the 108 Coy 12 of the 109 Coy in the blue line. Rations from the horse lines come up at 4.30 AM to WIELTJE in a limber, this being the quietest time.	
	9th		Situation heavy shelling reported, "D" section are relieved by A section and later C section are relieved by B section. The guns are worked in teams of 4 each. All surplus men remaining in BRGE TRENCH just behind WIELTJE	

Instructions regarding War Diaries and Intelligence Summaries are contained in F. S. Regs., Part II. and the Staff Manual respectively. Title pages will be prepared in manuscript.

WAR DIARY
or
INTELLIGENCE SUMMARY.
(Erase heading not required.)

Army Form C. 2118.

3

Place	Date	Hour	Summary of Events and Information	Remarks and references to Appendices
WIELTJE	10th		The guns of the company in the [illegible] line were heavily shelled most of the night	
DUGOUTS			and fired of 12000 rounds in response to the SOS call sent up from the	
			line. Our casualties from the line were two sick and two men admitted	
			to hospital with slight gas poisoning.	
	11th	2 AM	Preparations for the offensive. Lt Root with 13 mules carrying [illegible] of SAA	
			came from the horse lines to work at the emplacements, the work continued to	
			4 AM the position of the rockets 10000 23 D 82 80 Behind CARNATION Fm	
	12		2 AM 12th Lt Root gets 58000 rounds up to the limber [illegible] [illegible] During the night of the 11-12th 182, two guns were put out of action one	
			nearly receiving a direct hit from a 5.9 the other more slightly damaged	
			one man was slightly gassed and two wounded	
			During the morning of the 12th two more men were wounded	
G5c44	13th	1.30 AM	At 1.30 Captain [illegible] arrived and relieved Capt Mulholland [illegible]	
			who returned.	

A6945 Wt. W11422/M1160 350,000 12/16 D. D. & L. Forms/C./2118/14.

Instructions regarding War Diaries and Intelligence Summaries are contained in F. S. Regs., Part II. and the Staff Manual respectively. Title pages will be prepared in manuscript.

WAR DIARY
or
INTELLIGENCE SUMMARY.

(Erase heading not required.)

Army Form C. 2118.

August   Page 4

Place	Date	Hour	Summary of Events and Information	Remarks and references to Appendices
GERMAN TRENCH SYSTEM 500 yds NE of WIELTJE N of YPRES	16th	4.45 AM	Zero hour disposition of Guns: one subsection of A section 2/Lt Grant, one subsection of B section 2/Lt Idris detached from the company and attached to the 1st 5th Royal Inniskilling Fusiliers; positions in the front line, these guns moved forward with the wave of infantry C section with a subsection of A section under 2/Lt Webb formed "Y" battery and D section and ½ B section under 2/Lt Brown formed "U" battery under the "Divisional Machine Guns barrage Scheme" Both batteries being under the command of Lt Bowerbank at C 23 D 90 90. These guns had orders to fire a creeping barrage till Zero + 40.	[illegible]
			Narrative of the 12 Barrage guns: At Zero hour 4.45 the 12 Guns opened fire at the rate of a belt 250 rounds per five minutes and eventually slowed down to a belt per 10 minutes, rate of fire 1765 rounds per hour as laid down. The rate of fire was slow because there was not sufficient men to fill the belts.	MAP Reference FREZENBERG Sheet 1/10000
			After about 10 minutes a heavy barrage of 5.9 High explosive was put down by the Germans this became so heavy at Z+15 that it was impossible to continue the fire.	

2353 Wt. W2544/1454 700,000 5/15 D. D. & L. A.D.S.S./Forms/C. 2118.

Instructions regarding War Diaries and Intelligence Summaries are contained in F. S. Regs., Part II, and the Staff Manual respectively. Title pages will be prepared in manuscript.

WAR DIARY
or
~~INTELLIGENCE~~ SUMMARY.
(*Erase heading not required.*)

Army Form C. 2118.

August

Page 5.

Place	Date	Hour	Summary of Events and Information	Remarks and references to Appendices
C23C6080	AM 4.45	16th	The German barrage then slackened down and fire was started again at	MAP REF FREZENBERG
			Z+18 and continued to Z+40. under very heavy fire several guns were hit	1/10000
			but only one was put directly out of action. A lot of Ammunition	
			was burned and two casualties were received	
	AM 5.55		The guns got ready to move off to their new barrage positions and	
			the mule column under 2/Lt Wilgar moved up; owing to hostile fire	
			it was found impossible to move the ammunition any further up	
			so it was dumped at C23D9090 and the mules went back.	
			"V" battery moved off to its new position D13A 40 40	
			As soon as "V" Battery had moved off news reached Lt Bowerbank that	
			the objectives had not been taken; so under orders from Lt Cayley	
			he moved "V" battery to "CALL RESERVE" pending further information from the	
			front	
	AM 6.15		News was received that the attacking waves had met with large resistance and	
			were retiring on their old line.	

A6945 Wt. W11422/M1160 350,000 12/16 D. D. & L. Forms/C./2118/14.

Instructions regarding War Diaries and Intelligence Summaries are contained in F. S. Regs., Part II. and the Staff Manual respectively. Title pages will be prepared in manuscript.

WAR DIARY
or
INTELLIGENCE SUMMARY.
(Erase heading not required.)

Army Form C. 2118.

AUGUST

Place	Date	Hour	Summary of Events and Information	Remarks and references to Appendices
				MAP REF
C23C6080	16th	7AM	A telephone message was received from the 10th Royal Inniskillen Fusiliers that the final	FREZENBERG
			objective had been taken; this however proved to be faulty information	1/10000
			and reliable news was received that we were holding a line Hill 30, POND FM	
			under these circumstances "V" battery was not moved up as its destination should	
			have been "HINDU COTTAGE" some way behind the above line.	
		9.15	A report came back that we were retiring from Hill 35 to the original line	
			and that the enemy were following up: So "V" battery received orders to fire	
			if necessary on a barrage line in front of our supposed line	
			Parties of our infantry were seen retiring across the open.	
		11.30	A message came by runner from Sergeant France of "V" battery that 2/Lt Brown	
			had been wounded also 3 men of the teams: The runner was sent back	
			with orders for the battery to retire on to {C23C6080 CALL RESERVE} four men were sent from	
			"V" battery to assist the move	* This proved to be false
		11.45	Ptes McVittie & LILLEY report "That they have come back from the subsection of "B" Section	2/Lt Idiens was badly
			attached to the 11th R.F. that they are the sole unwounded survivors: that the	wounded
			officer 2/Lt Idiens* had been mortally wounded and both guns & all equipment lost	

Army Form C. 2118.

Instructions regarding War Diaries and Intelligence Summaries are contained in F. S. Regs., Part II. and the Staff Manual respectively. Title pages will be prepared in manuscript.

WAR DIARY
or
INTELLIGENCE SUMMARY.
(Erase heading not required.)

August   Page 7.

Place	Date	Hour	Summary of Events and Information	Remarks and references to Appendices
C23c6050	16th	11.45	[illegible] to Brigade if 2nd Lt Geard and 2/Lt R. [illegible] can be withdrawn from the Black line. This was agreed as it was considered that the presence of the two guns was necessary in the Blue line.	Map Ref FREZENBERG 1/10000
		PM 12·[illegible]	Y Battery returned from the Black line and are put into position for barrage work at C23c9050.	
		PM 2.30	A message was received from 2nd Lt Geard that he was short of ammunition and men. The four men under Lce Corporal Steadman with 8 boxes of belted ammunition were sent up to him, Lce Cpl Steadman and two men returned the remainder staying with 2nd Lt Geard.	
		9PM	Orders were received from the Divisional Machine Gun Officer to prepare to give a fresh barrage for an attack at dawn on the 14th. Also to withdraw 2nd Lt Geard's two guns from the front line.	
		9.15PM	Ordered 2nd Lt Geard by runner to withdraw to [illegible] reserve. (Coming back from the front line 2nd Lt Geard lost his way and arrived at WIELTJE on the morning of the 14th).	

A6945 Wt. W11422/M1160 350,000 12/16 D. D. & L. Forms/C./2118/14.

Army Form C. 2118.

Instructions regarding War Diaries and Intelligence Summaries are contained in F. S. Regs., Part II. and the Staff Manual respectively. Title pages will be prepared in manuscript.

WAR DIARY
or
INTELLIGENCE SUMMARY.
(Erase heading not required.)

August

Place	Date	Hour	Summary of Events and Information	Remarks and references to Appendices
C23C6050	16th	PM 1130	Everything now complete for barrage at Zero tomorrows dawn, the time of Zero not received yet	MAP REF. FREZENBERG 1/10000.
	17th	4AM	Stand to the guns crews of the eight barrage guns all loaded and ready to fire the moment the Artillery start, as the hour of Zero is not known	
		5AM	Still standing too, but as it is growing very light, the guns are dismounted to avoid been seen by the enemy.	
		6AM	Orders received dated 11PM 16th that the attack of the 17th is postponed. For the rest of the day nothing was done but at 7PM instructions were received about a relief	
	18th	AM 530	The company in the line was relieved by the 182nd Company and after breakfast at the horse lines the whole company less transport moved in motor lorries to the billeting area of WINNEZEELE, the transport move at the same time but arrived later	
WINNEZEELE	19th		Sunday; Brigade Massed Church parade. A section are equipped with gun equipment left in the Company	

A6945 Wt. W11422/M1160 350,000 12/16 D. D. & L. Forms/C./2118/14.

Instructions regarding War Diaries and Intelligence Summaries are contained in F. S. Regs., Part II. and the Staff Manual respectively. Title pages will be prepared in manuscript.

WAR DIARY
or
INTELLIGENCE SUMMARY.
(Erase heading not required.)

Army Form C. 2118.

August Page 9.

Place	Date	Hour	Summary of Events and Information	Remarks and references to Appendices
WINNEZEELE	Aug 20th		Sections overhaul and clean guns. All personal clothing inspected and list of deficiencies made. Thirty four reinforcements arrive from the base; these are equipped with rifle	
	21st		Training programme started: drill and inspection of Gas helmets and respirators. List of deficiencies handed into D.A.D.O.S. include 2 guns, 45 revolvers, 22 prs of glasses	
	22nd		Training programme, physical drill, Gas helmet drill, squad drill and an inspection of transport by the C.O. Several hostile aeroplanes flew overhead and a large number of bombs were dropped in the direction of HAZEBRUCK.	
	23rd		The Company marched off from WINNEZEELE area at 9.10 a.m. and entrained fairly comfortably at CAESTRE. The train for the SOUTH moved off at 2.5 p.m. The train journey was remarkable as we had plenty of room and as the train was up to time. We passed through the outskirts of ARRAS and arrived at BAPAUME, our detraining station at 10.30 p.m. Leaving the transport to detrain, the Company marched through BAPAUME and a five miles of desolate country to camp near BARASTRE, reaching there, very tired, about 1.30 a.m. (24th). The transport arrived an hour after. The atmosphere is one of peace and rumour says our line will be remarkably quiet. Very showery all day. En route, 2nd Lt S. MOOR (reinforcement) joined the Company at HAZEBRUCK.	HAZEBRUCK MAP. LENS MAP. (initials)

A6945 Wt. W11422/M1160 350,000 12/16 D. D. & L. Forms/C./2118/14.

Army Form C. 2118.

Instructions regarding War Diaries and Intelligence Summaries are contained in F. S. Regs., Part II. and the Staff Manual respectively. Title pages will be prepared in manuscript.

WAR DIARY
or
~~INTELLIGENCE SUMMARY.~~
(*Erase heading not required.*)

Page 10.

Place	Date	Hour	Summary of Events and Information	Remarks and references to Appendices
			REF. MAP. FRANCE. Sheet 57c	
	AUGUST.			
BARASTRE.	24th		Our new camp would be ideal if the tents were a bit better. The camp, which takes the whole Brigade is well arranged and beautifully situated: the country, being entirely desolate and the villages flat, resembles SALISBURY PLAIN. We squared up the camp.	Weather fine.
	25th		A fine day. Bath for the Company and lecture on Barrage Work, the new men being very ignorant after 6 months at GRANTHAM. Lt BOWERBANK and two sergeants are attached, till we take over the line, to the Company we shall relieve.	2nd Lt S. FOX reported for duty. D.W.
	26th		The Company attended a Brigade Church Parade held close to our camp. Capt MULHOLLAND assumed the duties of DMGO, temporarily. Lt WALKER went round the Sector we shall take over with O.C. 27th MGCoy and reported favourably on the state of the line, which is very quiet at present. A fine day.	D.W.
	27th		In the morning, the Company marched to BANCOURT to test the new guns etc. but the range intended for use could not be found. It rained all the afternoon.	
	28th		Last night was very uncomfortable as the tents are bad and the wind & rain were very heavy. We packed limbers this morning preparatory to moving and the Company marched off at 5.0 p.m., going through BARASTRE, BUS and LECHELLE to camp at P32. A.7, 2. Quarters not very good but we are only here for two nights. Weather – showery.	D.W.
			CSM. DE ROSE reported for duty on 27/8/17.	

A6945 Wt. W11422/M1160 350,000 12/16 D. D. & L. Forms/C./2118/14.

Instructions regarding War Diaries and Intelligence Summaries are contained in F. S. Regs., Part II. and the Staff Manual respectively. Title pages will be prepared in manuscript.

WAR DIARY
or
~~INTELLIGENCE SUMMARY~~.
(*Erase heading not required.*)

Army Form C. 2118.

PAGE 11.

Place	Date	Hour	Summary of Events and Information	Remarks and references to Appendices
YTRES AREA.	AUGUST. 29th		The Company paraded to fill belts and examine gun kit in preparation for the trenches. Heavy showers all day – unable to leave the huts in the afternoon.	
	30th		Parade for packing limbers etc. in the morning. In the evening, the Company moved up the line, marching off with gun kit etc. at 7.30 p.m. and entraining at 8.0 p.m. near YTRES. The transport and Coy HQ left camp at 5.0 p.m. and marched to BERTINCOURT. Here are situated the transport lines. HQ moved off again at 8.30 p.m. and marched to J21 D.40,30. Here Coy HQ is accomodated in a row of dugouts – quarters very good. C Section under 2nd Lt WEBB and D SECTION under Lt BOWERBANK and 2nd Lt FOX took over eight guns from 27th MGCoy. A Section took over three guns temporarily from 197th MGCoy (these last positions were abandoned on Aug 31st.) The gun positions are good on the whole though some must be altered. Weather fine but dull.	Ref Map. HERMIES 1/10,000. D.L.
J21 D.40,30.	31st		This sector is a wonderful contrast with the one we left at YPRES. Everything is very quiet. All parties are busy. A and B Sections at transport lines are starting work, putting up NISEN huts and making horse standings. These are hardly commenced. Men at Coy HQ are busy rebuilding certain dugouts. All the positions in the line and the dugouts need attention. Everybody wants to be ready for the Winter. All is quiet in the line. Weather – unsettled.	D.L.

A6945 Wt. W11422/M1160 350,000 12/16 D. D. & L. Forms/C./2118/14.

SECRET.

ADMINISTRATIVE INSTRUCTIONS

109th MACHINE GUN COMPANY

1. THE 36th DIVISION (LESS ARTILLERY) WILL MOVE TO THE 3RD ARMY AREA. THE JOURNEY BY TRAIN WILL TAKE ABOUT 9 HOURS.

2. BRIGADE ENTRAINING OFFICER, LIEUT W.G. GRIFFITHS.

3. BRIGADE HD QRS, SIGNAL SECTION, M.G. COY AND T.M. BTY. ENTRAIN ON THE 23RD ON [illegible] CAESTRE AT [illegible] 30

4. TRAIN CONSISTS OF (A) OFFICERS CARRIAGE
   (B) 17 FLATS EACH TO TAKE 4 AXLES
   (C) 30 COVERED TRUCKS EACH TO TAKE 8 H.D. OR 8 L.D. OR 40 MEN.

5. NO PERSONNEL OR STORES ARE ALLOWED IN THE BRAKE VAN AT THE END OF THE TRAIN. NO COVERED TRUCK WILL BE USED FOR BAGGAGE.

6. ALL TRANSPORT WILL REPORT TO THE BRIGADE ENTRAINING OFFICER 3 HOURS, AND ALL PERSONNEL 1½ HOURS BEFORE DEPARTURE OF TRAIN.

7. GOOD WATERING FACILITIES FOR MEN AND HORSES EXIST AT CAESTRE.

8. SUPPLY WAGGON WILL ACCOMPANY UNIT.

9. BREAST ROPES FOR HORSE TRUCKS WILL BE PROVIDED BY UNITS. ROPES FOR LASHING WAGGONS ON THE FLATS WILL BE SUPPLIED BY THE RAILWAY AUTHORITIES.

THE SUPPLY WAGGON OF THIS UNIT WILL REMAIN IN THIS CAMP TODAY, AND WILL BE LOADED WITH THE SADDLERS AND SHOEING SMITH'S KITS. ON ARRIVAL AT CAESTRE (THE REFILLING POINT) ON THE 23RD INST, THE SUPPLIES WILL BE LOADED ON TOP OF THE ABOVE KITS, THE WHOLE BEING LOADED ON THE FLATS.

11. RATIONS FOR THE DINNER MEAL MUST BE [illegible] AS THERE WILL BE NO OPPORTUNITY OF COOKING FRESH MEAT ON THE TRAIN.

12. REFILLING POINT FOR THE 24th & 25th DAYS WILL BE BAPAUME.

[illegible] Capt.
109th MACHINE GUN COY

[illegible] 22ND AUG 1917.

Van Draaij

SECRET   OPERATION ORDERS No. 1.   COPY No. 12.

109th MACHINE GUN COMPANY.

1. THE 109th M.G. COY WILL RELIEVE 5 GUNS OF THE 21st M.G. COY, AND 3 GUNS OF THE 197th M.G. COY IN THE LINE ON THE NIGHT OF THE 30th/31st.

2. "C" AND "D" SECTIONS WILL TAKE OVER THE 7 POSITIONS ON THE HERMIES – DEMICOURT LINE AND 1. AA POSITION IN A POST IMMEDIATELY IN REAR OF No. 1. GUN POSITION.

3. HEADQUARTERS   COMPANY – J. 21. D. 40. 40.

"C" SECTION – [illegible] 23. A. 30. 30 (APPROX)

[illegible] SECTION – [illegible] CENTRAL (")

4. CONTROL. O.C. "C" SECTION [illegible] GUNS [illegible] AND THE A.A. GUN (GUN No. [illegible] BEING MANNED BY A DETACHMENT FROM "D" SECTION.

O.C. "D" SECTION WILL CONTROL GUNS No. 5. 6 AND 7.

5. THE GUNS OF 197th M.G. COY WILL BE TAKEN OVER BY 3 DETACHMENTS OF "A" SECTION, THE REMAINING DETACHMENT OF THE SECTION BEING QUARTERED IN HEADQUARTERS DUGOUT [illegible]

6. O.C. "A" SECTION WILL HAVE HIS HEADQUARTERS AT COMPANY HQ. QRS.

7. SECTIONS WILL CARRY IN THE FOLLOWING EQUIPMENT:–

GUNS, TRIPODS, [illegible] BELT BOXES, SPARE PARTS [illegible] (2 PER DETACHMENT)

8. DRESS. FULL MARCHING ORDER (WATER BOTTLES FILLED) LESS HAVERSACKS WHICH WILL CONTAIN [illegible] [illegible] Q.M. STORES [illegible]

9. CARRYING PARTIES [illegible]

O.C. [illegible]

[illegible]

[illegible] WILL RENDEZVOUS AT THE RAILHEAD IN HERMIES WHERE THEY WILL [illegible] SGT HOLMES [illegible] BERTINCOURT [illegible]

10. GUIDES   THESE WILL MEET THE UNIT AT THE RAILHEAD IN HERMIES AT 9. P.M. [illegible]

"C" [illegible] PER GUN POSITION.

"A" [illegible] PER GUN POSITION.

11. [illegible]

12. [illegible] AT 5. PM [illegible] HERMIES AT [illegible]

13. [illegible] READY TO MOVE OFF AT 5 PM TO-DAY TO THE NEW WAGGON LINES IN BERTINCOURT.

14. THE HEADQUARTERS WAGGON, MESS CART AND WATER CART WILL BE GUIDED TO COY. HQ. QRS BY SGT. HOLMES FROM BERTINCOURT. SGT. HOLMES WILL THEN CARRY IN AS IN PARA. 9.

15. ALL TRENCH STORES WILL BE TAKEN OVER AND RECIEPTED. A COPY OF RECIEPTS WILL BE FORWARDED TO HEADQUARTERS WITHIN 12 HOURS OF COMPLETION OF RELIEF.

16. COMPLETION OF RELIEF WILL BE NOTIFIED BY RUNNER TO HQ. QRS.

17. ACKNOWLEDGE.

[illegible] Lt.

for O.C.

109th MACHINE GUN COY

Max [illegible]

SECRET ADMINISTRATIVE INSTRUCTIONS

109th MACHINE GUN COMPANY

REFERENCE: SHEET 28 [illegible]

1. PREPARATORY TO TAKING OVER A SECTOR IN THE LINE IN A FEW DAYS TIME, THE 109th MACHINE GUN COY WILL MOVE INTO THE YPRES AREA ON THURSDAY 23rd AUGUST 1917.

THE CAMP AT PRESENT OCCUPIED BY THE COMPANY AND TRANSPORT IN THE [illegible] AREA AND NOW OCCUPIED BY THE 109th [illegible] WILL BE LEFT IN CHARGE OF TWO CORPORALS WHO WILL BE RESPONSIBLE [illegible] THAT NOTHING IS TAKEN FROM THEIR CAMPS.

2. THE LIGHT [illegible] WILL BE [illegible] BY THIS UNIT. [illegible] WILL BE [illegible] WITH [illegible] BINOCULARS [illegible] EQUIPMENT [illegible] FOR WHICH HE WILL OBTAIN A RECEIPT FROM THE INCOMING UNIT. A COPY OF THE RECEIPT [illegible] WITHIN 24 HOURS OF HANDING OVER.

3. THE COMPANY IN FULL MARCHING ORDER WILL FORM UP AT [illegible] PM AT THE [illegible] AND WILL MARCH OFF AT [illegible] PM VIA [illegible] FOR THE YPRES SECTOR.

4. ON THE NIGHT OF 23/24th AUGUST, THE COMPANY WILL BE ACCOMMODATED IN HUTS AT [illegible]. THE TRANSPORT WILL "STAND OUT" CLOSE TO THESE HUTS.

DATE 22nd AUG 17

[illegible signature] Lt.
FOR O.C.
109th MACHINE GUN COY.

Vol 18

CONFIDENTIAL.

W A R   D I A R Y

of

109th MACHINE GUN COMPANY,

Period 1st September
to
30th September

1917.

Instructions regarding War Diaries and Intelligence Summaries are contained in F. S. Regs., Part II. and the Staff Manual respectively. Title pages will be prepared in manuscript.

Army Form C. 2118.

WAR DIARY
or
~~INTELLIGENCE SUMMARY.~~

(*Erase heading not required.*)

PAGE I.

Place	Date	Hour	Summary of Events and Information	Remarks and references to Appendices
			REF. MAPs. HERMIES 1/10000 and FRANCE 57C.	
HERMIES SECTOR. J21D.40,35.	SEPT. 1st		Reports from the line are very reassuring. There is very little artillery on either side.	
			Our guns carried out indirect fire during the night.	
			WorK at BERTINCOURT as per programme. Horse standings begun. Weather fine.	D.W.
	2nd		Another quiet night in the line. Machine guns on both sides were fairly active.	
			Sections out of the line worked by programme. Weather very fine looks settled.	
	3rd		Machine guns in the line maintain their activity. The HERMIES – HAVRINCOURT ROAD	
			is swept regularly. Pte JONES of "C" Section was slightly wounded there last night.	
			Training programme and working parties occupy the men out of the line. A draft	
			of 30 men arrived today. The Coy is up to strength. Weather still splendid.	D.W.
	4th		Our Brigade Front, which was quite two miles, has been materially reduced.	
			The Brigadier, DMGO and the C.O. have settled the gun positions. We shall have	
			ten guns in the line manned by two sections. A lot of worK to be done.	
			Artillery and aircraft rather more active in the line, but no serious activity and	
			machine guns were very much quieter last night. Our own were silent as	
			worK was being done on the positions. The LEFT SECTOR HQs were moved	
			to J24A.60,40; the RIGHT SECTOR HQs will remain at K25A.30,30.	
			Weather is magnificent and quite hot.	D.W.

A6945 Wt. W11422/M1160 350,000 12/16 D. D. & L. Forms/C./2118/14.

Instructions regarding War Diaries and Intelligence Summaries are contained in F. S. Regs., Part II. and the Staff Manual respectively. Title pages will be prepared in manuscript.

WAR DIARY
or
~~INTELLIGENCE SUMMARY.~~

(*Erase heading not required.*)

Army Form C. 2118.

PAGE II.

Place	Date	Hour	Summary of Events and Information	Remarks and references to Appendices
HERMIES SECTOR. J21D.40,35.	SEPT. 5th		Last night in the line was very quiet: machine gun activity at a minimum:- "Apparently hostile MG fire at night is regulated by our own." (Brigade Summary). Considerable aerial work today. The weather is hot and is settled. Work at BERTINCOURT as per training programme.	H.W.
	6th			

2353 Wt. W2544/1454 700,000 5/15 D. D. & L. A.D.S.S./Forms/C. 2118.

Instructions regarding War Diaries and Intelligence Summaries are contained in F. S. Regs., Part II. and the Staff Manual respectively. Title pages will be prepared in manuscript.

Ref 57c NE3 1/10000 HERMIES

WAR DIARY
or
INTELLIGENCE SUMMARY.
(Erase heading not required.)

Army Form C. 2118.

Place	Date	Hour	Summary of Events and Information	Remarks and references to Appendices
J22c	Sept 6th		Work on the line is at present taking the first place and no firing is being done except at hostile aircraft which does not often occur as few Boche aeroplanes come over our line.	
			C & D sections are in the line.	
	7th		At 7.30 PM / AB sections leave BERTINCOURT on the light railway as far as HERMIES the train waits for the outgoing sections and takes them back to BERTINCOURT.	
			C section is relieved by B section, D by A section.	
	8th		At ~~Bert~~ BERTINCOURT the winter quarters for the company are proceeding apace; the horse lines are 3/4 done and the space for the Nissen huts is cleared.	
	9th		A little rain fell today however not enough to matter, the enemy put a few shells into the HERMIES DEMICOURT Road, and two in the factory J133.	
			Work proceeds as usual during the night, none is possible by day	

Ref
57C NE 3 1/10000

HERMIES

Instructions regarding War Diaries and Intelligence Summaries are contained in F. S. Regs., Part II. and the Staff Manual respectively. Title pages will be prepared in manuscript.

WAR DIARY
or
INTELLIGENCE SUMMARY.
(Erase heading not required.)

Army Form C. 2118.

Place	Date	Hour	Summary of Events and Information	Remarks and references to Appendices
J22C	Sept 10th		Enemy shelled the sugar factory and HERMIES ~~LEMICOURT~~ road but this did not interfere with the work of the left section. 250 rounds were fired at an aeroplane by A section, 20 % of the shots fired were tracer ammunition and two tracer bullets were seen to pass through the planes tail	
	11th		Two Nissen huts have now been erected in the horse lines and headquarters. [illegible] of the Company at Bertincourt [illegible] two more huts are on their way for erection	
	12th		With the favourable weather we are having work is progressing well in the horselines and also in the line. The Company is 20 over strength. Training for [illegible] done by the sections out in the line now C section.	

2353 Wt. W2544/1454 700,000 5/15 D. D. & L. A.D.S.S./Forms/C. 2118.

Instructions regarding War Diaries and Intelligence Summaries are contained in F. S. Regs., Part II. and the Staff Manual respectively. Title pages will be prepared in manuscript.

REF S43 NE 3 1/10000 HERMIES

WAR DIARY
or
INTELLIGENCE SUMMARY.
(Erase heading not required.)

Army Form C. 2118.

Place	Date	Hour	Summary of Events and Information	Remarks and references to Appendices
J22c	13th		Weather still very fine, and no work is progressing fast, no firing has yet been done except at Aeroplanes.	
	14th		The C.O. Captain Mulholland and transport Officer go on leave from the date the former for three days and the latter for one. The 2nd in Command Lt Ogilby [illegible] attached MGC is temporarily in command. Lt Walker is acting 2nd in C and also transport officer.	
	15th		An indirect fire chart came in from the Division for harassing fire at night. 5000 rounds were fired by four guns during the night on enemy communications and especially on bridges across the Canal. Inter section relief.	

Instructions regarding War Diaries and Intelligence Summaries are contained in F. S. Regs., Part II. and the Staff Manual respectively. Title pages will be prepared in manuscript.

Ref SYCNE 3 1/10000 HERMIES

WAR DIARY
or
INTELLIGENCE SUMMARY.
(Erase heading not required.)

Army Form C. 2118.

Place	Date	Hour	Summary of Events and Information	Remarks and references to Appendices
J22C	16th		In conjunction with the left Group of the Divisional Artillery our harassing fire guns fired 5000 rounds on enemy communication. He retaliated by firing at the Mill J18B and HERMIES DEMICOURT road.	
	17th		Night firing with the Artillery programme. [illegible] firing of [illegible] [illegible] with the [illegible], but the firing of [illegible] [illegible] necessary.	
	18th		The four Nissen huts for the Company at BERTINCOURT are now erected; Cookhouse, orderly room etc. are now started building in progress by the bricklayers of the Company.	
	19th		Night firing as per programme from Divisional headquarters lasted all night; four guns were employed and five thousand rounds were expended. Work on the new position goes on during hours of darkness.	

2353 Wt. W2544/1454 700,000 5/15 D. D. & L. A.D.S.S./Forms/C. 2118.

REF 57C NE 3
HERMIES

Instructions regarding War Diaries and Intelligence Summaries are contained in F. S. Regs., Part II. and the Staff Manual respectively. Title pages will be prepared in manuscript.

WAR DIARY
or
INTELLIGENCE SUMMARY.
(Erase heading not required.)

Army Form C. 2118.

Place	Date	Hour	Summary of Events and Information	Remarks and references to Appendices
J22 c	Sept 20		The weather remaining fine a good deal of work was put in at the emplacements in the line [illegible] firing was done through the night by four guns on enemies communication	
	21st		Work went on as usual; the enemy shelled a [illegible] at J18 3 where no movement ever takes place, most probably he imagines this to be the emplacements for the indirect [illegible] fire	
	22nd		C and D sections on the line are working [illegible] the emplacement in K13c is now nearly completed, the enemy shelled the NE end of Hermies and at night the road [illegible] over to catch transport	
	23rd		Work in the [illegible] line is progressing, the [illegible] shelters are now finished having been [illegible] twice. the [illegible] huts [illegible] are [illegible] AB sections are [illegible]	

2353 Wt. W2544/1454 700,000 5/15 D. D. & L. A.D.S.S./Forms/C. 2118.

Instructions regarding War Diaries and Intelligence Summaries are contained in F. S. Regs., Part II. and the Staff Manual respectively. Title pages will be prepared in manuscript.

WAR DIARY
or
INTELLIGENCE SUMMARY.
(Erase heading not required.)

Army Form C. 2118.

Place	Date	Hour	Summary of Events and Information	Remarks and references to Appendices
J22 c	24th		Today was the day for inter-section relief in the line. A Section under 2/Lt Moore relieved D Section under 2Lt Bowman. Relief was completed by 4.30 PM. No guns were brought up and the relieved section went back to BERTINCOURT by train. In the night Lt Root of "C" Section was relieving the 2nd Gun of "B" section.	
	25th		General [illegible] G.O.C. 109 Brigade inspected the Bankhot and gave orders that it must be made much more open for the G.O.C. 36th Division's inspection on the 28th. Work on the line as usual.	
	26th		[illegible] in the [illegible] firing by the [illegible] guns fired 5000 rounds. The transport and rest of the company are preparing for Saturday's inspection.	

2353 Wt. W2544/1454 700,000 5/15 D. D. & L. A.D.S.S./Forms/C. 2118.

Army Form C. 2118.

WAR DIARY

or

INTELLIGENCE SUMMARY.

(Erase heading not required.)

Instructions regarding War Diaries and Intelligence Summaries are contained in F. S. Regs., Part II. and the Staff Manual respectively. Title pages will be prepared in manuscript.

573 [illegible]

HEBUTERNE [illegible]

Place	Date	Hour	Summary of Events and Information	Remarks and references to Appendices
[illegible]	27th		[illegible] by General Nugent [illegible]	
	28th		General Nugent [illegible]	
	29th		[illegible]	
	30th		Night time and work carried on with [illegible] advantage [illegible] condition of the [illegible] [illegible] the day [illegible]	

2353 Wt. W2544/1454 700,000 5/15 D. D. & L. A.D.S.S./Forms/C. 2118.

Vol 19

109th M.G. Coy

WAR DIARY.

for

OCTOBER. 1917.

Dunsmore Walker
Lt a/Adj.
109th M.G. Coy
3/11/17.

Instructions regarding War Diaries and Intelligence Summaries are contained in F. S. Regs., Part II. and the Staff Manual respectively. Title pages will be prepared in manuscript.

WAR DIARY
or
~~INTELLIGENCE SUMMARY.~~

(Erase heading not required.)

Army Form C. 2118.

Place	Date	Hour	Summary of Events and Information	Remarks and references to Appendices
[illegible]	1st		Owing to the [illegible] of [illegible] in the line, the [illegible] [illegible] of the Company being about 98 [illegible] the work in the line is progressing slowly. The [illegible] [illegible] they [illegible] [illegible] [illegible] of them to [illegible] the [illegible] of [illegible] for this purpose two Sappers and a [illegible] of [illegible] are attached from the 150th Coy R.E. [illegible] [illegible] in the line carried out by [illegible]	
	2		Night firing was carried out by the [illegible] guns [illegible] [illegible] rounds [illegible] fired in conjunction with the [illegible] [illegible] [illegible] [illegible] [illegible] the [illegible] [illegible] by the [illegible] [illegible].	
	3rd		Nothing happened today. Firing as usual was carried out. The enemy shelling was very light, [illegible] [illegible] [illegible] [illegible] through the night 5000 rounds being fired by the four [illegible] guns	

2353 Wt. W2544/1454 700,000 5/15 D. D. & L. A.D.S.S./Forms/C. 2118.

Instructions regarding War Diaries and Intelligence Summaries are contained in F. S. Regs., Part II. and the Staff Manual respectively. Title pages will be prepared in manuscript.

WAR DIARY
or
INTELLIGENCE SUMMARY.

(*Erase heading not required.*)

Army Form C. 2118.

[illegible pencilled note]

Place	Date	Hour	Summary of Events and Information	Remarks and references to Appendices
[illegible]	4th		[illegible handwritten entry]	
	5		[illegible handwritten entry]	
	6		[illegible handwritten entry]	
	7th		[illegible handwritten entry]	

Instructions regarding War Diaries and Intelligence Summaries are contained in F. S. Regs., Part II. and the Staff Manual respectively. Title pages will be prepared in manuscript.

WAR DIARY
or
INTELLIGENCE SUMMARY.

(Erase heading not required.)

Army Form C. 2118.

Place	Date	Hour	Summary of Events and Information	Remarks and references to Appendices
[illegible]	8th		[illegible]	
	9		[illegible]	
	10		[illegible]	
	11th		[illegible] ... the night	

2353 Wt. W2544/1454 700,000 5/15 D. D. & L. A.D.S.S./Forms/C. 2118.

Instructions regarding War Diaries and Intelligence Summaries are contained in F. S. Regs., Part II. and the Staff Manual respectively. Title pages will be prepared in manuscript.

WAR DIARY
or
INTELLIGENCE SUMMARY.

(*Erase heading not required.*)

Army Form C. 2118.

Place	Date	Hour	Summary of Events and Information	Remarks and references to Appendices
[illegible]	12		The winter accomodation for the Company [illegible] [illegible] and [illegible] for building.	
	13		[illegible] took over the Company from the 2nd in C. [illegible]	
	14		[illegible] for the [illegible].	
	15		[illegible]	
	16		[illegible] at [illegible] the [illegible]	

2353 Wt. W2544/1454 700,000 5/15 D. D. & L. A.D.S.S./Forms/C. 2118.

Instructions regarding War Diaries and Intelligence Summaries are contained in F. S. Regs., Part II. and the Staff Manual respectively. Title pages will be prepared in manuscript.

Army Form C. 2118.

WAR DIARY
or
INTELLIGENCE SUMMARY.
(Erase heading not required.)

[illegible] HERMIES [illegible]

Place	Date	Hour	Summary of Events and Information	Remarks and references to Appendices
JUNE	17th		Today was the 8th day in the line [illegible] HERMIES [illegible] section, the Battn kept the [illegible] at [illegible] completely by 9 PM. Night firing was carried on as usual.	
	18th		Night firing carried on [illegible] and [illegible] over 3000 rounds fired by [illegible] [illegible] some of [illegible]	
	19th		The 1st [illegible] [illegible] discovered [illegible] particulars	
	20th		The horse lines and new headquarters being [illegible] to transfer the Coy headquarters at present at [illegible] to BERTINCOURT	
	21st			

2353 Wt. W2544/1454 700,000 5/15 D. D. & L. A.D.S.S./Forms/C. 2118.

Instructions regarding War Diaries and Intelligence Summaries are contained in F. S. Regs., Part II. and the Staff Manual respectively. Title pages will be prepared in manuscript.

57CNE3
Ref HERMIES 1/20000

WAR DIARY
or
INTELLIGENCE SUMMARY.

(Erase heading not required.)

Army Form C. 2118.

Place	Date	Hour	Summary of Events and Information	Remarks and references to Appendices
J21D	21		The brigade on the left of our brigade sector the 16[illegible] Bde were to have done a raid that night; this was to have started at 3 AM; [illegible] of our guns in the left sector were to have participated, these [illegible] connected by special wire to Coy HQ [illegible] of the Right Coy Right Battalion [illegible]	
	22nd		Night firing carried out as usual, five thousand rounds were fired, some of the targets were in HAVRINCOURT Coy headquarters moved down to BERTINCOURT	
	23rd 24th		Night firing as usual, not sufficient [illegible]	
	25th		In order to prepare to fire on certain gaps in the enemy's wire of the [illegible] section [illegible], one was moved up into the front line, this fired off a few rounds into enemy working parties [illegible]. [illegible] was the relief of [illegible] sections, [illegible] section went up [illegible] the line, the relief was complete by 8.0 PM	
	26th		Night firing was carried out [illegible]	

2353 Wt. W2544/1454 700,000 5/15 D. D. & L. A.D.S.S./Forms/C. 2118.

Army Form C. 2118.

Instructions regarding War Diaries and Intelligence Summaries are contained in F. S. Regs., Part II. and the Staff Manual respectively. Title pages will be prepared in manuscript.

WAR DIARY
or
INTELLIGENCE SUMMARY.
(Erase heading not required.)

Place	Date	Hour	Summary of Events and Information	Remarks and references to Appendices
[illegible]	27		[illegible]	
	28th		The night was spent in the [illegible]	
	29th		[illegible] The C.O. returned to the [illegible]	
	30th		No firing last night as special work was being done [illegible]	
	31st		The usual night firing programme was carried out. [illegible] trouble.	

[illegible] Lt. Col. [illegible]

2353 Wt. W2544/1454 700,000 5/15 D. D. & L. A.D.S.S./Forms/C. 2118.

Vol 20

109th Machine Gun Coy.

W A R D I A R Y

for period from 1st to 30th November, 1917.

ORIGINAL.

WAR DIARY.

of

109th MGCo.

for

NOVEMBER, 1917.

[illegible] Lt. Adj.
109 MGCo.

Instructions regarding War Diaries and Intelligence Summaries are contained in F. S. Regs., Part II. and the Staff Manual respectively. Title pages will be prepared in manuscript.

WAR DIARY
or
INTELLIGENCE SUMMARY.
(Erase heading not required.)

Army Form C. 2118.

SHEET I.

Place	Date	Hour	Summary of Events and Information	Remarks and references to Appendices
BERTINCOURT. P7C. MAP of FRANCE SHEET 57C.	Nov.^R 1.st		Activity in the Line was normal during the night. Our guns carried out the usual harassing fire according to the programme. One hostile plane flew unusually low over No Man Land in the afternoon. Work on the camp is progressing very well. All the accomodation is completed and we have the best billets in BERTINCOURT.	
	2.nd		The good visibility brought out many planes today and artillery activity increased correspondingly. A company hairdresser has now been appointed and the institution is proving very useful. Work was continued on the camp in the afternoon – training in the morning.	
	3.rd		Nothing unusual happened in the Line – our guns fired according to the programme. Every morning now the enemy shells the old factory in J15D. This appears to be his target for registration. Nobody lives in the factory. Light are shewn there occasionally to deceive the Hun. In camp, training was continued and the Commanding Officer lectured NCOs and No I. on barrage work.	
	4th		A very successful raid was carried out on our right last night by the 9th Roy IRISH FUS. They killed a large number of the enemy. Our own sector was quite quiet. Most of the men went to Church Parades in the morning. The first match of the league was played in the afternoon. We combine with B^de HQ and the TMB. The 9th R. Innis Fus beat us today by 2 to 1. A very good game indeed.	
	5th		The usual night firing was carried out in the line. Shelling etc. is quite normal. The C.O. lectured again on Barrage Work. This gives the N.C.O.s some trouble. They find the calculations somewhat difficult to master but with practice, they will grasp the main ideas.	

D. D. & L., London, E.C. (A8001) Wt. W1771/M2031 750,000 5/17 Sch. 52 Forms/C2118/14

Instructions regarding War Diaries and Intelligence Summaries are contained in F. S. Regs., Part II. and the Staff Manual respectively. Title pages will be prepared in manuscript.

WAR DIARY
or
~~INTELLIGENCE~~ SUMMARY.

(Erase heading not required.)

SHEET II.

Army Form C. 2118.

Place	Date	Hour	Summary of Events and Information	Remarks and references to Appendices
	NOVEMBER			
	6th		Reports from both Sectors say that the line is extraordinarily quiet. Both sides have been quite inactive for 24-hours. The Section "out" bathed and worked in the camp.	
	7th		The Line is again abnormally quiet. Hostile MGs inactive. Ours carried out the usual harassing fire. One of our planes was night-flying very low at 8.0 p.m.	
	8th		Activity in the Line is quite normal. Our guns carried out firing according to programme. 2nd Lt T. G. WEALL reported yesterday and is posted sub-section officer to "A" Section. 2nd Lt F. MOOR is acting O.C. "A" Section. The men played football in the afternoon.	
	9th		Rather more activity is reported from the Line. Our guns fired by the programme. The good visibility brought out numerous aeroplanes. The hostile batteries round GRAINCOURT were active in the morning and our guns engaged them. In billets, the men worked at mechanism and immediate action.	
	10th		The weather has broken. Considerable rain and very low visibility kept things quiet in the Line. A and B Section relieve C and D in the line tonight. We are unable to get a train as the railways are heavily engaged in bringing up shells. Three officers and three sergeants attended a lecture today at Div HQ. on the new barrage work. They seem to have learnt very little there.	D.W.

2353 Wt. W2544/1454 700,000 5/15 D. D. & L. A.D.S.S./Forms/C. 2118.

Instructions regarding War Diaries and Intelligence Summaries are contained in F. S. Regs., Part II. and the Staff Manual respectively. Title pages will be prepared in manuscript.

WAR DIARY
or
~~INTELLIGENCE SUMMARY.~~

(*Erase heading not required.*)

Army Form C. 2118.

SHEET III.

Place	Date	Hour	Summary of Events and Information	Remarks and references to Appendices
	NOVEMBER. 11th		Activity in the line is normal. Our guns carried out their usual night firing. The sugar factory in J 18 D was shelled as usual. Yesterday, the enemy shelled LURGAN SWITCH, our new trench, and landed a 4'2 on the emplacement of C 1 gun. Luckily there was nobody there but we cannot find the tripod. Church Parades and Baths were ordered for the men. Another party went to Divn for barrage lecture.	
	12th		The enemy shelled LURGAN SWITCH again and scored three direct hits. Otherwise the Line is normally quiet. We fired on the indirect targets given in the programme. C Section went to an improvised range SW of VÉLU. D Section went for a route march. The remainder of the men were fitted with the new containers for SBRs. 32 men were attached to us from the battns yesterday. Rather poor material.	
	13th		Of the Sections out of the line, C went for a route march (2½ hours) and D went to the range, but a heavy mist forbade any shooting. The attached men are being taught how to fire the gun and belt filling. Activity in the Line is reported normal. LURGAN SWITCH was shelled again last night.	
	14th		The line has been very quiet for the last 24 hours — shelling at a minimum. Our guns fired 5000 rounds on indirect targets. Visibility was very low. In camp, all available officers and men passed through a lachrymatory chamber. This was essential as new containers (NC) have been fitted (locally) to all SBRs.	D.W.

D. D. & L., London, E.C.
(A8001) Wt. W1771/M2031 750,000 5/17 Sch. 52 Forms/C2118/14

Instructions regarding War Diaries and Intelligence Summaries are contained in F. S. Regs., Part II. and the Staff Manual respectively. Title pages will be prepared in manuscript.

WAR DIARY

or

~~INTELLIGENCE SUMMARY.~~

(*Erase heading not required.*)

Army Form C. 2118.

SHEET IV.

Place	Date	Hour	Summary of Events and Information	Remarks and references to Appendices
	NOVEMBER 15th		The night was quiet and the usual night firing programme was carried out. Today visibility is very low and the Line is quiet. There is an attack impending on this front and preparations are going on rapidly – the mist is helping us immensely and fresh battery positions are being made every day. Great secrecy is to be maintained.	
VÉLU WOOD J31d.00,30.	16th		Last night in the Line was quiet and today is misty. It becomes more evident every day that secrecy is the chief factor in the coming attack. Our guns, coming up in large numbers, will not register but all open at ZERO. Today has been very busy. We moved from our splendid quarters in BERTINCOURT – very sorry to leave as we had barely completed all the buildings. We handed over to the 208th Bty of the 62nd Divn. This Divn will attack on our right. We are in tents in VÉLU WOOD – very cold. All lights and movements are to be minimised. A relief in the line was carried out this evening – C and D Sections are now in.	
	17th		The mist still helps us – the continued low visibility is helping us enormously. "Heavies" are coming up every night and we hear that over 300 tanks will function. We are fitting out the teams for the battle and teaching the 32 attached men a little gun work. The Line is still quiet – our firing goes on as usual.	
	18th		The Line is still quiet and the mist still aids us. Preparations are going on very well and little can be seen in the daytime. The 107th Bde was raided last night and some men are missing. It is greatly feared that the attack may be suspected – a great deal depends on those prisoners.	

D. D. & L., London, E.C.
(A8001) Wt. W1771/M2031 750,000 5/17 Sch. 52 Forms/C2118/14

Instructions regarding War Diaries and Intelligence Summaries are contained in F. S. Regs., Part II. and the Staff Manual respectively. Title pages will be prepared in manuscript.

WAR DIARY
or
INTELLIGENCE SUMMARY.
(Erase heading not required.)

Army Form C. 2118.

SHEET V.

Place	Date	Hour	Summary of Events and Information	Remarks and references to Appendices
VÉLU WOOD	NOVEMBER. 18th	(Contd.)	All the battns are now in VÉLU WOOD except the 14th R.I.R. who hold the whole Bde front. Our operation orders will be finally issued today. What a wonderful surprise all this preparation should make – things will be on a big scale.	
	19th		This is Y day! Tomorrow the 3rd Army attacks towards CAMBRAI – this without any preliminary bombardment and with only about 10 days' silent preparation. The idea of the attack is as follows:– the IVth and Vth Corps attack the HINDENBURG LINE between HAVRINCOURT and the GOUZEAUCOURT – CAMBRAI road. The objective is over the BAPAUME – CAMBRAI road – the cavalry if possible to seize CAMBRAI and later, we threaten the German line between MŒUVRES and BULLECOURT. The whole operation depends on surprise and the strength of the enemy opposite to us. Over 300 tanks walk over the HINDENBURG wire and then – only the actual action can enlighten us. Only the 109th Bde of the 36th Divn takes part in the first day's operation. Our brigade keeps on the West side of the CANAL DU NORD and advances, after HAVRINCOURT falls, sideways up the HINDENBURG LINE. The point of entry is the large SLAG HEAP at K20C – thus, if all goes well, the HINDENBURG LINE and wire in K14, K8, K9, K2 and K3 loses its strength. Indeed, a frontal attack on that part of the line would be most difficult. The 14th R.I.R. are in reserve and the 10th R. INNIS. FUS. commence the attack. This battn advances from the SLAG HEAP to about HILL 90 in K8d. The 9th INNIS FUS. carry on from there to about K3C and the 11th Battn finish the operation of 2 day when they reach the CAMBRAI ROAD.	

D. D. & L., London, E.C.
(A8001) Wt. W1771/M2031 750,000 5/17 Sch. 52 Forms/C2118/14

Instructions regarding War Diaries and Intelligence Summaries are contained in F. S. Regs., Part II. and the Staff Manual respectively. Title pages will be prepared in manuscript.

WAR DIARY
or
INTELLIGENCE SUMMARY.
(*Erase heading not required.*)

Army Form C. 2118.

SHEET VI.

Place	Date	Hour	Summary of Events and Information	Remarks and references to Appendices
VELU WOOD	NOVEMBER. 19th	(Contd.)	The disposition of our guns is as follows:— the 8 guns of C and D Sections are attached to Div for the whole operation. Lt BOWERBANK is in command of the battery and with him are 2nd Lt FOX and 2nd Lt WEBB. These guns are under direct orders from the DMGO, who has eight guns from each MGC'y. Our Div guns put up a barrage from an already-prepared trench about K26a. central. This barrage is supporting the advance of the 62nd Div on the East of the canal, and it is maintained for 100 minutes. "A" ~~"B"~~ Section with 2 guns in LURGAN SWITCH, and the front line at K20a. 20,40 ~~swept~~ sweep the base of the SLAG HEAP for 3 minutes before the ZERO for the West of the canal – which is the main ZERO + 135 mins. These four guns then proceed to HILL 90 in K8d. to assist in the advance of the 9th Roy Innis Fus. "B" Section assemble in the front line at K20c. 10,40 and when the 10th Battn moves forward to the SLAG HEAP, this section takes up its position on the Eastern side of the HEAP to give overhead support to our Infantry advance.	
do.	20th/11/17.		Zero was at 6.15. A.M. During y/ night the enemy Trench Mortared our line severely three times, causing in all seven casualties to the 109th Brigade. At Zero the hostile barrage was noticeably weak. Operations were carried out according to programme, with the exception of a hold-up for about one hour in front of HILL 90 where a German Machine Gun and some bombers held out valiantly.	

D. D. & L., London, E.C.
(A8001) Wt. W1771/M2031 750,000 5/17 Sch. 52 Forms/C2118/14

Instructions regarding War Diaries and Intelligence Summaries are contained in F. S. Regs., Part II. and the Staff Manual respectively. Title pages will be prepared in manuscript.

WAR DIARY
or
INTELLIGENCE SUMMARY.
(Erase heading not required.)

SHEET VII

Army Form C. 2118.

Place	Date	Hour	Summary of Events and Information	Remarks and references to Appendices
VELU WOOD	21/11/17.		The Brigade was ordered to carry out an advance from the CAMBRAI ROAD toward MOEUVRES without any R.F.A. support, on the supposition and understanding that the enemy had evacuated the aforesaid village. The 14th R.I. RIFLES advanced as far as the trench in E 20.D up to and excluding LOCK 5 where some stout hearted GERMANS held out and impeded any further movement. This Battalion got in touch with the 56th DIV. on their left almost immediately who had entered his front line system via ALDGATE. An inter-Battalion relief took place this night.	
do.	22/11/17.		The Brigade held this line for the day and was relieved by the 108. Bde during the night.	
	23/11/17.		The Brigade came out to rest immediately in front of HERMIES and completed its fighting equipment.	
	24/11/17.		The Brigade relieved the 108th Brigade on night 24th/25th. Quiet relief.	
	25/11/17 26/11/17 27/11/17.		Numerous attacks took place on the new army front no signal successes taking place. The Guards Div were driven back to their assembly positions after making a very fine attack on FONTAINE NOTRE-DAME. On the night of the 27th/28th the 2nd Div relieved the 36th (ULSTER) DIV. less Machine Gun Companies who remained in action to support a projected attack on the Support line in E.22a.	

D. D. & L., London, E.C. (A8003) Wt. W1771/M2031 750,000 5/17 Sch. 52 Forms/C2118/14

Instructions regarding War Diaries and Intelligence Summaries are contained in F. S. Regs., Part II. and the Staff Manual respectively. Title pages will be prepared in manuscript.

WAR DIARY
or
INTELLIGENCE SUMMARY.
(*Erase heading not required.*)

SHEET. VIII.

Army Form C. 2118.

Place	Date	Hour	Summary of Events and Information	Remarks and references to Appendices
HERMIES	28/11/17.		A Conference was held at 2nd DIV H.Q. at YTRES to decide on the Artillery and M.G. support for the operation mentioned above. This Operation was cancelled owing to the failure of the 62nd DIV. to capture and retain BOURLON VILLAGE. It was then arranged that the 36th DIV. Machine Gun Companies should be relieved forthwith. This relief took place without casualties to the 109th M.G. Coy. although the relieving Company (6th) took about three. 29th inst. The Company arrived at BEAULENCOURT in Lorries at 3.30 AM. to find that the 109th Bde. Group were to entrain on the 29th morning.	
BEAULENCOURT.	29/11/17.		The Brigade entrained for RIVIÈRE in the ARRAS district arriving at its destination at 5.15 P.M. The Company marched to billets, a distance of 10. Kilos. to LAHELIÈRE.	
	30/11/17.		A Conference was held at Bde. H.Q. at GOUY at which the G.O.C. Div. questioned the C.O.s. on the preceding operation. In the middle of this conference a telephone message was received warning the 36th D.V. to stand by to move at short notice. The Brigade moved off at 2.30. P.M. via POMMIERE, BUCOY, to ACHIET-LE-PETIT where it rested for the night. The Company was encamped at SAPPERS CAMP	

D. D. & L., London, E.C.
(A8001) Wt. W1771/M2031 750,000 5/17 Sch. 52 Forms/C2118/14

14

WO 95/2503/6 36

Vol 21

109TH MACHINE GUN COMPANY.

W A R D I A R Y

FOR MONTH OF

D E C E M B E R, 1917.

Instructions regarding War Diaries and Intelligence Summaries are contained in F. S. Regs., Part II. and the Staff Manual respectively. Title pages will be prepared in manuscript.

WAR DIARY
or
INTELLIGENCE SUMMARY.
(*Erase heading not required.*)

Army Form C. 2118.

SHEET I.

Place	Date	Hour	Summary of Events and Information	Remarks and references to Appendices
ACHIET LE-PETIT.	December 1st		The night was very cold and the billets were bad. Paraded at 7.0 p.m. and marched through ACHIET LE GRAND and BAPAUME to a field near BANCOURT, here we were given a few tents. These were erected in the dark and another very cold night followed.	
BANCOURT.				
BERTINCOURT.	2nd		We left BANCOURT in the morning and arrived BERTINCOURT about 2.0 p.m. We occupy our old billets. Rumours of going in the line near GOUZEAUCOURT are about.	
	3rd		Spent the whole day here and very thankful for the full 24 hours. Barge refitting.	
TRESCAULT.	4th		We left BERTINCOURT at 9.0 a.m. and marched via ROYAULCOURT to the S.E. corner of HAVRINCOURT WOOD. The C.O. was visiting the line with DMGO and Lt BOWERBANK went to see the 184th MGCoy prior to taking over. We had dinner in the WOOD and moved off when it was dark for the line via TRESCAULT and RIBECOURT. We missed the guide on the road and after wandering about for a time, received instructions that the relief was cancelled and we marched back to TRESCAULT, spending a wretched night there, practically in the open as the village is ruined. A half limber was hit by a shell in RIBECOURT.	
LINE. R3C.50,80. (Coy HQ.)	5th		We left TRESCAULT at 8.0 p.m. and marched via RIBECOURT to a point R2B00,50 where we unloaded the limbers. The Coy relieved the 182nd MGCoy which defended the whole Sector of WELSH RIDGE to the EAST of the MARCOING VALLEY. There was no time to inspect the Positions prior to taking over and the guides took the team straight to the positions. We were holding over seven positions in the outpost line, from R4C50,90 to R4C00,00.	

2353 Wt. W2544/1454 700,000 5/15 D. D. & L. A.D.S.S./Forms/C. 2118.

Instructions regarding War Diaries and Intelligence Summaries are contained in F. S. Regs., Part II. and the Staff Manual respectively. Title pages will be prepared in manuscript.

WAR DIARY
or
INTELLIGENCE SUMMARY.
(Erase heading not required.)

Army Form C. 2118.

SHEET II.

Place	Date	Hour	Summary of Events and Information	Remarks and references to Appendices
	December.			
R3c.50,80. Coy HQ.	5th	Cont.	The C.O. was given the location of these guns on the map and the trench from R3.b.[illegible],2 to R3d.5,2. There was some shelling during relief but no casualties. A & B Sections took over the guns. C & D are in reserve at R2.b central. Lt LOWERBANK is in charge of the [illegible] in HAVRINCOURT WOOD and the rest of the transport and QM Stores are at SOREL LE GRAND near FINS.	
	6th		This morning at 8.0 a.m. the Germans bombed down the trenches and took the outpost line. The infantry were very short of bombs and some time elapsed before the enemy was driven out again. The outpost line was not strongly held and the guns were under [illegible] as the enemy kept to the trenches. Our casualties were very heavy — 20 all told — all four guns were temporarily lost. In the afternoon, most of the lost trenches were recovered and [illegible] guns retaken. For the night, a battery of guns were put on S.O.S. lines about R3 central. [illegible] the roads are shelled in the back areas and at certain times, there are [illegible].	
	7th		To-day, the shelling has been [illegible] a [illegible] of 4.2s [illegible]. Early this morning, the 11th Roy Irish Fus. recovered the whole of the lost ground and established [illegible] in the three main trenches of the HINDENBURG System.	
	8th		MG batteries are now being established. Lt ROG[illegible] with C Section [illegible] guns, is manning a position at R4c.10,70. This Section will just be able to manage with [illegible]. The four guns are near together and have a good dugout in an old [illegible] position.	

2353 Wt. W2544/1454 700,000 5/15 D. D. & L. A.D.S.S./Forms/C. 2118.

Instructions regarding War Diaries and Intelligence Summaries are contained in F. S. Regs., Part II. and the Staff Manual respectively. Title pages will be prepared in manuscript.

WAR DIARY
or
INTELLIGENCE SUMMARY.
(Erase heading not required.)

Army Form C. 2118.

Place	Date	Hour	Summary of Events and Information	Remarks and references to Appendices

2353 Wt. W2544/1454 700,000 5/15 D. D. & L. A.D.S.S./Forms/C. 2118.

Instructions regarding War Diaries and Intelligence Summaries are contained in F. S. Regs., Part II. and the Staff Manual respectively. Title pages will be prepared in manuscript.

WAR DIARY
or
INTELLIGENCE SUMMARY.
(Erase heading not required.)

Army Form C. 2118.

Sheet IV.

Place	Date	Hour	Summary of Events and Information	Remarks and references to Appendices
Line. (See Sheet III for the 13th)	December 12th		Visibility is very low today. Consequently things are very much quieter. Good [illegible] established now and the situation is better. All ranks are very tired. There seems to be considerably more activity behind our own lines. Hostile planes are absolutely [illegible] of [illegible].	
	14th		The 109th Bde moves off today and entrains at ETRICOURT. The 187th Bde with the 63rd Div (RND) relieve the 107th Bde in our sector tonight. The [illegible] officers of the 187th [illegible] visited the line this morning and practically took over. [illegible]	
	15th		[illegible] The relieving [illegible] were in VILLERS-PLOUICH by 3.30 p.m. and the relief was very rapid — the [illegible] assembled in the camp near FINS by 10.30 p.m. The march from the line through VILLERS, TRESCAULT and METZ was a very long one. The whole Bde is practically completely worn out with the line — very little spare time since Nov 20th. The [illegible]	
	16th		The men all had baths at SOREL-LE-GRAND and were fitted out with new uniforms.	
	17th		Heavy snow fell during the night — there are 5–6 ft drifts on the roads. The Bde marched off at 9.0 a.m. for ETRICOURT where we entrained at 11.30 a.m. A very cold journey of 7 hours duration [illegible] via BAPAUME and ARRAS to MONDICOURT. Thence we marched to CAUMESNIL-LES-ORVILLE, spending a cold night there with bad billets and little room [illegible]. All held up on the road. [illegible] Div [illegible] BERNAVILLE [illegible]	

2353 Wt. W2544/1454 700,000 5/15 D. D. & L. A.D.S.S./Forms/C. 2118.

Instructions regarding War Diaries and Intelligence Summaries are contained in F. S. Regs., Part II. and the Staff Manual respectively. Title pages will be prepared in manuscript.

WAR DIARY
or
INTELLIGENCE SUMMARY.
(Erase heading not required.)

Army Form C. 2118.

Sheet V.

Place	Date	Hour	Summary of Events and Information	Remarks and references to Appendices
	DECEMBER			
HUMBERCOURT	18th		The Bn travelled off from CAUMESNIL at 2.0 p.m. and marched [illegible] via HUMBERCOURT [illegible] The billets here are poor. [illegible] Traffic is fairly [illegible].	
	19th		Today [illegible] The [illegible] with [illegible] the [illegible] fairly the whole [illegible]. All [illegible] are billeted in the village as well as a battalion.	
	20th		The frost still holds [illegible] and the roads are almost impossible. [illegible]	
	21st		Frost [illegible] today. Mechanism [illegible]	
	22nd		The Div. [illegible] Officer [illegible] applications [illegible]	
	23rd		Church Parades in the morning. Very cold again. A draft of [illegible] men arrived. They are good on the whole but the men just out have no knowledge of horses.	
	24th		Several officers to DOULLENS to buy Xmas dinner for the men. We have hired a big barn room to seat the whole Co. Limbers were all cleaned [illegible] the morning. Some [illegible] Scott on Dec 27th. Very sad [illegible].	
	Xmas Day		A very [illegible] in the morning. Church parade of combined M.G. [illegible] in the evening. An excellent dinner for the men in the evening & everybody [illegible].	
	26th		Another [illegible] the Company in the morning.	
	27th		All the limbers [illegible] today. The frost still holds. Limbers packed in the afternoon preparatory to the transport moving off tomorrow. The Company following by bus on the following day.	[illegible initials]

2353 Wt. W2544/1454 700,000 5/15 D. D. & L. A.D.S.S./Forms/C. 2118.

Instructions regarding War Diaries and Intelligence Summaries are contained in F. S. Regs., Part II. and the Staff Manual respectively. Title pages will be prepared in manuscript.

WAR DIARY
or
INTELLIGENCE SUMMARY.
(Erase heading not required.)

Army Form C. 2118.

SHEET VI

Place	Date	Hour	Summary of Events and Information	Remarks and references to Appendices
HUMBERCOURT	28th		The Transport [illegible] moved off at 8.0 a.m. today. They go [illegible] via [illegible] and stop for the night at CONTAY. [illegible] BRIG. GENERAL THESSEY, originally with the 11th [illegible] has taken command of the 13th [illegible]	[illegible]
HANGARD	29th		The [illegible] left HUMBERCOURT at 7.30 a.m. [illegible] MONDICOURT [illegible] via DOULLENS and AMIENS to MOREUIL and [illegible] 3.30 p.m. The transport arrived [illegible]	AMIENS [illegible]
	30th		The [illegible] great improvement on HUMBERCOURT [illegible] It is [illegible]	
	31st		Considerably [illegible] from Bn. [illegible]	

[illegible]

2353 Wt. W2544/1454 700,000 5/15 D. D. & L. A.D.S.S./Forms/C. 2118.

17

109TH MACHINE GUN COMPANY.

Vol 22

W A R D I A R Y

for

MONTH OF JANUARY, 1918.

Instructions regarding War Diaries and Intelligence Summaries are contained in F. S. Regs., Part II. and the Staff Manual respectively. Title pages will be prepared in manuscript.

WAR DIARY
or
~~INTELLIGENCE~~ SUMMARY.

(*Erase heading not required.*)

Army Form C. 2118.

SHEET I.

Place	Date	Hour	Summary of Events and Information	Remarks and references to Appendices
	JANUARY			
HANGARD. (S.E. of AMIENS)	1st		The Company carried on with the Divn Training Programme today. The frost still holds.	
	2nd		Parades today according to programme, including T.O.E.T.. It is as cold today as ever.	
	3rd		The Training Programme was continued – A & B Section fired two practices in Part I and there was a snowball fight in the afternoon. Very cold still.	MAPS AMIENS, St QUENTIN 1/100,000.
	4th		Today, C & D Section went on the range – a very good one. We expect to move in about two days. Col. Place lectured to Officers and Sergeants. The frost holds.	
	5th		Capt MULHOLLAND, awarded the M.C. in the New Years Honours, left for the 51st M.G. Course at Camiers. It has been thawing today – not very much.	
	6th		Today, limbers were packed in preparation for the move and an advanced party under Lt ROOT went off to billet at ~~BIARRE~~ FRESNOY in the ~~NESLE~~ BEAUCAMP AREA. Late in the day, the thaw set in properly.	
	7th		The Company paraded at 9.15 a.m. and marched to FRESNOY EN CHAUSSÉE, just off the main road to ROYE. Quite good billets in the village which we shared with the 150th Coy R.E. The thaw continues today.	
	8th		The billetting party went on to BIARRE in the NESLE AREA. A lorry took our S.A.A. on at the same time. At night, the destination was changed. We are now to go to BALÂTRE, the next village to BIARRE.	D.W.

2353 Wt. W2544/1454 700,000 5/15 D. D. & L. A.D.S.S./Forms/C. 2118.

Instructions regarding War Diaries and Intelligence Summaries are contained in F. S. Regs., Part II. and the Staff Manual respectively. Title pages will be prepared in manuscript.

WAR DIARY
or
~~INTELLIGENCE~~ SUMMARY.
(Erase heading not required.)

SHEET II.

Army Form C. 2118.

Place	Date	Hour	Summary of Events and Information	Remarks and references to Appendices
	JANUARY.			
BALÂTRE.	9th		The Company left FRESNOY at 8'0 a.m. and marched along the main road into ROYE, close to which town we had dinner. We reached BALÂTRE at 2'30 p.m. and proceeded to billet ourselves. The village was almost ruined though a few civilians remained. 2nd Lt SLOAN reported for duty. Very cold today.	
	10th		The billeting party went off to CUGNY in the French Area. The Company repacked the limbers – we are close to a large French aerodrome.	
	11th		The Company marched off at 9'0 a.m. through SOLENTE and HAM to CUGNY. We had dinner on the road and reached our billets, very good ones, at dusk.	
	12th		A party of 4 officers and 16 NCOs moved off early to inspect the line. Instructions were obtained from the French Regimental Commander. The French MGs are in Companies attached to the Batt^ns and two separate groups had to be arranged. The 16 NCOs remained in the Line for the night.	
	13th		The Company moved off at 10'0 a.m. from CUGNY and rested for dinner at ARTEMPS. Sections moved off independently about 3'30 p.m. for the Line. The guides were splendid and with no trouble, all the positions were occupied by 8'0 p.m. The transport remain in ARTEMPS temporarily. All sixteen guns are in the Line, divided into two groups – A and D under Lt BOWERBANK on the right and B and C under Lt ROUT on the left. Coy HQ. at B.14c.30,70.	D.H.

2353 Wt. W2544/1454 700,000 5/15 D. D. & L. A.D.S.S./Forms/C. 2118.

Instructions regarding War Diaries and Intelligence Summaries are contained in F. S. Regs., Part II. and the Staff Manual respectively. Title pages will be prepared in manuscript.

WAR DIARY
or
~~INTELLIGENCE SUMMARY.~~

(Erase heading not required.)

Army Form C. 2118.

SHEET. III.

Place	Date	Hour	Summary of Events and Information	Remarks and references to Appendices
In the Line.	14th		As the French had 48 guns in the line – a form of Hotchkiss on a long-legged tripod – they handed over to us the 16 positions they considered most important – these were distributed along the French front and support lines to a maximum depth of about 400x. This would not appear to be very sound and the majority will have to be moved. The Line is quiet – the only artillery activity is devoted to back areas – counter battery.	
MAP. FRANCE. SHEET 66c NW.	15th		Hostile MGs are very active by day and night. The valley in B14 c and d is continually swept. At 5.0 p.m. today, the guns at M6 and M21 were withdrawn to M10 and M11 – reserve positions.	
	16th		The night was quiet. Artillery is still fairly active on back areas. Our own guns are taking over gradually. At 5.0 p.m. today, M5 was evacuated and M9 occupied. We now have 6 guns back on the reserve line. The Left Sector looks much better.	
	17th		The night was normal, only MGs being active. M2 guns moved to M8 today. All the positions have 2 guns in them, which is very sound.	
	18th		The night was normal but at 6.0 a.m. this morning, the enemy opened heavily on the trenches in B16 b and d; the junction of the French and English. Our guns at M1 fired across the French front. The position was heavily mortared but no casualties resulted. No hostile attack developed. Today, M23 was evacuated and two positions were occupied in TRENCH DE LA VILLE GOZE[illegible] at B15 a. 00, 40. The final disposition of the Left Sector is almost complete now.	

2353 Wt. W2544/1454 700,000 5/15 D. D. & L. A.D.S.S./Forms/C. 2118.

Instructions regarding War Diaries and Intelligence Summaries are contained in F. S. Regs., Part II. and the Staff Manual respectively. Title pages will be prepared in manuscript.

WAR DIARY
or
INTELLIGENCE SUMMARY.
(Erase heading not required.)

Army Form C. 2118.

SHEET IV.

Place	Date	Hour	Summary of Events and Information	Remarks and references to Appendices
B25b.30,50	19th		Coy HQ moved to this reference the evening. This is much nearer to Brigade HQ and more convenient in every way. The site is an old French battery position. Hostile MGs were very active throughout the night. Considerable aircraft activity today.	
	20th		Last night at 6.0 p.m. a heavy barrage was put down from B16d. central to B17c.3,2. The French S.O.S. was fired but no attack developed and the guns at M1 did not fire. Our own artillery is mostly in position now and registration is in progress.	
	21st		Very much quieter during the last 24 hours. There was a stand-to at 5.0 a.m. as some hostile operation was expected. All was quiet.	
	22nd		The Line is very quiet. A heavy mist precluded aircraft activity – observation nil. Today, M4 was evacuated and M7 position was occupied. The following positions are now manned. M1, M3, M8, GOZET, M7, M9, M10 and M11. All have 2 guns.	
	23rd		Activity normal. Our heavies were active in the evening.	
	24th		Very heavy fog. No observation possible. 24 hours very quiet. The trenches are very bad owing to the thaw – the French had no revetting done.	
	25th		Activity below normal. The Line is remarkably quiet.	
	26th		The fog has cleared and there has been a recrudescence of activity in consequence. Aircraft very busy on both sides. MG fire heavy.	

2353 Wt. W2544/1454 700,000 5/15 D. D. & L. A.D.S.S./Forms/C. 2118.

Instructions regarding War Diaries and Intelligence Summaries are contained in F. S. Regs., Part II. and the Staff Manual respectively. Title pages will be prepared in manuscript.

WAR DIARY
or
INTELLIGENCE SUMMARY.
(*Erase heading not required.*)

Army Form C. 2118.

SHEET. V

Place	Date	Hour	Summary of Events and Information	Remarks and references to Appendices
B25b.30,50.	27th		Very heavy mist again. Only about 20x of ground visible all day. The line dead quiet in consequence — no activity whatsoever. M10 position was evacuated in favour of M8 where a four gun battery is to be installed. There will be a four gun battery at M7 when M1 is vacated. Except for the last proposed move, the final disposition of guns is complete.	
	28th		The last 24 hours have been very quiet. Arrangements for relief are all complete. The 108th MGC'y relieves us tonight commencing at 6'0 p.m.	
HAPPENCOURT.	29th		Reliefs were carried out very satisfactorily last night. It was very quiet. The Company reached HAPPENCOURT finally at 11'0 p.m. Several miles from the line. The village is completely wrecked — the transport have been here 10 days. We have taken over billets from the 108th MGC'y — not too bad but very cold.	
	30th		Baths for the Company today in SERAUCOURT — very good baths. Guns etc. cleaned. We have two AA guns here. Football in the afternoon.	
	31st		Another batt parade this morning. All the Company is finished now. This afternoon, about 50 men were inoculated. This will prevent any strenuous training for a few days. Revolver practice was carried out in the afternoon. The weather is remarkably cold.	

DR

2353 Wt. W2544/1454 700,000 5/15 D. D. & L. A.D.S.S./Forms/C. 2118.

www.ingramcontent.com/pod-product-compliance
Lightning Source LLC
Chambersburg PA
CBHW080859230426
43663CB00013B/2581
* 9 7 8 1 4 7 4 5 1 7 9 7 3 *